Business Management
Study and Revision Guide

Paul Hoang

HODDER
EDUCATION
AN HACHETTE UK COMPANY

Dedication

This book is dedicated to Mrs Smith, my wonderful primary school teacher who taught at Fonthill Junior School, Bristol, UK.

Acknowledgements

My deepest thanks and love to Kin, Jake and Luke for always being there for me.

My heartfelt thanks to So-Shan Au, my Publisher and a fellow Arsenal fan, for her dedication, support and guidance throughout the many projects we have worked on.

Finally, my sincere gratitude also goes to Anson Miu and Joyce Tong, outstanding students who provided me with invaluable feedback from the perspective of IB learners.

The Publishers would like to thank the following for permission to reproduce copyright material:

Photo credits

p.11 © Sean Gallup/Getty Images; **p.24** © Yu/Thinkstock/iStock/Getty Images; **p.28** © Graham Oliver/Alamy Stock Photo; **p.44** © Monkey Business – Fotolia; **p.55** © Monkey Business – Fotolia; **p.64** Photo from Pixabay.com, CC0 Public Domain; **p.73** © Global Integration Ltd (www.global-integration.com); **p.75** © xPACIFICA/Alamy Stock Photo; **p.76** © Carsten Reisinger/Fotolia; **p.85** © Steve Rosset/iStockphoto.com; **p.134** © karandaev – Fotolia.com; **p.151** © Imagestate Media (John Foxx); **p.167** © iStockphoto/silkwayrain; **p.172** © Aleksandr Kurganov – Fotolia.

Text credits

pp.vi-vii, **p.87**, **p.89** From *Business Management Guide* © International Baccalaureate Organization 2014; **p.38** *Business Review*, February 2013, © Philip Allan Publisher Ltd 2013.

This work has been developed independently from and is not endorsed by the International Baccalaureate (IB).

All brand names are protected by their respective trademarks and are acknowledged.

Although every effort has been made to ensure that website addresses are correct at time of going to press, Hodder Education cannot be held responsible for the content of any website mentioned in this book. It is sometimes possible to find a relocated web page by typing in the address of the home page for a website in the URL window of your browser.

Hachette UK's policy is to use papers that are natural, renewable and recyclable products and made from wood grown in sustainable forests. The logging and manufacturing processes are expected to conform to the environmental regulations of the country of origin.

Orders: please contact Bookpoint Ltd, 130 Park Drive, Milton Park, Abingdon, Oxon. OX14 4SE. Telephone: (44) 01235 827720. Fax: (44) 01235 400454. Email education@bookpoint.co.uk. Lines are open from 9 a.m. to 5 p.m., Monday to Saturday, with a 24-hour message answering service. You can also order through our website: www.hoddereducation.com

© Paul Hoang 2016

First published in 2016 by

Hodder Education,

An Hachette UK Company

Carmelite House

50 Victoria Embankment

London EC4Y 0DZ

www.hoddereducation.com

Impression number   6

Year   2019

Cover photo © Pavlina/istockphoto.com

Illustrations by Aptara

Typeset in GoudyStd, 10/12 pts by Aptara Inc.

Printed in India

A catalogue record for this title is available from the British Library.

ISBN: **978 147 186842 9**

Contents

Unit 4 Marketing

Unit 5 Operations management

Glossary

How to use this study and revision guide

Welcome to the *Business Management for the IB Diploma Revision and Study Guide*!

This book will help you plan your revision and work through it in a methodological way. The guide follows the Business Management syllabus topic by topic, with revision and exam practice questions to help you check your understanding.

■ Features to help you succeed

CUEGIS CONCEPTS

These provide you with activities and essay questions to help prepare you for the Paper 2 Section C component of the final examination. Have a go at these to consolidate your understanding and application of the conceptual lenses used in Business Management – change, culture, ethics, globalization, innovation and strategy.

EXAM PRACTICE

Exam practice is given for both Papers and for the type of questions you might get – short data questions, definitions, and mathematical calculations, and extended response questions, with suggested answers online. Use these to consolidate your revision and to practise your exam skills.

Expert tip

These tips give advice that will help you boost your final grade.

Keyword definitions

The definitions of essential key terms are provided on the page where they appear. These are words that you can be expected to define in exams.

You can keep track of your revision by ticking off each topic heading in the book. Use a checklist to record progress as you revise. Tick each box when you have:

■ revised and understood a topic

■ used the **Exam practice questions** and gone online to check your answers.

Use this book as the cornerstone of your revision. Don't hesitate to write in it and personalize your notes. Use a highlighter to identify areas that need further work. You may find it helpful to add your own notes as you work through each topic. Good luck!

Getting to know the exam

Exam paper	Duration	Format	Topics	Weighting	Total marks
Paper 1 (SL)	1 hour 15 mins	Pre-release case study	All	30	40
Paper 2 (SL)	1 hour 45 mins	Structured questions	All	45	50
Paper 1 (HL)	2 hours 15 mins	Pre-release case study	All	35	60
Paper 2 (HL)	2 hours 15 mins	Structured questions	All	40	70

At the end of your Business Management course you will sit two papers – Paper 1 and Paper 2. The external exams (Paper 1 and Paper 2) account for 75% of the final marks. The other assessed part of the course (25%) is the Internal Assessment (IA) which is marked by your teacher, but externally moderated by an examiner.

Here is some general advice for the exams:

- Make sure you have learnt the command terms (e.g. evaluate, explain, outline, etc.); there is a tendency to focus on the content in the question rather than the command term, but if you do not address what the command term is asking of you, then you will not be awarded full marks. Command terms are covered below.

- If you run out of room on the page, use continuation sheets and indicate clearly that you have done this on the cover sheet.

- The fact that the question continues on another sheet of paper needs to be clearly indicated in the text box provided.

- Plan your time carefully *before* the exams.

Assessment objectives and command terms

To successfully complete the course, you have to achieve certain assessment objectives. The following table shows all of the command terms, with an indication of the depth required from your written answers.

Command term	AO	Assessment objective	Description
Define	AO1	**Assessment objective 1** Demonstrate knowledge and understanding	These command terms require students to learn and comprehend the meaning of information.
Describe	AO1		
Outline	AO1		
State	AO1		
Apply	AO2	**Assessment objective 2** Demonstrate application and analysis	These command terms require students to use their knowledge and skills to break down ideas into simpler parts and to see how the parts relate
Comment	AO2		
Demonstrate	AO2		
Distinguish	AO2		
Explain	AO2		
Suggest	AO2		
Compare	AO3	**Assessment objective 3** Demonstrate synthesis and evaluation	These command terms require students to rearrange component ideas into a new whole and make judgements based on evidence or a set of criteria
Compare and contrast	AO3		
Contrast	AO3		
Discuss	AO3		
Evaluate	AO3		
Examine	AO3		
Justify	AO3		
Recommend	AO3		
To what extent	AO3		

Expert tip

SL students must include documentary evidence of their three to five supporting documents in the IA, otherwise you will score zero marks in Criteria A and C.

Expert tip

Spend time learning the key terms featured in the case study as definition questions will appear in the Paper 1 examination. Also, use the Business Management syllabus to guide you in determining the topics that are likely to be tested in your Paper 1 examination.

Expert tip

Students do get a formulae sheet in the final exams, but it is still worth spending revision time learning the formulae for all quantitative elements of the syllabus, such as ratio analysis (Unit 3.5 and 3.6). For HL students, the relevant discount factors will be provided in the final examination if an investment appraisal question (see Unit 3.8) is asked.

Annotate	AO4	**Assessment objective 4**	These command terms
Calculate	AO4	Demonstrate a variety of appropriate skills	require students to demonstrate the selection and use of subject-specific skills and techniques.
Complete	AO4		
Construct	AO4		
Determine	AO4		
Draw	AO4		
Identify	AO4		
Label	AO4		
Plot	AO4		
Prepare	AO4		

Source: *IB Diploma Business Management Guide 2014*

Each section in this study and revision guide starts with the syllabus content and the relevant assessment objectives (AO1 to AO4). Use these as a guideline to the level of depth needed when studying and revising the various components of the Business Management Guide.

Command terms indicate the depth of treatment required for a given assessment statement. Assessment objectives 1 and 2 address simpler skills, assessment objective 3 relates to higher-order skills, whilst assessment objective 4 refers to the skills of selecting, using and applying Business Management skills and techniques.

It is essential that you are familiar with these terms, so that you are able to recognize the type of response you are expected to provide as well as the depth your response should be.

Countdown to the exams

Four to eight weeks to go

- Start by looking at the Business Management syllabus and make sure you know exactly what you need to revise.
- Work out a realistic revision plan that breaks down the material you need to revise into manageable pieces. Each session should be around 25–40 minutes with breaks in between. The plan should include time for relaxation.
- Read through the relevant sections of this book and refer to the expert tips, CUEGIS concepts boxes, key definitions and worked examples.
- Tick off the topics that you feel confident about, and highlight the ones that need further work.
- Look at past papers. They are one of the best ways to check knowledge and practise exam skills. They will help you identify areas that need further work.
- Try different revision methods, e.g. summary notes, mind maps and flash cards.
- Test your understanding of each topic by working through the exam practice questions.
- Make notes of any problem areas as you revise, and ask a teacher to go over them in class.

One week to go

- Aim to fit in at least one more timed practice of entire past papers, comparing your work closely with the mark scheme.
- Examine the contents list of this revision guide carefully to make sure you haven't missed any of the topics.
- Tackle any final problems by getting help from your teacher or talking them over with a friend.

The day before the examination

- Look through this book one final time. Look carefully through the information about each exam paper to remind yourself what to expect, including timings and the number of questions to be answered in each section of the examination paper.
- Check the exact time and place of your exams.
- Make sure you have all the equipment you need (e.g. extra pens, pencil and ruler for diagrams, tissues and water). Make sure you have a GDC calculator (or a simple four-function calculator) for both examination papers.
- Allow some time to relax and have an early night so you are rested and ready for the exams. There is a huge opportunity cost if you are not refreshed!

My exams

Paper 1

Date:...................................

Time:...................................

Location:...............................

Paper 2

Date:...................................

Time:...................................

Location:...............................

1.1 Introduction to business management Revised ☐

The role of businesses in combining human, physical and financial resources to create goods and services (AO2) Revised ☐

- A **business** is any organization set up to provide goods and/or services.

- Businesses aim to satisfy the needs and desires of their customers by selling a good or providing a service.

- To produce goods and services, a business needs to combine human, physical, financial, and entrepreneurial resources. These resources are referred to as the **factors of production**, comprising land, labour, capital and enterprise:

  ☐ Land – Natural resources used in the production process, e.g. wood, water, physical land, fish, water, metal ores and minerals.

  ☐ Labour – Physical human effort and psychological intellect used in the production process.

  ☐ Capital – Non-natural (manufactured) resources used to further the production process, e.g. tools, equipment, machinery, vehicles and buildings.

  ☐ Enterprise – An individual with the necessary skills and ability to take risks in organizing the other factors of production to generate output in a profitable way.

- The production process adds value to the final goods and services sold to customers. **Value added** is the process of creating a product that is worth more than the cost of the inputs used to produce it, e.g. bottled orange juice is worth more than the original oranges grown on a farm.

- Businesses strive to add value to a good or service so that the product better meets the needs and wants of their customers.

- Value added is measured as the difference between the cost of the inputs in the production process and the price of the final output.

> **Expert tip**
>
> **Consumers** are the people who use a good or service. **Customers** are the buyers of a good or service. Buyers and users are not necessarily the same.

The main business functions and their roles (AO2) Revised ☐

■ Human resources

- Human resource management oversees staffing (personnel) within an organization.

- It handles human resource (HR) issues such as recruitment, dismissal, training and development, redundancies, appraisals, performance management, career planning and the general welfare (wellbeing) of the firm's employees.

- The HR department must comply with employment legislation (labour laws), e.g. minimum wage legislation, regulations about working hours, equal opportunities laws, and anti-discrimination acts.

■ Finance and accounts

- The function of the finance department is to manage the organization's money.

- It processes payments for its bills (e.g. suppliers and the tax authorities) and financial compensation to the organization's employees.

- It prepares the final accounts such as income statements and balance sheets (see Unit 3.4) and the various budgets of the organization (see Unit 3.9) in order to improve its financial control.

■ Marketing

- The marketing department is responsible for identifying the needs and wants of its customers, and ensuring the organization's goods and services meet these demands in a profitable way.

- It conducts market research to identify the changing needs of the organization's customers.

- It arranges promotional activities to sell the firm's products at appropriate prices, distributed to customers at the right place and time.

■ Operations

- Operations, or production, covers the process of making products from the available resources of the business.

- The operations department is responsible for manufacturing finished goods or providing services to the organization's customers.

- It is responsible for meeting production targets and deadlines, stock control management, research and development (innovation), and meeting quality standards.

Primary, secondary, tertiary and quaternary sectors, and the nature of business activity in each sector and the impact of sectoral change on business activity (AO2)

Revised ☐

■ The primary sector

- The primary sector is the first stage of production. It refers to businesses involved in the extraction of natural resources and raw materials, e.g. farming (agriculture), fishing, forestry and mining.

- In less economically developed (low income) economies, the majority of people are employed in the primary sector.

- Value added in the primary sector is relatively low compared to the other sectors.

■ The secondary sector

- The secondary sector refers to businesses engaged in manufacturing and construction to create finished, usable products.

- It involves businesses using and transforming primary products and components into finished goods for sale, e.g. car making, aerospace manufacturing, construction (road building and other forms of infrastructure), breweries and bottlers, engineering, and ship building.

- In many parts of the world, the use of mechanisation and automation has caused a decline in employment in the secondary sector.

The tertiary sector

- The tertiary sector refers to businesses that focus on providing a service to consumers and other businesses, e.g. banking, insurance, security, catering, education, healthcare, retail, transportation, news media, law, leisure and tourism, and entertainment.

- The tertiary sector accounts for the largest sector (in terms of employment and the value of output) in economically developed (high income) countries.

The quaternary sector

- The quaternary sector refers to businesses engaged in the creation or sharing of knowledge or information.

- Value added is high in both the tertiary and quaternary sectors.

- Sectoral change happens over time because, as a country develops, it shifts the majority of output from the primary sector, to manufacturing and then eventually to the tertiary sector and quaternary sectors.

> **Expert tip**
>
> It is wrong to assume that those working in the tertiary sector are paid more than those in the primary or secondary sectors. Whilst value added is higher in the tertiary sector, plenty of people working in the tertiary sector, such as in the retail and fast-food industries, earn minimum wages. Engineers in the secondary sector and fishermen or miners in the primary sector are often very well paid.

The role of entrepreneurship and intrapreneurship in overall business activity (AO3)

`Revised` ☐

- **Entrepreneurship** is the term for the activity undertaken by individuals who take calculated risks and initiative in the start-up of a new business or commercial project.

- An **entrepreneur** is someone who is willing to take financial risks by investing in a business idea. Entrepreneurs are usually self-employed and develop new products or services mainly for their own benefit.

- The entrepreneur brings together the factors of production necessary to produce goods and services to meet the needs and desires of customers.

- The economic success of countries worldwide is largely the result of encouraging and rewarding an entrepreneurial culture. It is entrepreneurs who take the risk of business management in search of profit. They provide employment opportunities, satisfying the needs of customers and contribute to overall economic prosperity.

- Entrepreneurs are unique in that they are capable of bringing together the necessary finance, manufacturing facilities, land and buildings facilities, and skilled labour required to produce a good or service. They are also capable of planning, executing and managing the marketing of that particular good or service.

- Entrepreneurship is a rare trait that requires a profound skill set: time management, creativity, communications, leadership, teamwork, business planning, and risk management.

- An **intrapreneur** is someone who develops new products or services within an organization, usually a large one, for the benefit of the firm and its employers.

- Intrapreneurs are important to a business as their creative skills and innovative thinking can give the organization a competitive edge over its rivals. Intrapreneurs provide the right environment to support sustainable innovation over time.

- Intrapreneurs possess the same kind of skills set and competencies and behaviours found in entrepreneurs and business leaders. These assets can undoubtedly help businesses to thrive as they implement new growth initiatives and strategies.

- Intrapreneurs are change agents who initiate and implement change for improvement. Their level of involvement in the organization is such that it can inspire and motivate others.

Reasons for starting up a business or an enterprise (AO2)

Table 1.1 Reasons for starting up a business/enterprise

To be your own boss	<ul><li>'Wanting to work for yourself' is a key reason many people start up their own business</li><li>Some people don't like working for others and natural-born entrepreneurs feel that they aren't able to work for someone else</li><li>They prefer the freedom of decision making by being their own boss</li><li>This can help individuals to meet their self-actualization needs on Maslow's hierarchy of needs (see Unit 2.4)</li></ul>
Challenges	<ul><li>Setting up a business involves obstacles and opportunities that employees would not otherwise face if they work for someone else</li><li>Some people are motivated by and thrive on personal challenges. They enjoy gaining knowledge and developing new skills</li></ul>
Interest and enjoyment	<ul><li>Some people have a desire to follow a personal interest and pursue this as a business opportunity</li><li>Doing something you are passionate about every day is a key reason for the motivation of entrepreneurs</li><li>The aim is not always primarily to make a profit</li></ul>
Niche market opportunities	<ul><li>Some people identify business opportunities or gaps in the market so start their own business, e.g. Stelios Haji-Ioannou (easyJet) and Tony Ryan (Ryanair) saw huge business opportunities in the low-budget European airline industry</li><li>Recognizing a niche in the market helps the business to gain a first mover advantage</li></ul>
Family tradition	<ul><li>Being entrepreneurial is often a family trait, e.g. the Trump family (Trump Organization), the Walton family (Walmart) and the Hilton family (Hilton Hotels)</li></ul>
Flexibility (autonomy)	<ul><li>Setting up and running your own business means the owners can set their own deadlines and get things done in their own way</li></ul>
Money	<ul><li>The key driver for starting up a business or an enterprise is the potential to earn a lot of money through hard work and sheer determination</li></ul>

Common steps in the process of starting up a business or an enterprise (AO2)

Table 1.2 Steps to starting up a business

Have an idea	Entrepreneurs identify and develop market opportunities. Many new businesses start from the innovative and creative ideas of entrepreneurs, such as Red Bull, Alibaba.com and the Walt Disney Company
Conduct relevant research	This helps to determine the likelihood of success, e.g. size of the potential market, set-up costs, cash flow forecasts, barriers to entry, and a competitor analysis. A suitable business location also needs to be determined
Produce a business plan	A business plan is created, outlining the firm's mission, goals, resources, personnel, finances and budgets, marketing plans and overall business strategy. A business plan is important if the firm wishes to seek external finance from banks and investors
Determine a business structure	The owner(s) need to decide on the legal structure of the business, e.g. a sole trader, partnership or limited liability company (see Unit 1.2). The owner(s) should also decide on an appropriate business name
Meet legal requirements	Business registration is important to get formal certification, permits and licenses to trade. The owner(s) must make necessary payment to solicitors for legal fees. Insurance needs to be sorted out for employees and the business itself

Once these steps have been completed, the business can set up its premises in order to trade. The business will need to be managed effectively in terms of human resources, operations management, marketing and finance.

Problems that a new business or enterprise may face (AO2)

Table 1.3 Problems that a new business may face

Planning	Poor market research can result in the business idea being flawed as the product fails to meet the needs and wants of customers. The set-up procedures can be time-consuming, especially with complicated legal aspects to deal with
Finance	Inability to raise sufficient start-up finance or to maintain liquidity in the business (see Unit 3.7) can cause financial problems. Start-up businesses often struggle to secure external sources of finance from banks and other lenders to fund their operations. In some cases, set-up costs can prove to be unaffordable
Marketing	Start-ups have a limited budget available for promotion and advertising. The product might lack differentiation or a distinctive selling point, so fails to gain recognition and market share. A small customer base is likely to cause liquidity issues
Human resources	New, unestablished businesses may struggle to recruit suitable and experienced employees
Operations management	New businesses lack an established relationship with suppliers, which can cause delivery and distribution problems. They lack necessary finance to fund research and development, so are at a disadvantage against established businesses
Strategic thinking	Entrepreneurs may lack the necessary experience in strategic decision making, causing major problems for the start-up business. Their business plans are often not convincing or detailed enough to secure the necessary finance to get the business started

The elements of a business plan (AO2)

Table 1.4 Elements of a business plan

Executive summary	An overview of the business, its objectives and strategies. It is essentially a summary of the business plan
Business description	Description of the business, its legal status and ownership, and the goals and objectives. It may also include the firm's mission or vision statement (see Unit 1.3). For larger firms, the plan might also include details of the management team
Business environment	Details of the market or industry in which the firm operates, e.g. market leaders or market share data. This section is likely to include a SWOT analysis (see Unit 1.3) or a STEEPLE analysis (see Unit 1.5)
Product description	Details of the product offering (goods and/or services) to prospective customers. The plan should identify what makes the product unique or distinguishable from others that might be available on the market
Marketing	This section details the state of the market, including projected sales figures and marketing opportunities. It may include information about market research, branding, prices, distribution channels, promotions and advertising, and online processes
Finance	This part outlines the finances of the organization, including its balance sheet and income statement (see Unit 3.4), thus defining the financial status of the firm. Business plans are often used to attract funds from banks, venture capitalists or other investors
Operations	Production processes and operational costs appear in this section. It may include sections on quality assurance, stock control (inventory management), supply-chain management (see Unit 5.5) and supplier networks
Human resources	This section contains information about staffing and may include an organizational chart

Keyword definition

A **business plan** is a formal document that details how an organization intends to meet its objectives. It adds substance to a business idea and helps with strategic thinking and decision-making.

CUEGIS CONCEPTS

For an organization of your choice, explore how the concepts of change and innovation have impacted on its business start-up.

1.2 Types of organization

Revised ☐

Distinction between the private and the public sectors (AO2)

Revised ☐

- The **private sector** is the commercial sector of the economy, mainly owned and run by private individuals and organizations that typically strive for a profit.

- Examples of private sector businesses include: sole traders, partnerships, limited liability companies, franchises (see Unit 1.6) and multinational corporations (see Unit 1.6).

- Organizations in the **public sector** are controlled by regional and/or national governments.

- The public sector **provides goods** and services deemed to be essential and of benefit to its citizens, e.g. transport and communications networks, healthcare services, education and national defence.

The main features of the following types of for-profit (commercial) organizations (AO3)

Revised ☐

■ Sole traders

- A sole trader (or **sole proprietorship**) is a commercial business owned by a single person (known as the sole trader). S/he can employ as many people as required, but remains the only owner of the business.

- It is run as an unincorporated business, i.e. there is no legal separation between the owner and the business itself. Hence, a sole trader has unlimited liability and is responsible (liable) for any debt of the business which may be paid from the sole trader's personal assets.

- Finance to run the business is provided by the owner.

- Legally, a sole trader and the business are considered as one, i.e. the owner is not a separate legal entity from the owner.

- The individual owner accepts all the risks of running the business, including possible losses or business failure, but receives all profits if the business succeeds.

> **Keyword definition**
> **Unlimited liability** means that the owner of a business is personally liable for all of its debts. This means s/he may need to pay for the debts by selling off their personal assets.

Table 1.5 Advantages and disadvantages of sole traders

Advantages of sole traders	Disadvantages of sole traders
• A sole trader is quick to create, without long and expensive set-up procedures; it is the easiest form of business organization to set up	• The sole trader bears all risks and has unlimited liability as the firm's finances are not separate from the owner's
• The owner has complete control and is free to make decisions without any consultation with others	• Finance is limited as the main source is provided by the owner; access to external finance is difficult as the firm represents high risk, so expansion is difficult
• Decision making is therefore quick	• There is no one else to share ideas, burdens or responsibilities, limiting the extent to which sole traders can benefit from specialization and division of labour
• The owner enjoys tax advantages as a small business	
• The owner enjoys privacy as the business does not need to publish its financial accounts to the general public (only the tax authorities need to see these)	• Added workload and stress from having to run the business as a sole owner, often having to work long hours
• Flexibility as the sole trader can introduce new trading activities or change what the business does with relative ease	• The lack of continuity if the owner is sick or wishes to go on holiday as the business will struggle to continue
• Motivational as owners have a sense of achievement from running their own business	• Inability to exploit economies of scale which means that a sole trader struggles to gain cost advantages so has to charge higher prices for their products

◼ Partnerships

- ◼ A partnership is a commercial business organization owned by two or more people. In an **ordinary partnership**, there are usually between 2 to 20 owners (depending on the country's laws on partnerships). These owners are called **partners**.

- ◼ As an unincorporated business, at least one partner will have unlimited liability, although it is usual for all the partners to share responsibility for any losses made by the partnership.

- ◼ It is possible for some businesses, such as law firms and health clinics, to operate with more than 20 partners.

- ◼ To prevent potential misunderstandings and conflict, most partnerships draw up a legal contract between the partners, known as a **deed of partnership**, stating their responsibilities, voting rights, and how profits are to be shared between the owners.

- ◼ Partnerships are usually found in professional services (such as doctors, solicitors, dentists and accountants) and in family-run businesses.

Table 1.6 Advantages and disadvantages of partnerships

Advantages of partnerships	Disadvantages of partnerships
• With up to 20 owners (depending on the country), partners are able to raise more finance than sole traders	• As there is more than one owner, there might be disagreements and conflict between the partners, which can undoubtedly harm the running of the firm
• The partners can benefit from having more ideas and expertise, along with shared workloads and responsibilities	• Any profits made must be shared between all the partners
• They can also benefit from specialization and the division of labour	• The death or departure of a partner can cause the organization to cease until a new partnership agreement is legally created
• Business affairs are kept confidential, so only the tax authorities need to know about the financial position of the partnership	• In most cases, partners have unlimited liability (sleeping partners are exempt)
• There is improved continuity as the partnership can remain in business if a partner is ill or goes on holiday	• Limited ability to raise capital compared with limited liability companies; access to finance is constrained by the number of partners
• Silent partners (or sleeping partners) can provide additional capital without having an active role in the running of the business	

◼ Companies/corporations

- ◼ Companies (or corporations) are commercial businesses with limited liability and owned by their shareholders. Hence, any profits must be distributed among shareholders.

- ◼ As incorporated businesses, there is a **divorce of ownership and control** (a legal difference between the owners of a company and the business itself), so shareholders have the benefit of limited liability.

- ◼ Limited liability protects shareholders who, in the event of the company going bankrupt, cannot lose more than the amount they invested in the company.

- ◼ Typically, to set up a limited liability company, the owners must submit two important documents:

    - ☐ **The Memorandum of Association** – a relatively short document that records the name of the company, its registered business address, the amount of share capital and an outline of the company's operations (what it does).

    - ☐ **The Articles of Association** – a longer document that contains information about:

        - – The details and duties of the directors of the company

        - – Shareholders' voting rights

        - – The transferability of shares

        - – Details and procedures for the Annual General Meeting

        - – How profits are to be distributed (dividend policy)

        - – Procedures for winding up (closing) the company.

- Once the authorities are satisfied with the paperwork, a Certificate of Incorporation is issued to the limited company so that it can begin trading.

- The shareholders elect a Board of Directors (BOD) to take charge of the strategic direction of the company on behalf of its owners.

- There are two types of limited companies: private limited companies and public limited companies (see Table 1.7).

Table 1.7 Features of private limited companies and public limited companies

Features of private limited companies	Features of public limited companies
• Usually smaller businesses than public limited companies	• Shares in a public limited company can be bought by and sold to any member of the public or institution
• Shares can only be transferred (bought or sold) privately, and all shareholders must agree on the sale/transfer	• The first time that shares in a public limited company are sold via a stock exchange is called an initial public offer (IPO)
• Typically, shares are owned by family, relatives and close friends	• There is no legal maximum number of shareholders; the company can have as many shareholders as its share capital can accommodate
• The shares cannot be advertised for sale or sold via a stock exchange	• Public limited companies tend to be the largest type of business organizations
• Examples include Mars and IKEA	• They are strictly regulated and are required by law to publish their complete financial accounts (see Unit 3.4) on a yearly basis
	• Examples include Google, Toyota and Samsung

Table 1.8 Advantages and disadvantages of private limited companies

Advantages of private limited companies	Disadvantages of private limited companies
• Control of the company cannot be lost as shares cannot be bought without the agreement of existing shareholders	• Shares cannot be sold to the general public, restricting finance compared with a public limited company
• More finance can be raised compared with a sole trader or a partnership	• Legal fees and auditing fees mean it is more expensive to set up compared to a sole trader or partnership
• Private limited companies tend to have more privacy than public limited companies	• The company can become vulnerable to a takeover by a larger company
• There is continuity in the event of the death of one of the main shareholders	• There is a lack of privacy as financial accounts must be made available upon request
• Owners have limited liability so can only lose up to the sum of their investment	

Table 1.9 Advantages and disadvantages of public limited companies

Advantages of public limited companies	Disadvantages of public limited companies
• It is easier to obtain finance for growth and evolution (see Unit 1.6) by selling additional share capital	• The financial information becomes public as people have access to the final accounts of a public limited company
• It is also easier for large public limited companies to secure external sources of finance from banks and other investors or financiers	• They are the most administratively difficult, time consuming and expensive type of commercial business to set up
• They can enjoy the benefits of being large, e.g. economies of scale, market power and market dominance	• There are high costs of complying with the rules of the **stock exchange**
• Owners enjoy limited liability	• There is the potential threat of a takeover by a rival company
• As with private limited companies, there is continuity, even if one of the principal shareholders dies	• There is the possibility that the firm becomes too large to manage efficiently so suffers from diseconomies of scale i.e. higher average costs of production

> **Keyword definition**
>
> A **stock exchange** (or **stock market**) is the marketplace where people and businesses buy and sell second-hand company stocks and shares, e.g. the New York Stock Exchange.

Types of for-profit social enterprises (AO3)

- A social enterprise is an organization that uses commercial business practices to improve communities, the environment and human well-being rather than focusing on profits for external shareholders.

- Some social enterprises are run for profit (e.g. cooperatives, microfinance providers and public–private partnerships), whilst others are run as non-profit organizations (e.g. non-governmental organizations and charities).

- Non-profit organizations can earn a surplus from selling goods and services but reinvest this back into the business and/or local community.

■ Cooperatives

- Cooperatives are for-profit social enterprises owned and run by their members, such as employees, managers and customers. Cooperatives strive to provide a service and to create value for their members, rather than a financial return for their member-owners.

- Like a limited liability company, a cooperative is a separate legal entity. Shareholders, directors, managers and employees have limited liability so are not personally liable for any debts incurred by the business.

- All members have equal voting rights irrespective of their position in the organization or their level of investment.

- All shareholders are expected to help run the business.

- They promote a democratic style of managing the organization, with a culture of promoting the concepts of sharing resources and delegation to increase competitiveness.

Table 1.10 Advantages and disadvantages of cooperatives

Advantages of cooperatives	Disadvantages of cooperatives
• It is usually straightforward and inexpensive to set up a cooperative	• It can be difficult to attract potential members/shareholders as cooperatives are not formed to generate a financial return on investment
• All members and shareholders must be active stakeholders of the cooperative, making it more likely to succeed	• Limited resources as the financial strength of cooperatives depends on the capital contributed by its members (membership fees are limited so they are unable to raise large amounts of finance)
• Shareholders have equal voting rights (all members are equally important for the cooperative), making the organization more democratic and harmonious	• Employees and managers may not be highly motivated due to the absence of financial rewards and benefits
• Members have limited liability	• As cooperatives are managed by their members only, employees may not have any managerial skills so inefficiencies can hinder the success of the business
• Members own and control the business rather than being governed by external investors	• Although some members have more responsibilities, they still only get one vote, which may be deemed as unfair
• Any surplus is spent on the welfare of the members and a portion is kept for reserves as an internal source of finance	
• Governments often provide special financial assistance to help cooperatives	

■ Microfinance providers

- Microfinance providers are a type of banking service provided to unemployed or low-income earners who would otherwise struggle to gain external finance, e.g. savings, insurance, loans and remittance transfers.

- Microfinance gives these people, women in particular, the opportunity to become self-sufficient by providing small loans, savings and other basic financial services.

- Microfinance providers charge interest on loans, although the rates are generally lower than those offered by commercial banks.

Table 1.11 Advantages and disadvantages of microfinance providers

Advantages of microfinance providers	Disadvantages of microfinance providers
• Helps those living in poverty to become financially independent • Empowers entrepreneurs (especially females) of small businesses • As around half of the world's population survives on less than $2 a day, microfinance provides poverty relief • They generate social benefits, e.g. health, education, clean water, and job creation • Helps to build and encourage a culture of economic responsibility	• Critics of microfinance condemn the system for earning profits from the poor, so is regarded as being unethical • Microfinance is small scale, so is insufficient to transform communities and societies • Microcredit loans can prove to be too expensive for some borrowers as it is difficult for them to earn enough profit to sustain the loan repayments

Public–private partnerships (PPPs)

■ Public–private partnerships (PPPs) are organizations jointly established by the government and at least one private sector organization, e.g. the Hong Kong government owns 51% of the stake in Hong Kong Disneyland whilst the Walt Disney Company owns the other 49% stake.

■ PPPs have been used for a wide range of projects that benefit local communities and society, e.g. schools, hospitals and health care services, bridges, roads, public transportation networks, prisons, parks and convention centres.

■ They are suitable when the capital to finance a public project from public funding is insufficient or not available, e.g. a government might be heavily indebted but collaborates with a private sector firm in exchange for receiving some of the operating profits from the project.

■ Once the project is built or complete, it is usually maintained by the private sector contractor on a medium to long term basis (up to 30 years), after which time there is the option to renew the partnership or the asset returns to public ownership.

■ According to the World Bank, more than half the countries around the world now use PPPs.

■ Find more about PPPs on the World Bank website (**http://goo.gl/fm62u3**), which includes an introductory video on Vimeo: **https://vimeo.com/47015729**

Table 1.12 Advantages and disadvantages of public–private partnerships (PPPs)

Advantages of PPPs	Disadvantages of PPPs
• Both private and public sectors contribute financial resources towards the project and share some of the risks • They are run more efficiently than traditional bureaucratic public sector organizations • They provide a solution to the funding shortfall of many governments • Similarly, government funding can help private firms to reduce the amount of money they need for investment projects • Private sector management skills and financial support help to create better value for money for taxpayers (who help to fund the PPP) • PPPs have positive impacts on employment and economic growth	• There is always an opportunity cost of public sector finances and resources; by engaging in a PPP, the government forgoes (turns down) other projects or areas of expenditure • As PPPs tend to be large projects and involve vast sums of money and high operational costs for a long period of time, they are high risk investments • There is the potential danger of conflict of interests between stakeholders of the PPP, e.g. private sector managers need to act in the interest of their shareholders whilst the government has alternative priorities • Private investors might be put off due to the difficulty in estimating financial outcomes of the PPP over such long time periods

Types of non-profit social enterprises (AO3)

Revised ☐

■ Social enterprises are organizations that generate revenue but act with community objectives (for the well-being of others) at the core of their operations.

■ A non-profit organization acts in a business-like way but does not distribute profits to its owners or shareholders, but instead uses the surplus to pursue its mission or vision.

■ Examples of non-profit social enterprises include non-government organizations and charities, such as UNICEF, Human Rights Watch, Greenpeace, Ronald McDonald House Charities, and World Wildlife Fund.

Figure 1.1 Greenpeace is a non-profit social enterprise

Table 1.13 Advantages and disadvantages of non-profit social enterprises

Advantages of non-profit social enterprises	Disadvantages of non-profit social enterprises
• They are exempt from paying income taxes and corporate taxes	• In order to protect the general public, there are strict restrictions and guidelines that must be followed, including the types of trading activities allowed
• They qualify for government grants and subsidies	• Earnings of workers are often lower as it would be regarded as unethical if workers were paid similar wages to those in for-profit firms
• They exist for the benefit of local communities and societies, which can assist fundraising and donations	• They are often reliant on donations and external support in order to survive
• As part of government incentives to encourage donors, non-profit social enterprises qualify for tax reductions on their donations	• Cost and financial control may not be stringent as there is no expectation to earn a profit

Non-governmental organizations (NGOs)

- A non-governmental organization (NGO) is a type of non-profit social enterprise that is neither part of a government nor a traditional for-profit business but run by voluntary groups.

- They may be funded by governments, international organizations, charities, commercial businesses or private individuals.

- NGOs can operate at a local, national or international level but are not usually affiliated with any government.

- The majority of NGOs are run to promote a social cause, e.g. human rights, animal rights, environmental protection, disaster relief, and development assistance.

- Examples include: Oxfam, the Wikimedia Foundation, Amnesty International, Doctors Without Borders and World Vision International.

- They exert pressure and influence on government policies to support their cause and/or a wide range of global issues.

Charities

- Charities are not-for-profit organizations that operate in an altruistic way with the objectives of promoting a worthwhile cause, e.g. child protection or anti-whaling.

- They predominantly operate in the private sector.

- As with all non-profit social enterprises, charities are run for the benefit of others in society.

- Charities get their finance from a limited range of sources, e.g. donations, fund-raising events and selling goods.

- Whilst they do not always necessarily sell goods, they operate to promote and raise money for social causes.

Expert tip

Be sure to know the difference between charities and NGOs. Whilst both are non-profit organizations (NPOs), not all NPOs are charities. To be a charity, the organization must be registered with the respective Charity Commission. This is why organizations can be charities in some countries (such as Oxfam and VSO in the UK) yet be NGOs in other countries.

1.3 Organizational objectives

Vision statement and mission statement (AO2)

> **Keyword definitions**
>
> A **vision statement** is an optimistic and inspiring declaration that defines the purpose and values of an organization and where it wants to be in the future.
>
> A **mission statement** is a clear and concise declaration of an organization's fundamental purpose, i.e. a succinct description of what the organization does, in order to become what it wants to be.

Table 1.14 Vision and mission statements

Vision statement	Mission statement
• Abstract statement that outlines what the organization ultimately wants to be or do	• A concrete and practical statement intended to state the purpose and guide the actions of an organization
• Concentrates on the future direction of the organization	• A declaration of an organization's reason for existence, i.e. *why* it exists
• A source of inspiration (driving force) for internal stakeholders	• Symbolizes an organization's philosophies, goals and ambitions
• A statement of the purpose of the organization, in terms of its core values or ideals	• Enables the organization's stakeholders to understand the desired level of performance
• Provides guiding beliefs about how things should be done within the organization	• Incorporates meaningful and measurable criteria, e.g. expectations of growth and profitability
• Informs strategic planning, i.e. where the organization wants to be	• Describes how an organization will execute its vision, i.e. the tactics that make the vision a reality
• Does not change, even as business models adapt over time	• Narrow and specific statements
• Broad statements	

Expert tip

Not all businesses have separate vision and mission statements. For example, Facebook combines its vision and mission as '… to give people the power to share and make the world more open and connected'. Amazon's vision and mission statements are also combined as 'To be earth's most customer centric company; to build a place where people can come to find and discover anything they might want to buy online.'

CUEGIS CONCEPTS

For an organization of your choice, investigate how the vision and mission statements have impacted on its organizational culture and strategy.

Aims, objectives, strategies and tactics, and their relationships (AO3)

■ Aims

- Aims are long-term goals of an organization, formulated by the senior management team.

- The aims of a business are often found in its mission statement.

■ Objectives

- Objectives are the targets an organization is trying to achieve, e.g. to maximize shareholder value.

- Objectives can be *strategic* (long term), *tactical* (medium term) or *operational* (short term).

- They are often set as SMART goals (specific, measureable, achievable, realistic and time constrained), e.g. to achieve sales growth of $250 m by 2023, or increase market share by 3% within five years.

- They can give a sense of direction to employees, managers, departments and the whole organization.

- Objectives can define both the purpose and the aims of an organization.

- They can be communicated through the organization's mission statement.

Expert tip

Objectives are vital for any business organization so that stakeholders know where it is going, and be able to measure its progress towards it. Objectives give departments and the organization a sense of common purpose, making it easier to create a team spirit and coordinate the business.

■ Strategies

- Strategies are how an organization intends to achieve its aims and strategic objectives.
- They are usually long-term, overall corporate decisions made by senior management.
- Examples of strategic decisions include decisions to expand overseas or to change location or product lines in order to develop competitive advantages.

■ Tactics

- Tactics are short-term, smaller-scale or routine decisions about how an organization intends to achieve its aims and objectives on a day-to-day basis. The responsibility of making these decisions is usually delegated to employees lower down in the hierarchy to motivate and inspire workers.
- Tactics are concerned with reaching more limited and measurable goals.
- Tactical objectives have specific targets and timelines, enabling managers to assess if or when these have been achieved.
- They are set to facilitate the strategies of the organization.

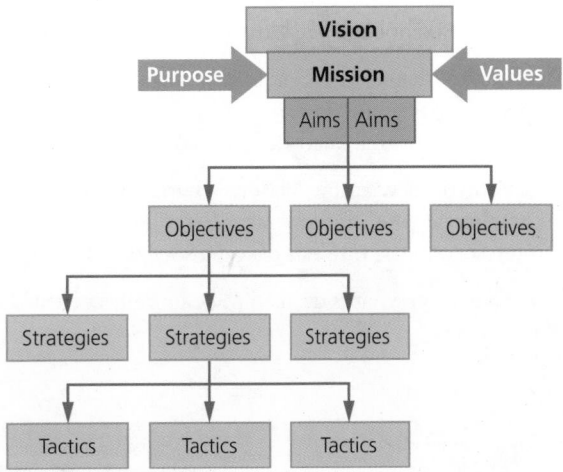

Figure 1.2 The relationship between aims, objectives, strategies and tactics

The need for organizations to change objectives and innovate in response to changes in internal and external environments (AO3)

Revised

Internal factors are those within the control of an organization.

- *Corporate culture* – the traditions and norms within an organization. Businesses that have a dynamic and adaptable corporate culture (such as Google or Apple) are likely to have changing and innovative objectives.
- *Growth and size of the organization* – New businesses tend to aim for break-even and survival, whereas established businesses might aim for greater market share. Inorganic growth through mergers and acquisitions (see Unit 1.6) is likely to create a change in corporate objectives.
- *A change in senior management* – Individuals have the capacity to change the corporate culture of an organization (see Unit 2.5). Hence, a change in leadership can result in changing business objectives. An ambitious leader is more likely to strive for innovative practices.
- *Crisis management* – A business that experiences an internal crisis (see Unit 5.7) such as working capital issues (see Unit 3.7) or a major product recall (see Units 5.7 and 5.3) will need to focus on maintaining its market position and corporate image.

External factors are those beyond the control of an organization.

- *Business cycle* – Organizational objectives change depending on the business cycle (see Unit 1.5), e.g. during a recession (when consumer spending is low and unemployment is high), there are few opportunities. Change and innovation become vital for business survival.
- *Laws and regulations* – Changes in the legal system (see Unit 1.5) can constrain business activity, e.g. complying with employment laws and ethical codes of practice can lead to higher costs.
- *Social trends* – Environmental pressure groups (see Unit 1.4) can cause businesses to change their objectives and practices, such as being socially responsible to their stakeholders.
- *Technological changes* – Technological progress and innovations can lead to many new opportunities, thereby changing the firm's corporate objectives, e.g. internet technologies have led to the growing popularity of e-commerce (see Unit 4.8).

Ethical objectives and corporate social responsibility (CSR) (AO1)

- Corporate social responsibility (CSR) refers to the concern and obligation of a business in committing to behaving ethically and responsibly towards its various stakeholders (see Unit 1.4).

- Examples include improving the quality of work life for the employees, adopting green practices to protect the natural environment, and using socially responsible marketing strategies (see Unit 4.1).

- CSR involves voluntary actions a business can take, over and above compliance with minimum legal requirements in order to address competitive interests and the interests of wider society.

- It is based on what is deemed to be morally correct according to societal norms and values.

> **Keyword definition**
>
> **Corporate social responsibility** (CSR) refers to an organization's duties to its internal and external stakeholders by behaving in a way that positively impacts society as a whole.

The reasons why organizations set ethical objectives and the impact of implementing them (AO3)

- Organizations are increasingly setting ethical objectives as they are more aware of their corporate social responsibilities (CSR).

- Setting and pursuing ethical objectives can increase employee motivation and productivity. Businesses might also find it easier to recruit and retain employees.

- It can reduce negative publicity from news media and pressure groups.

- The growing use of social media makes it easier for the general public to demand transparency and ethical business behaviour.

- Having a good corporate image with customers and a good corporate reputation with the government enables the organization to gain competitive advantages. Hence, CSR can be profitable (the ultimate aim of for-profit organizations).

- Pursuing ethical objectives is a form of self-discipline which avoids government intervention.

However, there can be negative impacts of implementing ethical objective, such as:

- The **compliance costs** of acting in a socially responsible way and the extra management time required to execute ethical business practices places the organization at a competitive disadvantage.

- This can mean lower profits being available to be distributed to shareholders in the form of dividends. This might therefore create some resentment with investors.

- Furthermore, as competitors are in pursuit of similar ethical objectives and practices, any unique selling point (USP) might not be sustainable.

> **Expert tip**
>
> It is incorrect to assume or state that only non-profit organizations (NPOs) set ethical objectives such as corporate social responsibility. NPOs may have different objectives (as they are not profit seeking), but it can be for humanitarian and altruistic reasons that for-profit organizations set ethical business objectives.

The evolving role and nature of CSR (AO3)

- As a business becomes more established and grows, the scale of its operations enlarges. For example, more workers are needed. As a result, organizational objectives and priorities may change.

- For example, the opportunity cost for a large multinational company that doesn't act ethically is potentially huge, especially when compared to a small sole trader operating in a remote town.

- Modern business practice in many countries has shown that CSR has an important role in determining the market position (see Unit 4.2) of an organization.

- Attitudes towards CSR can change over time. What was previously considered socially acceptable, such as smoking in public areas, may no longer be the case. Environmental protection was not a major corporate priority until the 1980s.

- Hence, changes in societal norms, expectations and values mean that organizations may need to review their CSR policies and practices occasionally.

- Media exposure, pressure group action and educational awareness have ensured that an increasing number of businesses are actively implementing ethical objectives.

SWOT analysis of a given organization (AO3, AO4)

Revised

A **SWOT analysis** is a management tool to assess where a business is at the present time and how it is affected by the external business environment. It is sometimes referred to as **situational analysis** as it examines the position of an organization at one point in time. SWOT stands for:

- Strengths – Internal factors that reveal what the organization does well compared to its rivals, e.g. high market share.

- Weaknesses – Internal factors that reveal what the organization does not do so well compared to its rivals, e.g. poor customer service or low employee motivation.

- Opportunities – External factors that may enable the organization to develop and prosper, e.g. an economic boom (see Unit 1.5).

- Threats – External factors that may hinder the organization's ability to achieve its aims, e.g. higher interest rates (see Unit 1.5) or increasing competition in the industry.

Table 1.15 Example of SWOT analysis

Strengths	Weaknesses
Dedicated and productive workforce	High labour turnover (demotivated staff)
High market share	Low profit margins
Brand loyalty/brand reputation	High wastage rate
Customer loyalty	Poor customer service

Opportunities	Threats
Internet technologies	Higher raw material costs
New overseas markets	Economic recession
The collapse of a major competitor	Protests from pressure groups
Demographic changes	Demographic changes

Table 1.16 Advantages and disadvantages of SWOT analysis

Advantages of SWOT analysis	Disadvantages of SWOT analysis
A useful visual tool to assist managers in the planning process	It is only a snapshot of the current situation for the organization
A decision-making tool which can give a good picture of the organization's actual position in the market	It may need to be revised regularly, accounting for changes in the internal and external business environment
It encourages an examination of strategic opportunities for an organization, e.g. growth (expansion) or relocation	It is subject to some bias as the analysis is based on opinions, not only facts and figures

Ansoff Matrix for different growth strategies of a given organization (AO3, AO4)

■ The Ansoff Matrix is a management growth tool, first published in an article titled 'Strategies for Diversification', featured in the *Harvard Business Review* (1957).

■ It is used by businesses to identify and decide their product and market growth strategies (see Figure 1.3).

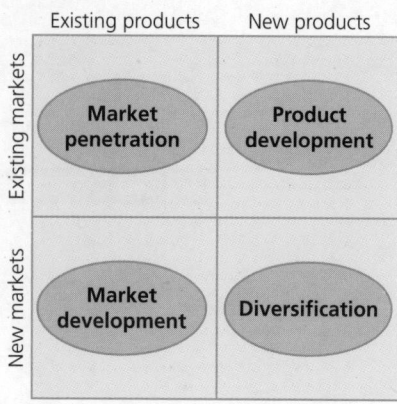

Figure 1.3 The Ansoff Matrix

Market penetration

■ Market penetration focuses on existing markets and existing products, i.e. the firm focuses on what it knows and does well.

■ It is a low-risk strategy so requires little, if any, investment in new market research as the organization aims to increase revenues by focusing on its existing products to existing customers.

■ The strategy concentrates on increasing the organization's sales revenue or market share of its existing products, e.g. by using competitive pricing strategies, introducing customer loyalty schemes, widening distribution channels or using a more effective promotional campaign.

Market development

■ Market development is the growth strategy where a business sells its existing products into new markets, i.e. the product remains the same, but it is sold to a new group of customers.

■ An example would be car manufacturers that export their cars to overseas markets or have production plants in various countries.

■ There is an element of risk with market development because customer tastes may vary in different regions and countries. There is also the added cost of market research. In the case of foreign direct investment, market development presents even higher financial risks.

■ Nevertheless, the business knows their products well so should be familiar with customer needs. This helps to minimize some of the risks involved with market development.

Product development

- Product development is a growth strategy where a business introduces new products into existing markets, i.e. it targets new products at existing customers.

- It is common for businesses, such as carmakers, to develop and innovate new products to replace their existing ones. These new products are then marketed to existing customers.

- An example is Apple's introduction of the iPhone, iPad and iPad Mini, and Apple Watch.

- Product development often involves a business developing modified products as part of its product extension strategy.

- It is a medium-risk strategy as product development often involves significant investment in research and development (R&D).

Diversification

- Diversification involves businesses marketing completely new products to new customers. It is a high-risk growth strategy as the business enters markets in which it has little or no experience.

- Related diversification means that organizations remain in a market (industry) that they are familiar with. Unrelated diversification involves businesses entering new industries, i.e. in which they have no previous market experience.

- For example, Honda launched its HondaJet (aircraft) division in 2015. Lenovo introduced smartphones, watches and sports shoes in 2015.

Table 1.17 Examples of diversification

Company	Original business	Company	Original business
American Express	Postal services	Peugeot	Toolmaker
Shell	Collectable shells	Nintendo	Playing cards
Nokia	Rubber and paper	Lamborghini	Tractors
Wrigley's	Soap and baking powder	Mitsubishi	Shipping

Table 1.18 Summary of the Ansoff Matrix

Market penetration	Product development	Market development	Diversification
Same products for existing customers	New products for existing customers	New customers for existing products	New products for new customers
Familiar markets	Product extension strategies and product development	Familiar products	Spreading of risks
Minimal risk	Moderate risk	Moderate risk	High risk
Seek to maintain or raise market share	Innovation to replace existing products	Entering overseas markets	Spreading of risks
Intense competition	Product improvements	New distribution channels	Use of subsidiaries and strategic business units
Changing marketing mix	Brand extension strategies	Changing marketing mix	Less focus on core markets and competencies

CUEGIS CONCEPTS

The needs of customers change over time. Investigate how the Ansoff Matrix is connected to the concepts of change and innovation for an organization of your choice.

1.4 Stakeholders

Revised ☐

The interests of internal stakeholders (AO2)

Revised ☐

> **Keyword definitions**
>
> **Stakeholders** are individuals, organizations or groups with a direct interest in the operations and performance of a particular business or organization. They have varying degrees of influence on the organization.
>
> **Internal stakeholders** are members of the organization, such as employees, managers, directors and shareholders (the owners of the business).

- **Employees** are the people who work within an organization. They can have significant influence on the organization, such as their level of motivation and productivity. Employees seek to improve the terms and conditions of employment, e.g. competitive levels of pay, job security, good working conditions and opportunities for professional advancement.

- **Managers** and **directors** are people hired to be in charge of certain departments or operations within an organization. They may aim to maximize profits, improve operational efficiency and enhance customer relations. They also strive to improve their own conditions of employment and financial rewards, such as bonuses, share ownership schemes, performance-related pay, and fringe benefits (see Unit 2.4).

- **Shareholders** are individuals or organizations that buy shares in a company, thereby owning a part of the business. As part-owners of the company, they have rights to a share of any profits earned (such payments are known as **dividends**), and voting rights at the company's Annual General Meeting (AGM) to decide who serves on the company's Board of Directors. They also expect the company to earn an acceptable return on their investment.

> **Expert tip**
>
> Shareholders can be classified as both internal and external stakeholders. For example, employees and directors may hold shares in the company so are internal stakeholders. However, the general public and other organizations may also own shares in the company but these stakeholders are external to the business.

> **Expert tip**
>
> Do not confuse the terms 'shareholders' with 'stakeholders'. The latter is a much broader term and includes more than shareholders. All shareholders of a business are stakeholders, but not all stakeholders are shareholders.

The interests of external stakeholders (AO2)

Revised ☐

- **Customers** are the clients of a business. They want overall value for money, i.e. prices that reflect the quality of the goods and services received, products that are safe and fit for their purpose, good customer care and the provision of after-sales support.

- **Suppliers** provide the goods and support services for other businesses, e.g. Coca-Cola supplies supermarkets with soft drinks and McKey's supplies McDonald's restaurants in Hong Kong and Southern China with its Chicken McNuggets. Suppliers are important stakeholders as they can decide what credit terms or discounts (if any) are offered to the business. They are interested in securing reasonable prices for their goods and services, regular orders and prompt payment from their business clients.

- **Competitors** are the rivals of a particular business. As external stakeholders, they are interested in the business operating in a fair and honest way. Competitors set their own targets and strategies based on the actions of other firms in the industry.

- The **local community** is interested in businesses acting in a socially responsible way, such as creating job opportunities, protecting the environment, and supporting local residents and events such as sponsorship of public events.

- **Pressure groups** are organizations or groups of people who have a common interest. They try to influence governments and public opinion in favour of their cause, such as environmental protection, fair trade or human rights. Therefore, these special interest groups put pressure on businesses to work in a socially responsible and ethical way (see Unit 1.3).

> **Keyword definition**
>
> **External stakeholders** are not members of a business or organization, yet have a direct stake (interest) in its operations and performance. Examples include customers, suppliers, competitors, the local community, pressure groups, financiers and the government.

- **Financiers** are banks and other creditors that provide sources of finance for businesses (see Unit 3.1). They are external stakeholders interested in the financial well-being of a business to assess its ability to repay debts such as bank loans and mortgages using quantitative factors such as liquidity (see Unit 3.7) and investment appraisal (see Unit 3.8).

- The **government** is a key external stakeholder of all businesses. It is keen to see that firms operate legally and in a socially responsible way. The government affects businesses directly by its policies, such as tax rates, employment legislation, consumer protection rights and environmental protection laws.

Possible areas of mutual benefit and conflict between stakeholders' interests (AO3)

Revised ☐

As outlined in the sections above, each stakeholder group has different interests in the various activities of a business. In practice, it is difficult to satisfy all stakeholder groups all of the time. There may be areas of mutual benefits, but there may also be disagreements or differences in opinions with others. For example, business growth can create jobs, thus creating positive impacts on the local community, such as creating more choice for consumers. However, business expansion in the local community might create traffic congestion and cause more pollution which defies the interest of pressure groups. Other examples of possible conflict between stakeholders' interests include:

- Owners of the business may be reluctant to pay higher wages to employees as they seek to use the surplus to distribute profits instead.

- Directors may want large bonuses but this may conflict with the desire of shareholders to have higher dividend pay outs.

- In general, customers may want lower prices, but shareholders may prefer higher prices as this would generate greater profit margins.

- In the pursuit of efficiency and productivity gains, employers may invest in new machinery, but this may result in redundancies (job losses) for employees (see Unit 2.1).

- Shareholders may demand a greater proportion of profits to be distributed as dividends, yet this leaves less funds for management to use on marketing, product development or to improve working conditions for their employees.

- Pressure groups might deem the corporate profits of some large multinational companies to be too high, although the management team would argue the profits are necessary to remain competitive.

- Acting in a socially responsible way, such as reducing and recycling waste, may help to please the local community but could upset directors and shareholders due to the high costs of compliance and implementation.

To some extent, stakeholder conflict is always likely to exist, so the varying interests of stakeholders must always be carefully managed. In order to deal with potential stakeholder conflict, businesses often use stakeholder mapping (see Figure 1.4) as a management tool to determine the key stakeholders. Stakeholder mapping (or stakeholder analysis) involves organizing the various stakeholders of the business into a matrix, based on their degree of power (influence) and their level of interest in the business.

The stakeholder groups with a high degree of power *and* interest are known as the **key stakeholders**. Successful businesses strive to fulfil as many of the needs and interests of various stakeholder groups as possible, but give priority to satisfying the needs and interests of their key stakeholders. Due to the complexities of operating large businesses, managing stakeholder interests in smaller businesses tends to be simpler.

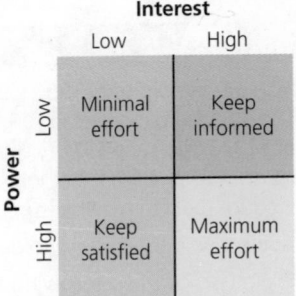

Figure 1.4 Stakeholder mapping

> **Keyword definition**
>
> **Stakeholder mapping** (or **stakeholder analysis**) is a management tool used to determine the key stakeholders of an organization based on the varying degrees of power and interest of the various stakeholder groups.

Potential solutions in handling stakeholder conflicts include the following:

- Use a **conciliation** service (see Unit 2.6) to align the conflicting interests of different stakeholder groups.

- Use an **arbitrator** to assess the conflicting interests, with the stakeholder groups agreeing to accept the judgment of the independent arbitrator (see Unit 2.6).

- Hiring **public relations** (PR) consultants (or use an internal PR team) to communicate with the local community and to keep other stakeholders informed of the positive aspects of the organization's operations or planned changes.

- Improved **communications** with the various stakeholder groups, i.e. keeping stakeholders informed of new developments and communicating the rationale for change.

- The use of **financial rewards** linked to employee productivity gains. This helps to motivate workers to perform more effectively, thereby enabling the business to earn more profits. Shareholders would also be content as higher profits should lead to higher dividends payments and increased share prices.

- Ensuring wider representation of stakeholders in the decision-making process, e.g. the involvement of a trade union representative in strategic decision making or including an employee representative at a Board of Directors' meeting.

In resolving conflict, the outcome of negotiations is largely influenced by the relative bargaining power of the various stakeholder groups. For example, employees who are backed by powerful labour unions may be in a better position to secure improved terms and conditions of employment. International pressure groups, such as Greenpeace and Friends of the Earth, can exert huge pressure on businesses, because they have greater backing of the general public and media.

However, it is possible to have mutual benefits between stakeholders' interests rather than conflict. For example, offering competitive financial rewards and good terms and conditions of employment for all workers can result in a highly motivated, loyal and productive workforce. This leads to lower staff turnover (see Unit 2.1) and greater output. It can also result in an improved corporate image, thereby helping with the firm's marketing and its recruitment. By contrast, conflict between management and the workforce can lead to industrial action such as strikes (see Unit 2.6). Ultimately, resolving the potential conflict between stakeholders leads to improved efficiency and higher profits.

Expert tip

Whilst different stakeholder groups have different aims and objectives, some stakeholders belong to multiple groups, e.g. managers are employees of the organization and might also be shareholders in the company. Hence, stakeholder analysis is a difficult balancing act of trying to meet the interests of most stakeholder groups.

EXAM PRACTICE

1 In 2015, HSBC announced 25 000 jobs losses around the world, including the sale of its troubled businesses in Turkey and Brazil (where it reported losses in 2014 of $232 million and $377 million respectively). The cuts would allow the banking giant to save $4.5–5 billion per year. Analysts suggested the news would reduce the return on investment for shareholders, at least in the short run.

   a Identify two internal stakeholders of HSBC.   [2]

   b Explain two conflicts following HSBC's decision to reduce its global workforce.   [4]

CUEGIS CONCEPTS

Investigate how the various stakeholder groups in an organization of your choice have influenced corporate culture and business strategy.

1.5 External environment

STEEPLE analysis of a given organization
(AO2, AO4)

- As a brainstorming framework, STEEPLE analysis is quite simple to construct and interpret.

- It can help managers be more objective, proactive and comprehensive in their analysis of external opportunities and threats for the business.

- Hence, the tool enables managers to be more informed and better prepared to deal with changes in the external business environment.

- The STEEPLE factors in the section below can provide both opportunities and threats for businesses.

> **Keyword definition**
> A **STEEPLE analysis** examines the influences in the external environment in which a business operates, i.e. social, technological, economic, ethical, political, legal, and environmental factors.

Social factors

Demographic changes are classified as a social factor. Changes in fashions and trends are also social factors affecting businesses. Other examples are shown below, which may not necessarily apply to all countries or regions of the world.

- An increasing number of people now live in single-person households.

- In many parts of the world such as France, the UK and Japan, there has been an increase in the retirement age.

- An ageing population is common in many economically developed countries, which has affected recruitment practices in these nations. Similarly, there is an increasing number of older and retired people living in these countries.

- Women in modern societies are choosing to have children at a later age due to the higher costs of raising children and due to the desire to advance their careers.

- A common trend is the increasing movement of young workers to cities away from rural areas.

Technological factors

- The increasing use of mobile devices and internet technologies provides huge opportunities for businesses engaged in e-commerce.

- The increasing number of businesses that strive to have a greater online presence by developing their e-commerce strategies.

- Advances in automation and industrial technologies that improve efficiency and productivity in the manufacturing process.

- Unemployment in certain industries due to the use of automation and more capital-intensive methods of production.

- The increasing ability to communicate with customers all around the world, using social networks and social media.

Economic factors

- The level of consumer confidence influences the level of demand in an economy.

- Higher costs of production will tend to force prices to go up. Higher prices will also tend to damage a country's international competitiveness.

- A currency appreciation reduces the competitiveness of an exporter's prices, e.g. an appreciation of the US dollar against the yen will tend to lead to a fall in US exports to Japan.

- An increase in interest rates makes borrowing more expensive, thus discourages investment expenditure. In addition, firms with existing loans have larger repayments.

- An economic boom is associated with an expanding economy, i.e. high levels of consumption, income and investment, creating many opportunities for businesses (see Figure 1.5).

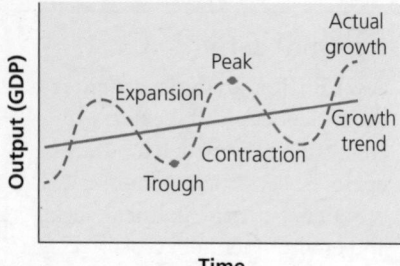

Figure 1.5 The business cycle

- By contrast, an economic recession occurs when the level of economic activity contracts for at least two consecutive quarters (half a year), caused by lower levels of consumption and investment expenditure in the economy.

Table 1.19 Phases in the business cycle

	Trough (Slump)	Expansion (Recovery)	Peak (Boom)	Contraction (Recession)
Consumer and business confidence	Very low confidence (pessimistic)	Increasing levels of confidence	Very high (optimistic)	Low and falling confidence levels
Consumer spending	Very low	Increasing	High	Falling
Economic growth	Negative GDP growth	Rising levels of GDP	Positive growth, high GDP	GDP begins to fall
Unemployment	Very high	Falling	Low	Rising
Inflation	Low or negative (deflation)	Rising prices	High price levels	Price levels begin to fall
Number of firms failing	High	Falling	Low	Rising
Business investment	Very low, if any	Rising	High	Falling

EXAM PRACTICE

2   Bristol Cars, a specialist British car maker, sells its sports cars at an average price of £120000 to customers in America. Calculate the change in the price paid by American customers if the US dollar depreciates from £1 = $1.6 to £1 = $1.8.   [2]

Environmental factors

- The depletion of renewable resources raises concerns about the sustainability of business activity (see Unit 5.1).

- Inclement weather and climate change are environmental factors that can cause major threats to businesses, e.g. severe flooding, droughts, typhoons, tsunamis and snowstorms.

- An increasing number of businesses use green technologies as part of their operations in order to conserve the planet, e.g. renewable energy sources or cradle to cradle design and manufacturing (see Unit 5.3).

- Firms also have to consider their ecological footprint, i.e. the impact of their business activities such as waste production on the natural environment. Firms that take an active approach can benefit from having a positive corporate image, whilst those that do not may face financial penalties.

Political factors

- Political instability due to regional conflict can be a major threat to business activity.

- The government might use the rate of income tax to manage the economy, e.g. countries such as Bahrain, Brunei, Kuwait and the Bahamas have a zero rate of income tax to attract a migration of workers.

- Laws such as censorship or bans on the production or sale of certain goods and services can be a threat to business operations.

- Some governments use trade protectionist measures to safeguard domestic businesses and jobs, e.g. a tariff on imported cars protects the domestic car industry.

- Similarly, governments may impose quotas (quantitative limits) on the number of foreign products sold in the country, e.g. Hollywood movies released in Hong Kong to protect the local film industry.

- Governments also provide subsidies as a form of protection for certain domestic industries, e.g. the French government for farmers and the Chinese government for the film (movie) industry.

- The government itself is a large consumer with its various forms of expenditure, e.g. education and health care services, and thus provides huge opportunities for some businesses.

Legal factors

- Businesses must meet certain legal standards that help to reduce any adverse effects from a company's operations, corporate image and profits.

- Many countries have data protection laws as a form of consumer protection.

- Businesses must operate within the constraints of employment laws, e.g. a National Minimum Wage, laws on maximum working hours, health and safety regulations, and anti-discrimination employment legislation.

- Smoking bans in restaurants, shopping malls and public parks can have a significant impact on businesses.

- Environmental protection legislation can impact on the production and investment decisions of businesses.

Ethical factors

- Businesses need to consider the impact of their activities on society and the environment.

- Ethical factors consider doing what is right or morally correct.

- Businesses are often presented with ethical dilemmas, e.g. determining how much of the firm's profits to keep for investment purposes or to distribute to shareholders.

- Bribery, fraud, embezzlement and theft are examples of unethical and illegal practices.

- Businesses choose to adopt environmental practices and to meet their corporate social responsibilities.

> **Expert tip**
>
> It is not always easy to classify external factors into the STEEPLE categories. For example, an increase in the tax on cigarettes can be regarded as a political, legal or economic factor. What matters is how you justify your answer.

Consequences of a change in any of the STEEPLE factors for a business's objectives and strategy (AO3)

- Oil prices around the world increased by 110% between 2007 and 2008.

- The global financial crisis of 2008 caused many countries to go into recession for several years. Countries were hit by another round of financial turmoil in late 2015 when Chinese, US and European stock markets crashed.

- In 2009, China overtook the USA as the world's largest car market by sales. This has a significant impact on the marketing strategies of all car makers around the world.

- Severe flooding in Kaohsiung, Taiwan (September 2010) cost the economy $211m.

- The devastating 9.0-magnitude earthquake followed by the tsunami that hit Japan on 11 March 2011 was the worst in Japanese history.

- Indonesian authorities outlawed Lady Gaga's *Born This Way Ball* concert tour in Jakarta (May 2012), following concerns from Islamists and local community leaders about her inappropriate image, dress code and use of language. More than 50 000 tickets had been sold.

- The Twitter feeds of several high profile companies were hacked into in February 2013, including Burger King and Jeep.

- In February 2013, frozen meat producer Findus had all its beef lasagne products withdrawn from UK supermarkets after horsemeat was found in some products.

> **Expert tip**
>
> The contextualized nature of the Business Management course means that you will need to be able to examine how changes in any combination of the STEEPLE factors impacts on the objectives and strategies of a particular basis. Some examples that you might choose to investigate further are outlined in this section.

> **CUEGIS CONCEPTS**
>
> Investigate how changes in the STEEPLE factors have affected the objectives and strategy for an organization of your choice.

Figure 1.6 Car wash firms struggle on a snowy day

1.6 Growth and evolution

Economies and diseconomies of scale (AO2)

- **Economies of scale** are the cost-saving benefits of operating on a large scale, i.e. the reduction in unit costs of production as an organization grows.

- By contrast, **diseconomies of scale** arise when unit costs increase due to the organization being too large and inefficient, e.g. problems with communication and coordination.

- Internal economies of scale are generated and enjoyed within the organization when it operates on a larger scale. Examples include:

  ☐ *Financial economies* – larger firms can obtain finance easier and at better lending rates due to their relatively lower risk.

  ☐ *Managerial economies* – larger organizations can afford greater numbers of specialized managers, thereby boosting productivity and output.

  ☐ *Production economies* – fixed costs of production are spread out over a larger volume of output, thereby reducing average fixed costs of production.

  ☐ *Marketing economies* – marketing costs per unit fall when sales volume grows as the larger firm can market its entire product range.

  ☐ *Purchasing economies* – bulk purchase and delivery of raw materials, components and stock reduces average costs of production.

- External economies of scale arise from having specialized back-up services available in a particular region where firms are located, e.g. Silicon Valley in California is home to many of the best-known technology companies.

- Diseconomies of scale occur when an organization becomes too large to manage effectively so its unit costs begin to increase, e.g. a firm increases its factor inputs by 50% but the subsequent output only increases by 20%.

- Internal diseconomies of scale are caused by problems of coordination, control and communication within a firm. For example:

  ☐ As firms get larger, managers find it more difficult to coordinate, control and communicate with a larger workforce, resulting in higher unit costs.

  ☐ It also occurs when fixed costs increase, such as the purchase of additional premises as a firm grows but this substantially increases its average costs of production.

- External diseconomies of scale (those that affect all firms in an industry) include:

  ☐ Traffic congestion causing costs to increase.

  ☐ Higher rent costs due to the high demand for firms locating in a particular area.

  ☐ Labour shortages in a certain area, thus leading to increased labour costs.

Keyword definitions

Internal economies of scale refers to the fall in unit costs of production for a single organization as it experiences growth, e.g. managerial and financial economies of scale.

External economies of scale refers to the fall in unit costs of production for all organizations as the industry experiences growth.

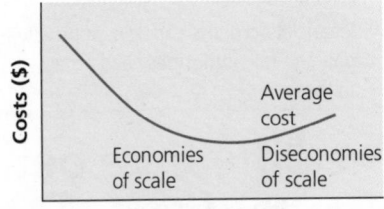

Figure 1.7 Economies and diseconomies of scale

Expert tip

Students often state that costs of production will fall as a firm increases the scale of its operations. This is not quite correct – clearly it is cheaper to produce 1000 cans of Coca-Cola than it is to produce 500 000 cans. However, it is cheaper to produce each can of Coca-Cola on a larger scale, i.e. economies of scale reduce the *average* costs of production.

EXAM PRACTICE

3 Armstrong's Candies has monthly fixed costs of $4800 and average variable costs of $1.50. Demand for its candies is 4000 units each month. The average unit price is $4.

  a Distinguish between internal and external economies of scale. [3]

  b Calculate the average costs for Armstrong's Candies each month. [2]

  c Calculate the profit made by Armstrong's Candies each month. [2]

Expert tip

Candidates need to demonstrate they clearly understand the distinction between internal economies of scale (which relate to a specific firm) and external economies of scale (which relate to the whole industry).

The merits of small versus large organizations (AO3)

Table 1.20 Merits of small versus large organizations

Merits of small organizations	Merits of large organizations
• Small businesses are easier to set up and at a much lower cost	• Greater access to financial resources; having more capital than their rivals means larger firms have scope for further growth
• Owners of small businesses enjoy independence in decision making, i.e. the freedom to operate independently from demands of directors and shareholders	• They can attract better skilled staff as they can offer better career development and remuneration packages
• Greater control and ownership of the business	• Customers tend to be attracted to larger, well known brand names as they recognize and trust these names more
• Greater ease in introducing new goods and/or services quickly, and typically more flexible in responding to changes in the marketplace	• Large firms are less likely to fail so represent lower risk for owners, investors and financiers; small firms are more vulnerable during an economic recession
• They can serve specialized niche markets that are potentially highly profitable	• Larger firms benefit from economies of scale so may be able to offer lower prices yet offer greater choice to customers
• Small businesses tend to have a closer relationship with their customers	• These advantages can give larger firms a competitive edge over smaller rivals
• Financial accounts can be kept private; only the tax authorities need access to these	

Expert tip

Students are not expected to give a definitive verdict about small versus large organizations. Both large and small businesses can thrive; the important thing is to consider size in a critical way and in the context of the organization. There are other factors to consider, e.g. size might not matter as much as the firm's vision and the organizational culture.

The difference between internal and external growth (AO2)

- **Internal growth** (also known as **organic growth**) occurs when an organization expands using its own resources, without involving other organizations, e.g. using Ansoff's Matrix strategies such as market penetration and product development (see Unit 1.3).

- **External growth** (also known as **inorganic growth**) occurs when a business relies on third party organizations for growth, e.g. mergers, acquisitions, and franchising.

- Key indicators of growth include an increase in an organization's sales revenue, its market share (see Unit 4.1), and the number of employees hired.

Table 1.21 Differences between internal and external growth

External growth	Internal growth
• External growth is usually the quickest form of growth	• Brand identity and corporate culture can be maintained
• Ordinarily requires external sources of finance (see Unit 3.1)	• Less risky, especially if financed by using retained profits (see Unit 3.1)
• Often results in the dilution of ownership	• Often involves expanding the range of products and/or locations
• Far more bureaucratic, especially with mergers and acquisitions (M&As)	
• Involves greater financial risk	
• In the case of M&As, external growth reduces or eliminates competition	

Methods of external growth (AO3)

Methods of external growth include: mergers and acquisitions (M&As), takeovers, joint ventures, strategic alliances, and franchising.

Mergers and acquisitions (M&As) and takeovers

- A takeover is a form of external growth that occurs when one company buys a controlling interest in another company, i.e. it purchases enough shares in the company to own a majority stake.

- For example, in July 2015 British publishing giant Pearson sold the *Financial Times* to Japanese media firm Nikkei for £844 million ($1.27 billion) in cash. Interestingly, the *FT* was founded through a merger in 1888.

■ Takeovers are often hostile, i.e. the target company does not wish to be bought out by the purchasing company.

■ Takeovers (also called acquisitions) often result in redundancies (job losses) of the target firm due to cost savings desired by the purchasing company.

Table 1.22 Advantages and disadvantages of M&As

Advantages of M&As	Disadvantages of M&As
● A range of economies of scale gained through external growth	● Resistance from employees, trade unions, managers and shareholders (who are unwilling to sell their shares)
● Enables the larger firm to spread costs, expertise and risks	● M&As are not always successful, especially when firms pursue a diversification strategy
● Quick way for the firm to enter new industries and geographic markets	● M&As are generally very expensive, especially if there are delays in the process; in some cases the purchase price ends up being unaffordable
● Instantaneous growth as M&As are quicker than methods of organic growth	
● The cutting of costs and synergies from M&As allow the business to earn higher profits and/or gain market share	● Corporate culture clashes, such as contrasting management styles and organizational structures, cause huge problems for M&As
● The newly formed business gains market power to influence prices and output in the industry	● Diseconomies of scale may occur due to a firm's loss of cost control and the loss of focus of its core activities
● A merger or takeover could be the only way that a business can survive due to its poor cash flow or financial difficulties	

■ Joint ventures

■ A joint venture (JV) is an arrangement between two or more separate parties to pool their resources together to form a new legal entity.

■ An example is Hong Kong Disneyland, a joint venture between the Hong Kong government (which owns 51% of the JV) and the Walt Disney Company (with a 49% stake).

■ The companies engaged in a JV seek profit, sharing resources (financial, capital and human), such as personnel, assets, costs and revenues.

Table 1.23 Advantages and disadvantages of joint ventures

Advantages of joint ventures	Disadvantages of joint ventures
● The firms combine their resources, such as technology and capital, creating synergies and strengthening their position in the market	● Possible conflicts and disagreements due to different corporate cultures and management styles of the partner firms
● Financial risks of the project are shared between the partner companies	● Compromises are often made with JVs and this can lead to suboptimal outcomes for both parent companies
● Local firms can enable the partner to overcome cultural difficulties that a foreign company may encounter	● Execution of business strategy is more decisive with acquisitions and takeovers
● JVs enable companies to become larger and thus benefit from economies of scale	● Diseconomies of scale may occur due to operations on a larger scale, e.g. extra meetings and administrative processes, and communication problems
● The partner firms enjoy the advantages of growth without losing their identities	● JVs are generally more difficult to terminate due to the lawfully binding obligations of the newly created legal entity
● Firms in the JV avoid high legal and administrative costs associated with M&As	

■ Strategic alliances

■ Strategic alliances (SAs) are formed when two or more businesses join forces to benefit from growth without any fundamental changes to their own long-term strategies.

■ Unlike joint ventures, the formation of a strategic alliance does not create a new organization.

■ Examples include the SA between Starbucks and Barnes & Noble (coffee shop chain and bookstore) which started in 1993. Apple has partnered with Sony, Motorola, Phillips, and AT&T. The Star Alliance consists of 27 airlines, forming the world's largest global SA in the airline industry.

Table 1.24 Advantages and disadvantages of strategic alliances

Advantages of strategic alliances	Disadvantages of strategic alliances
● Like JVs, firms in a strategic alliance can benefit by sharing expertise and resources with other firms in the SA	● Unlike joint ventures, strategic alliances are easier to enter and exit so can be less stable
● Businesses in the SA remain separate legal entities, without the relatively high costs of forming a new company	● Strategic alliances are sometimes only short term, temporary agreements
● Synergies and economies of scale can be gained by the partner firms in the SA	● It can make a business vulnerable to mistakes or malpractice made by partner firms in the SA

■ Franchising

■ Franchising refers to an agreement between a business (the franchisor) giving the legal rights to other organizations (the franchisees) to sell products under the franchisor's brand name.

■ Examples of multinational companies that use franchising include: McDonald's, Subway, Starbucks, Pizza Hut, KFC and Holiday Inn.

Figure 1.8 McDonald's is a multinational company that uses franchising

Table 1.25 Advantages and disadvantages of franchising

Advantages of franchising	Disadvantages of franchising
● The franchisor can expand the business without the need to raise finance and invest their own funds to make the business grow (as the franchisee pays for the expansion); hence it is a cheaper method of expansion than organic growth	● Not all businesses have the expertise to properly manage the franchising model in terms of quality control and marketing activities
● The franchisor receives royalties based on a predetermined percentage of the franchisee's sales revenues	● It can be very expensive for the franchisee in terms of start-up costs and running costs as it has to pay a percentage of its sales revenues to the franchisor
● It is a relatively fast method of external growth which can strengthen the brand name quickly	● The franchisee is also usually charged an annual fee by the franchisor, so this can substantially cut the franchisee's profit margin
● The franchisor does not need to closely monitor or control the day-to-day operations of the franchisee (whereas monitoring and control must take place with directly-owned stores)	● The franchisee lacks flexibility in decision making as it needs to follow the corporate rules and policies of the franchisor, including what it can and cannot sell, and the marketing used to promote the firm's goods and services
● The franchising model is usually a tried and tested one, so the success rate is high; hence, there can be large profits made for the franchisee and franchisor	● Diseconomies of scale can arise, even with franchises, especially if the franchise over expands in too short a time scale
● Economies of scale, such as purchasing economies of scale, can be gained and passed onto franchisees when buying products to be sold	● Incompetent, substandard or dishonest franchisees can easily damage the corporate image and reputation of the franchisor's brand
● The franchisee receives ongoing support from the franchisor, e.g. marketing, market research, staff training, and distribution networks	

The role and impact of globalization on the growth and evolution of businesses (AO3)

Revised

- **Globalization** is the growing degree of integration and interdependence of the world's economies. Decisions and actions taken in one part of the world have a direct impact on those in other parts of the world.

- A major contributing factor to globalization is the growth and expansion of multinational companies (MNCs). There is increasing pressure for MNCs to market their brands to a worldwide audience.

- Cultural exports, such as Hollywood movies or American fast food, have led to increased globalization. This creates business opportunities for firms looking to grow and evolve.

- Globalization has both positive and negative effects on businesses, e.g. it stimulates competition as there are more foreign firms and products competing in the domestic market.

- A lack of international business etiquette can cause offence to others. Habits, fashions and tastes may differ in overseas countries so different customs may need to be considered.

- The deregulation of trade restrictions around the world has allowed domestic businesses to enter overseas markets, thereby enabling these firms to benefit from economies of scale and a larger customer base.

- Internet technologies have also contributed to globalization, with social media making it increasingly easier for people and businesses around the world to connect. E-commerce (see Unit 4.8) has improved consumer access to a huge range of markets.

- Advocates of globalization argue that it has increased job opportunities around the world, so has significantly reduced the number of people living in poverty.

Reasons for the growth of multinational companies (MNCs) (AO3)

Revised

Reasons for the growth of MNCs include:

- MNCs benefit from access to larger markets in foreign countries.

- They usually benefit from economies of scale.

- They spread risks by operating in other markets, not just within their own country.

- MNCs often operate on a large, global scale with powerful brand names.

- MNCs expand overseas as a market development strategy (see Ansoff's Matrix, Unit 1.3), when other markets are saturated.

- They can exploit the potential growth opportunities in certain overseas markets that are still untapped.

- Cost-saving benefits of operating in overseas countries, e.g. cheaper labour, lower tax rates, access to cheaper raw materials and components, or being closer to global customers.

Keyword definition

A **multinational company (MNC)** is an organization that operates, owns, or controls production and/ or service facilities in two or more countries.

Expert tip

MNCs are not without their complications and limitations. They are, for example, exposed to additional risks when operating in overseas markets, e.g. cultural differences in business practices, legal differences, political risks and volatility with fluctuating foreign exchange rates.

The impact of MNCs on the host countries (AO3)

Positive impacts of MNCs on the host countries include the following:

■ MNCs provide a significant number of employment opportunities, helping to raise the quality of the labour force in the host country.

■ MNCs are likely to buy local raw materials and components, thus providing extra revenue for local suppliers and supporting local industries (such as packaging and distribution).

■ Consumers in the host country do not have to rely only on local suppliers as they have more choice from MNCs, thus helping to raise standards of living.

■ Similarly, increased competition from MNCs can force local firms to improve their operational efficiency, quality, customer care and prices.

■ The transfer of technical knowledge and benchmarking practices (see Unit 5.3) from MNCs can also benefit local firms.

■ Profitable MNCs will be taxed by the host government, thus providing added tax revenue to benefit the host economy.

Negative impacts of MNCs on the host countries include the following:

■ Local businesses may lose customers, market share and profit to foreign MNCs.

■ Foreign companies may not be socially responsible, especially if rules and regulations are more relaxed in overseas markets, which might result in employees being exploited, scarce resources being depleted or increasing pollution levels.

■ The existence of large and powerful MNCs can destroy local competitors as they do not have the resources to compete.

■ Not all local people and businesses will welcome the presence of foreign companies, especially if it results in a cultural shift in the way of life, and may result in social tension.

CUEGIS CONCEPTS

Investigate how globalization has impacted on the growth and evolution for a business of your choice.

EXAM PRACTICE

4   In 2015 Kraft Foods Group Inc., merged with H.J. Heinz Co. to form the world's fifth-largest food and beverage company. Heinz is a global brand, famous for its tomato ketchup, sauces, soups, beans, pasta and infant foods. Kraft is one of North America's largest consumer packaged food and beverage companies, with annual sales revenues of more than $18 billion and over 22 000 employees in the USA.

   a   Define the term merger.   [2]

   b   Examine the possible reasons for the merger between Kraft and Heinz.   [6]

1.7 Organizational planning tools (*HL only*)

Revised ☐

Planning tools (AO2, AO4) and their value to an organization (AO3)

Revised ☐

Planning is an essential element of business management. There are a number of planning tools available to help managers in the process. Strategic planning is about the direction of the business and is fundamental to the setting of goals, targets and objectives (see Unit 1.3).

■ Fishbone diagram

- The fishbone diagram (also known as the **Cause and Effect** model) is a visual decision-making tool devised by the Japanese guru on quality, Professor Kaoru Ishikawa.

- It is used to identify the root causes (shown as bones) of a problem or issue (shown as the 'head' of the fish).

- A business might face a problem, for example, of high labour turnover (i.e. the proportion of its workforce that leaves the organization during the year). An example is shown in Figure 1.9.

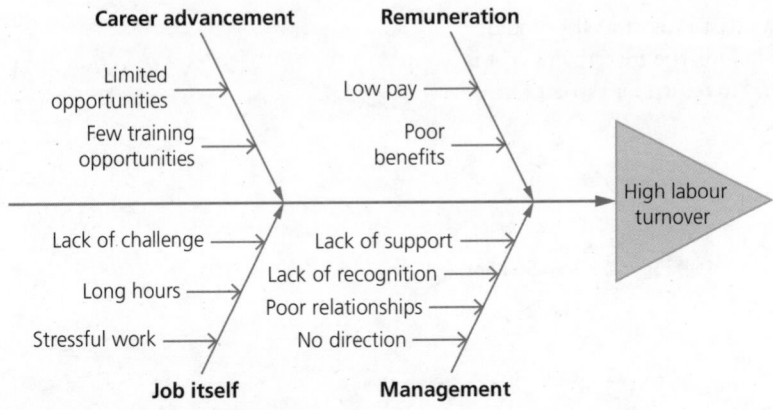

Figure 1.9 Fishbone diagram

Table 1.26 Advantages and disadvantages of the fishbone diagram

Advantages of the fishbone diagram	Disadvantages of the fishbone diagram
• It shows a variety of probable causes of a given problem in a succinct way	• Causes and effects are not always interrelated, making the construction of the fishbone more difficult and less meaningful
• As a visual tool, it is easy to follow in order to determine the root causes and consequences of a problem or issue	• As a qualitative decision-making tool, it does not include any quantifiable data so it is difficult to ascertain how much each factor actually contributes to the problem
• It organizes the causes of a problem by themes, such as communication issues or motivation problems, thus aiding the decision-making process	• Similarly, it does not show which decisions or actions need to be prioritized

■ Decision trees

- A decision tree is a quantitative and systematic decision-making tool that allows managers to visualize possible options and their probable outcomes.

- In a decision tree, a circle represents a chance node. A square represents a choice or decision.

- Probabilities of the various outcomes are shown, e.g. 0.35 means there is a 35% chance (likelihood) of the outcome actually materializing. Probabilities for each chance node must add up to 1.0, i.e. 100% likelihood.

- Figure 1.10 illustrates the decision of a firm to pursue either Project Chicago (which costs $55m) or Project Delhi (which costs $51m). The following can be seen from the decision tree:

  - There is a 65% chance of success if the firm chooses Project Chicago, which would gain the firm $70m in sales revenue. Thus, the likely outcome is $70m × 0.65 = $45.5m.

  - There is a 35% chance of failure for Project Chicago, with expected revenues of only $45m. Hence, the probable outcome is $45m × 0.35 = $15.75m.

  - Therefore, the combined outcome for Project Chicago is $45.5m + $15.75m = $61.25m. After the costs of the project are accounted for, the likely yield (return) of Project Chicago is $61.25m – $55m = $6.25m.

  - For Project Delhi, there is a 55% chance of success in earning $80m. Hence, the likely outcome is $80m × 0.55 = $44m.

  - If the project fails, the likely outcome of earning $35m in sales revenue is $35m × 0.45 = $15.75m.

  - Hence, the combined likely outcome is $44m + $15.75m = $59.75m. The likely profit is therefore $59.75m – $51m = $8.75m.

- Two parallel lines that cross through a branch represent the options that are rejected based on quantitative grounds.

- Examining the decision tree in Figure 1.10 shows that Project Delhi should be pursued. Despite the relatively higher risk of failure, the investment cost is lower and the likely yield is an extra $2.5m ($8.75m return for Project Delhi compared to $6.25m for Project Chicago).

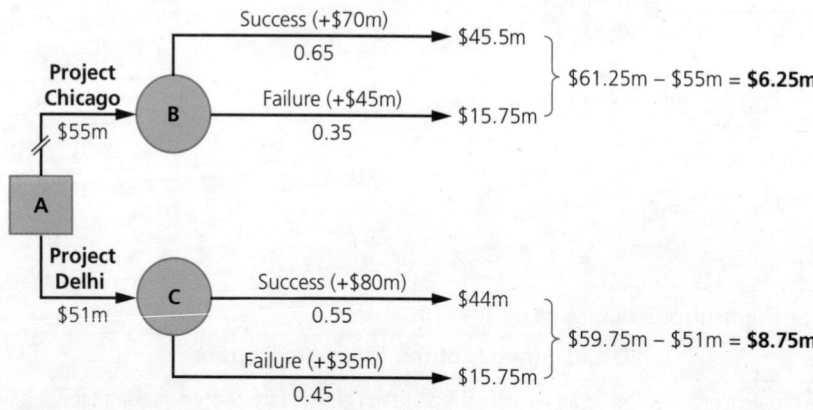

Figure 1.10 Example of a decision tree

Table 1.27 Advantages and disadvantages of decision trees

Advantages of decision trees	Disadvantages of decision trees
• Formalizes the decision-making process and makes it more impartial as outcomes can be compared objectively	• Qualitative factors affecting decision making are ignored, e.g. business objectives and stakeholder views
• Offers a visual and logical representation of various decisions with quantifiable outcomes, thus making things easier to follow	• Data on likely outcomes are only forecasts so actual outcomes can be quite different
• Management is forced to consider the risks of different options	• Data can become out of date by the time a decision is actually taken
	• External factors and non-financial information are ignored in the diagram

EXAM PRACTICE

5 Kingmans Educational Resources (KER) is considering expanding into one of three locations. The expected costs and revenues are shown in the table below. KER only has the resources to pursue one of these growth options.

Using the data in the table, construct a decision tree showing which project is best on financial grounds. Show all your workings and include an appropriate key in your diagram. [6]

Project	Probability (%)	Cost ($m)	Revenue ($m)
Ashtown		100	
Success	50		215
Failure	50		80
Brigcity		80	
Success	65		180
Failure	35		75
Centrapolis		90	
Success	60		175
Failure	40		90

▇ Force field analysis

- Force field analysis (FFA) was devised by German-American psychologist Kurt Lewin as a planning and decision-making framework for examining the factors for and against change.

- The factors (or forces) that support change towards a goal are called driving forces, whereas those that block or hinder change are called restraining forces.

- These forces are numerically weighted in order to calculate the relative strengths of driving and restraining forces, thereby aiding decision making in an objective and quantifiable way.

- In Figure 1.11, the weights range from 1 to 5, with 5 being of most significance to the business. In the example, as the driving forces outweigh the restraining forces, the objective decision is to relocate the business.

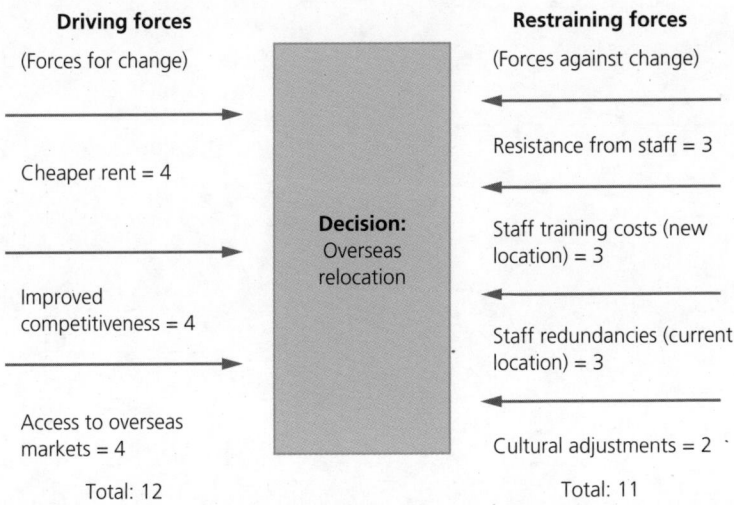

Figure 1.11 Force field analysis for overseas relocation

Table 1.28 Advantages and disadvantages of force field analysis

Advantages of FFA	Disadvantages of FFA
• As a quantitative planning tool, it makes the decision-making process more objective and logical	• Qualitative factors affecting decision making are ignored and/or difficult to quantify
• It offers a simple visual representation of the forces for and against change	• The omission of certain driving or restraining forces can alter the outcome quite drastically
• Weighting (numerical values) the forces makes managers consider the relative importance of factors affecting the decision	• The weighting of the forces is subjective, leaving room for potential bias

Expert tip

HL students who choose to use force field analysis in their Internal Assessment are reminded to consult the management of the organization to weight the driving and restraining forces. There is no significance in students assigning the weights as this adds no value to management.

Gantt chart

■ A Gantt chart, devised by American engineer Henry L. Gantt, is a visual planning tool that illustrates the sequencing and schedule of a particular project.

■ Links established between dependent tasks allow managers to sequence the various activities (tasks) of a particular project, i.e. it shows what must be completed before the next task(s) can begin.

■ The required time and resources can then be linked to each of the tasks in the project.

■ Ultimately, a Gantt chart helps project managers to determine how long a project should take to complete.

■ An example of a Gantt chart using the data in Table 1.29 is shown in Figure 1.12.

Table 1.29 Activities for Project X

Activity	Preceded by	Duration (days)
A	–	3
B	–	3
C	–	3
D	A	2
E	B	4
F	C	3
G	D, E and F	7

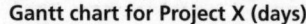

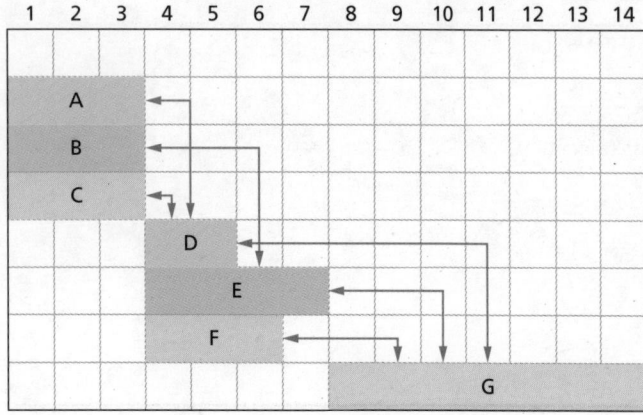

Figure 1.12 Example of a Gantt chart

Table 1.30 Advantages and disadvantages of Gantt charts

Advantages of Gantt charts	Disadvantages of Gantt charts
• Show the dependencies between different activities in order to minimize the time needed to complete a project	• The length of time (each bar) does not necessarily correlate with the amount of work or resources involved for each activity
• There are wide applications, e.g. scheduling production processes, employee work rosters, and holiday schedules	• Need to be monitored and may need regular updating
• Help managers to set realistic deadlines for the various activities of a project	• Complex projects may be difficult to display on a one-page Gantt chart
• Simple to interpret and understand	• Its simplicity means that a Gantt chart may not provide enough detail or information for complex projects
• Allow managers to monitor progress and take corrective measures	• Based on and reliant on the estimates of the timings of each task

Expert tip

HL students can produce a Gantt chart for the Action Plan of their Internal Assessment. Not only can this provide a neat and succinct visual of the intended activities for the IA, it also helps with the 500-word limit for the Research Proposal and Action Plan.

EXAM PRACTICE

6   Construct a Gantt chart from the data given in the table below
    for Project A.   [4]

Activity	Order	Duration (weeks)
A	–	3
B	A	2
C	A	1
D	B	3
E	C	2
F	D & E	5

Expert tip

Whilst quantitative techniques such as force field analysis, decision trees and Gantt charts provide quantifiable answers to complex decisions, it is important to remember that managers also consider qualitative factors in the process, e.g. the impact of decisions on the workforce and whether the decision is in line with organizational objectives.

2.1 Functions and evolution of human resource management

Human resource planning (workforce planning) (AO1)

- **Workforce planning** involves analysing and forecasting the numbers of workers and the skills of those workers that will be needed by the organization, e.g. new recruits are needed as a business expands or because current employees leave.

- Human resource (HR) planning aims for the effective management of an organization's workforce in order to achieve its objectives.

- Human resource planning functions include recruitment, induction (of new staff), retention, dismissal, redundancies, training and performance appraisals. It also involves monitoring and maintaining professional relations between employees and employers.

- Workforce planning involves an analysis of historical data relating to the size of the workforce, the workload and mobility (flexibility) of employees, labour turnover rates, and demographic trends in society.

- HR planning is also needed to deal with instances of **absenteeism**. This refers to the number of staff away from work as a percentage of the firm's total workforce, per time period.

- Successful workforce planning helps a firm to develop a competitive advantage by matching human resource needs to the organization's strategic direction. It enables workers to be properly trained and highly motivated so that they perform at their best.

> **Keyword definition**
>
> **Human resource planning** is the management process of anticipating and meeting an organization's current and future staffing needs.

Labour turnover (AO2)

- Labour turnover is calculated using the formula:

$$\frac{\text{Number of staff leaving per year}}{\text{Average number of staff}} \times 100$$

- It is inevitable in an organization as some employees leave for personal or professional reasons, e.g. to have a baby or spend more time with their young children, to retire or to pursue a promotional post in another organization.

- Retaining staff in the organization is important as there are significant costs to recruiting new staff, training them and getting them acclimatized to the organizational culture.

- Causes of high labour turnover include:

  - ☐ Better pay and working conditions offered by rival firms.

  - ☐ An unhappy and discontented workforce.

  - ☐ Staff being inadequately trained so feel incompetent and demotivated.

- Businesses try to avoid having a high labour turnover rate because this would lead to higher costs of recruitment (and retention). It also uses up a large amount of management time.

- Having a large number of new workers also means there is greater down-time when employees are less productive simply because they have yet to acclimatize to their new working environment, policies, procedures and processes.

- High labour turnover also raises concerns about stability and continuity in the business.

> **Keyword definition**
>
> **Labour turnover** measures the rate of change of human resources within an organization, per period of time.

EXAM PRACTICE

1 Duffy & Wong Ltd hire 86 people. Thirteen of the employees resign within the year. Calculate the firm's labour turnover rate. [2]

Internal and external factors that influence human resource planning (AO3)

Revised ☐

■ Demographic change

■ Demographic change refers to developments and trends in the population that influence workforce planning, e.g. the average age of the population, gender distribution, educational attainment levels and average household income.

■ In some countries, such as France and Britain, the official retirement age has been raised due to the longer life expectancy of workers.

■ The combination of lower birth rates, falling death rates and increased life expectancy in many economically developed countries has led to an **ageing population** (an increase in the average age of the population). This has several implications on workforce planning:

  ☐ reduced labour mobility

  ☐ lower labour productivity levels

  ☐ changing consumption patterns.

■ In many countries, there has been an increased number of women in the workforce. More females are choosing to have children at a later stage in their lives, opting instead to participate in the workforce and pursue their professional aspirations.

■ Change in labour mobility

■ **Occupational mobility** refers to the ease and flexibility of workers in moving from one job to another due to their ability and willingness to switch.

■ By contrast, occupational immobility is the inability of workers to move from one job to another, due to a lack of skills, expertise or qualifications.

■ **Geographical mobility** refers to the extent to which workers are able and willing to relocate to another area for employment purposes.

■ Geographical immobility is the reluctance of workers to move to another location. This might be due to personal reasons (such as family ties) or financial factors (such as relocation costs, property prices, or the higher costs of living in new locations).

■ International labour mobility is even more difficult to achieve. Expatriate workers are often highly remunerated as an incentive for them to relocate overseas.

■ Labour mobility can be improved by the business offering training and development programmes to its employees.

■ New communications technologies

■ New communications technologies make it easier for larger businesses to recruit globally through their websites and video-conferencing facilities, resulting in reduced costs of online advertising, recruitment and interviews.

■ Improved computer and mobile technologies also mean that flexitime, homeworking and teleworking become more attractive and accessible to workers.

■ The technologies make it possible to train and develop employees in a more efficient manner, e.g. online training courses or webinars. A large number of employees can be trained very quickly at the same time.

■ The use of computerized testing programs helps firms to assess the understanding and progress of trainees.

■ New communications technologies reduce the costs of business meetings and seminars due to the growing use of high-quality video-conferencing.

Common steps in the process of recruitment (AO2)

Revised

- **Job analysis** is the process of identifying what a particular job entails, e.g. the tasks, roles, responsibilities and skills required. From the analysis, the job description and person specification can be created.

- A **job description** is a document that provides details of a particular job, e.g. the job title, roles, duties and responsibilities.

- The **person specification** is a document that gives the profile of the ideal candidate for a job, e.g. a description of the qualifications, skills, experience, knowledge and other attributes. This is used as part of the selection process for shortlisting candidates for interview.

- Job advertisements are typically released after the job analysis has been completed and the job description and person specification produced.

- Candidates usually have to complete an application form for the job. They may also need to include a curriculum vitae (or résumé) – a document which outlines the applicant's educational achievements, professional qualifications, employment history, skills, accomplishments, hobbies and interests.

- **Shortlisting** is the systematic process of identifying and selecting the few most suitable candidates from all the applicants for an interview, because they best fit the profiles in the job description and person specification. Shortlisting eliminates unsuitable candidates from the recruitment process.

- Shortlisted candidates are then invited for interviews and (in some cases) testing in order to select the most suitable candidate for the job.

- Testing is used for some jobs to ensure the best candidate is recruited. Examples include:

    - **Aptitude testing:** a method of assessing the skills and ability of a candidate to do a particular job, e.g. typing speed for a receptionist or driving ability for a driving instructor.

    - **Psychometric tests:** used to assess the attitudes and personality traits of candidates, e.g. their level of drive (or motivation) and their ability to deal with stressful situations. These are used to ensure the chosen candidate is a good match with the organizational culture.

    - **Trade tests:** industry-specific assessments used to examine the candidate's skills and expertise in a specific profession.

    - **Intelligence tests:** used to assess a candidate's skills of numeracy, literacy and general knowledge.

- Background checks are made with **referees** (one of whom is likely to be the current or last employer) to ensure information declared by the applicant is truthful and to get a character reference so the business can assess the suitability of the candidate.

- A **job offer** is made to the most suitable candidate prior to issuing a contract of employment.

■ Internal recruitment

- Internal recruitment is the hiring of people from within the organization to fill a job vacancy.

- It is commonly used for targeting suitable employees for supervisory or management positions.

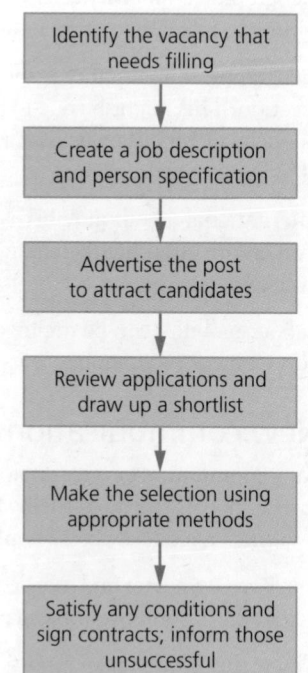

Figure 2.1 The recruitment process

Source: *Business Review*, February 2013

Table 2.1 Advantages and disadvantages of internal recruitment

Advantages of internal recruitment	Disadvantages of internal recruitment
• Lower risks as the employer already knows the strengths and suitability of the existing worker	• 'Dead wood' (outdated practices) might exist in the organization so an external candidate could bring in new ideas
• Relatively lower costs of recruitment compared to external recruitment	• Similarly, external candidates may be more skilled or better qualified
• It is generally faster than external recruitment	• A lower number of applicants can mean the employer has fewer candidates to choose from
• It strengthens the loyalty of employees as there are career development opportunities within the organization	• It can create unnecessary internal competition and conflict between existing workers who apply for a particular job
• It reduces or eliminates the need for induction as existing workers are already familiar with the practices and organizational culture	• Hiring someone internally means there is a vacancy created, so another person still has to be recruited

■ External recruitment

■ External recruitment is the hiring of people from outside of the organization.

■ It requires placing job advertisements using a range of media to attract potential applicants, e.g. newspapers, websites and trade magazines.

■ Interviews are the main method of selection for both internal and external recruitment.

■ In some cases, specialist recruitment agencies in a particular industry take responsibility for advertising, interviewing, selecting and hiring suitable people. In return, they charge a fee for their services.

■ The advantages and disadvantages of external recruitment are the opposite to those of internal recruitment (see Table 2.1), e.g. it can be difficult to determine the suitability of an external candidate to fit into the culture of the organization.

Types of training (AO2)

Revised ☐

■ Training is the process of teaching a particular new skill or knowledge in order to develop a person's competence in the workplace. The purpose is to match the skills of employees with the needs of the organization.

■ It is important as it improves the productivity of workers, boosts motivation and reduces labour turnover. Training can also help to improve customer service and customer relations.

■ A business that invests in its people can benefit from an improved reputation, which helps to attract good quality candidates in the recruitment process.

■ The main types of training are on the job, off the job, cognitive and behavioural.

■ On the job (including induction and mentoring)

■ **Induction** – This type of training is intended for employees who are new to the organization. It aims to support new staff in getting acquainted with the people, plans, policies and processes of the firm.

> ☐ It can help new workers to avoid costly mistakes by familiarizing themselves with standard procedures, formalities and codes of conduct.

> ☐ Induction training can be costly as it uses up valuable management time to set up and run the training for new staff.

■ **Mentoring** – This is the process of an adviser or trainer (the mentor) providing support to less experienced colleagues (the mentees) in various aspects of their job role, e.g. a head of department providing advice and training to new employees.

> **Keyword definition** ·
> **On-the-job training** is training conducted within the workplace whilst the employee is working.

Table 2.2 Advantages and disadvantages of on-the-job training

Advantages of on-the-job training	Disadvantages of on-the-job training
• Cheapest form of training if the firm uses in-house specialists to provide the training	• Trainees may pick up bad working habits from the trainer
• Training is relevant as it is targeted at specific issues related to the firm's needs	• Internal staff may lack the necessary skills, confidence and experience to deliver the training
• Fewer disruptions to daily operations as the trainee is still at work	• Internal trainers cannot get their own work done whilst planning or delivering the training
• Can help to build better relationships at work due to team working	

Off the job

- **Day release** – Employees take time off work to attend training at a local college, training centre or conference centre, e.g. IB teachers attend three-day workshops as part of their professional reflection and development.

- **Distance learning** – Employees undertake self-study courses to improve their skills and qualifications, perhaps by attending evening classes or following an online training course.

- **Seminars** – Staff attend a lecture or meeting as part of their professional learning and training.

> **Keyword definition**
> **Off-the-job training** is training conducted by specialists away from the workplace.

Table 2.3 Advantages and disadvantages of off-the-job training

Advantages of off-the-job training	Disadvantages of off-the-job training
• A wider range of skills and qualifications can be obtained	• It is more expensive than on-the-job training, e.g. training course fees
• Staff can learn from outside specialists or experts who may not exist within the organization	• Lost productivity during time when staff attend the training
• Employees are not distracted from the daily operations in the workplace	• Employees gaining new skills and qualifications may decide to leave the firm for better jobs elsewhere

Cognitive training

- Cognitive training refers to exercising and developing the mental skills of employees so as to improve their performance and productivity.

- Cognition is the brain's ability to learn and think, so cognitive thinking helps to develop the learning and thinking skills of employees.

- It focuses on improving memory, attention, perception, reasoning, judgement and general learning skills.

- Research has shown that cognitive training can lead to improvements in the self-esteem, self-confidence and emotional stability of employees.

Behavioural training

- Behavioural training seeks to change or improve the patterns of behaviour at work based on the desired outcomes.

- Examples of such behaviours include: team building, conflict resolution training, anger management, stress management, leadership training, mindfulness, emotional intelligence courses, or health and safety training.

- An important aspect of behavioural training is to identify the functional issues that could be hindering performance. Case studies and role plays are often used to facilitate this.

- Essentially, behavioural training strives to improve both personal and professional effectiveness.

Types of appraisal (AO2)

- Appraisals are conducted for several reasons, including:

  ☐ assessing an employee's performance against pre-agreed targets

  ☐ identify training needs of the individual employee

  ☐ helping the management to reward high achieving employees.

- Target setting is an integral part of appraisals. Targets should be SMART: specific, measureable, achievable, realistic and time bound.

- If an employee's performance is deemed to be less than satisfactory, it should be followed by providing relevant training or counselling. Such appraisals do not necessarily result in severe or demotivating measures such as warning letters or dismissal.

- Different organizations use different appraisal systems, such as: formative, summative, 360-degree feedback, and self-appraisal.

> **Keyword definition**
>
> **Appraisal** refers to the formal assessment of an employee's performance with reference to the roles and responsibilities set out in the job description.

Formative appraisal

- Formative appraisal takes place on an on-going basis to enable employees to improve their job performance.

- It helps to identify an employee's strengths and weaknesses in a specific role or the progress made in a particular task or project.

- It helps the organization to identify the training needs of an individual employee.

Summative appraisal

- Summative appraisals take place periodically, such as quarterly or annually, conducted by the line manager who summarizes the personal performance and achievements of the appraisee.

- The appraisee is held accountable for the outcome of his or her work, including identifying any areas for improvement.

360-degree feedback

- 360-degree feedback is an appraisal system that involves getting comments, opinions and information about an appraisee from the various groups of people who work with that person, e.g. peers, line managers and subordinates.

- 360-degree feedback is usually obtained using questionnaires, surveys, observations or interviews.

- In some cultures, such an approach to appraisal (where a senior member of staff is appraised by a junior colleague) would be deemed inappropriate and might not produce open and truthful discussions.

Self-appraisal

- Self-appraisal involves employees evaluating themselves against a predetermined set of criteria. The appraisee reflects on their strengths and weaknesses in order to set new targets for themselves.

- To avoid potential bias and any inconsistencies, self-appraisals are often used in conjunction with an appraisal conducted by the line manager.

Common steps in the processes of dismissal and redundancy (AO1)

- Dismissal is fair if an employee loses his/her job due to incompetence or gross misconduct in the workplace, e.g. theft, fraud, drunkenness, violence or sleeping on the job.

- Managers have to handle dismissals very carefully. There needs to be very definitive and comprehensive reasons for dismissing a worker to prevent any legal challenges being made in a court of law.

- In most cases, dismissal based on race, religion, age, gender, or sexual preferences is regarded as unfair dismissal.

- In general, dismissals go through a three-stage process: issuing the staff member an initial verbal warning, followed by a formal written warning, and finally termination of contract if the employee fails to meet the agreed targets.

- Redundancy occurs when a firm can no longer afford to employ a worker, when a job ceases to exist due to the completion of a project, or a lack of available work.

- Redundancies can be voluntary or compulsory. Voluntary redundancies are often associated with generous compensation packages (severance pay). Involuntary redundancies happen as a last resort, often causing low staff morale and instability in the organization.

- It can be difficult for a business to decide which workers to make involuntarily redundant. This needs to be done objectively, e.g. based on a last-in-first-out system (number of years of service with the organization).

> **Keyword definitions**
>
> **Dismissal** refers to the termination of a worker's employment due to their incompetence or breach of employment contract.
>
> **Redundancy** occurs when a business can no longer afford to hire a certain number or group of workers or because the job ceases to exist, perhaps due to seasonal or technological factors.

How work patterns, practices and preferences change and how they affect the employer and employees (AO2)

■ Teleworking

- Teleworking refers to employees working away from the office by using electronic forms of communication, e.g. telephone, the internet or mobile technologies.

- Homeworking is an example of teleworking, where staff work from home.

- Advancements in telecommunications and internet technologies, as well as rising office rents, have increased the number of businesses choosing to use teleworking.

- Teleworkers can benefit from autonomy in decision making and the absence of strict company policies, such as dress codes.

- However, productivity can be an issue due to the distractions at home or the lack of control when working outside of an office environment.

■ Flexitime

- Flexitime is a variable work schedule requiring employees to work a set number of hours but giving employees the right to choose when they work. There is normally a core (peak) period during the day when employees must be at work. This is common in the tech industry.

- Flexitime and part-time workers have led to a fall in the numbers of full-time workers in several industries, e.g. supermarkets and fast food.

- Such practices help to improve employee morale and productivity by improving the way they operate.

- Flexitime has cost implications for the business as managers need to supervise and monitor the hours actually worked by all flexitime employees.

■ Migration for work

■ Migrants usually move to other countries in search of employment opportunities.

■ Recruiting more immigrant and temporary workers can help employers to fill short-term gaps such as during seasonal or peak trading periods.

■ Highly skilled workers are more likely to be able and willing to migrate as they have a greater chance of securing well-paid jobs overseas.

■ The migration of skilled workers has increased due to globalization (such as the widespread growth of multinational corporations) and internet technologies enabling better flows of information to workers looking for job opportunities overseas.

■ Part time

■ Part time is an employment practice that hires workers for fewer hours per week than those with a full-time job.

■ Part-time staff work in shifts but may remain on call (standby) while off duty to cover for full-time staff who might be off sick, attending a training course or on annual holiday leave.

■ Part-time and shift workers give employers greater flexibility in their operational hours.

■ Whilst part-time work might suit some people (such as mothers with young children or full-time students in higher education), they do not qualify for the same employment perks (benefits) as those on full-time contracts.

Outsourcing, offshoring and re-shoring as human resource strategies (AO3)

Revised ☐

■ **Outsourcing** is the use of external providers for certain non-core business activities, e.g. cleaning, catering and security.

  ☐ Many businesses outsource their non-core activities to third party firms to reduce costs and to focus on their main business functions in which they have core competencies.

  ☐ The outsourced firm provides specialist services on a contract basis and at highly competitive prices. They are also used due to the improved quality standards provided.

■ **Offshoring** is the practice of relocating business functions or activities abroad.

  ☐ It is pursued mainly because of lower production costs by using cheaper labour in less economically developed countries.

  ☐ Cost savings also arise due to lower operational costs, e.g. fewer fringe benefits and lower training costs.

  ☐ Countries such as India, Vietnam and the Philippines have seen a sharp rise in multinational firms choosing to offshore their operations, e.g. customer service call centres, accountancy services and computer software development.

■ **Re-shoring** is the transfer and relocation of a firm's overseas operations back to its country of origin due to cost or competitive advantages (see Unit 5.4).

  ☐ There has been a surge in re-shoring in countries such as the UK and USA due to incentives offered by domestic governments for relocating production back to the home country.

  ☐ It also occurs when offshoring no longer offers cost savings, e.g. increased wage costs in countries such as China and Mexico have driven some multinational companies to re-shore their operations.

- ☐ Unethical labour practices in many off-shored countries (such as the exploitation of female workers and child labour) have given firms a reason to re-shore.

- ☐ The increasing cases of product recalls and low quality output from offshored production units has damaged the reputation of multinational companies, thus forcing them to pull out of their overseas operations.

How innovation, ethical considerations and cultural differences may influence human resource practices and strategies in an organization (AO3)

`Revised` ☐

Examples of how the concepts of innovation, ethics and culture may influence human resource practices and strategies are outlined below.

■ **Innovation**

- ☐ Human resource managers are increasingly relying on the use of information communications technologies (ICT) in workforce planning, e.g. the use of company websites to advertise job vacancies or video-conferencing facilities to conduct job interviews around the world.

- ☐ Social media and networks such as LinkedIn and Facebook are also used as part of the recruitment process.

■ **Ethics**

- ☐ The use of part-time and flexitime workers has raised some concerns about employers who take advantage of these employees yet gain from having lower operational costs.

- ☐ The unethical treatment of people in the workplace has huge consequences, e.g. lower staff morale, negative corporate image and costs of possible lawsuits.

- ☐ Unethical business practices of some offshored firms, such as the use of child labour, mean that more businesses are choosing to re-shore their operations.

■ **Culture**

- ☐ Firms with high rates of labour turnover may suffer from poor human resource management and a weak or fragmented corporate culture.

- ☐ The culture of some firms is such that human resources are viewed as a long-term investment so training and development become integral to their business strategy.

- ☐ Although 360-degree feedback is used in some countries, the act of subordinates appraising their senior colleagues in an organization is unacceptable in other countries.

> **CUEGIS CONCEPTS**
>
> Investigate how innovation, culture and ethics have impacted on human resource planning for an organization of your choice.

Figure 2.2 Culture impacts on how appraisals are conducted

2.2 Organizational structure

Revised ☐

Terminology to facilitate understanding of different types of organizational structures (AO1)

Revised ☐

■ Small businesses are often characterized by informal organizational structures while larger businesses need to adopt more formal structures due to the larger numbers of staff involved.

■ As a business grows, it needs to organize staff into formal organizational structures to ensure effective communications, increased efficiency, and clear expectations of accountability and responsibility.

■ The following terms help to facilitate understanding of different types of organizational structures: delegation, span of control, levels of hierarchy, chain of command, bureaucracy, centralization, decentralization, and de-layering.

■ Delegation

■ As a business grows, it becomes inevitable that managers need to relinquish some of their roles and responsibilities. This is known as delegation.

■ It involves passing on control and authority by the line manager while still holding the subordinate accountable for his or her actions. The overall responsibility still remains with the line manager.

■ Delegation makes people accountable for their actions. Accountability is the extent to which a particular individual is held responsible for the success or failure of a job role or activity.

■ Decision making can be delegated but responsibility remains with the executive directors as they are ultimately responsible for the organization's strategy.

■ It can be a motivational tool for employees as it recognizes their talent, ability and potential. Staff who are empowered may feel inspired to perform well. They feel a sense of achievement and pride in their work. Morale is high as they feel trusted and valued by management.

■ Delegation can, but does not always, come with extra financial rewards, e.g. pay rises.

■ Successful delegation frees up managers to attend to other important tasks such as strategic decision making.

> **Keyword definition**
>
> **Delegation** is the process of entrusting and empowering a subordinate to successfully complete a task, project or job role.

> **Expert tip**
>
> Whilst delegation empowers a worker with decision-making rights and authority, responsibility cannot be delegated – the line manager remains responsible for the work or tasks delegated to others.

■ Span of control

■ The span of control is inversely proportional to the number of hierarchical layers in an organization.

■ Having a narrow span of control can improve communication and control of the team.

■ A wide span of control means a manager is responsible for many subordinates, while a narrow span of control indicates fewer workers who directly report to the line manager.

■ The wider the span of control, the greater the need for strong leadership and clear lines of communication.

■ A wider span of control makes the organization flatter.

■ Organizations with wider spans of control require fewer managers, which lowers their costs.

> **Keyword definition**
>
> The **span of control** describes the number of subordinates who are directly accountable to a manager.

Levels of hierarchy

- Hierarchical structures show where each person within an organization fits and hence his or her roles and responsibilities.

- Hierarchical structures can be tall, with a narrow span of control but many levels in the hierarchy.

- Alternatively, organizations can be flat, with wider spans of control but with fewer levels in the hierarchical structure.

Chain of command

- The chain of command in an organizational structure is usually shown as a vertical line of authority indicating how decisions and responsibility are passed down the hierarchical layers.

- Instructions and commands flow downward along the chain of command whilst accountability flows upward in the organizational structure.

- The clearer the chain of command, the more effective the decision making tends to be.

- A clear and established chain of command improves the efficiency of communications in the workplace.

- Businesses with fewer levels in the hierarchy (flat structures) have a shorter chain of command.

Bureaucracy

- Bureaucratic organizational structures have a number of layers of management, with decisions passed down from senior executives to regional managers, departmental managers, supervisors and operative workers.

- In bureaucratic organizations, authority and decision making are generally centralized. Hence, strategic decisions can be made faster as fewer people are involved in decision making.

- Bureaucracy often leads to excessive administration, paperwork and other formalities.

- It encourages a culture focused on rules and standards, where daily operations are rigidly controlled with close supervision and accountability.

- Rigidity means that bureaucratic organizations are often slow to react to changes in the external environment. It also discourages creativity and innovation.

- This reduces flexibility and discourages progress in the organization, and thus leads to inefficiencies and slower decision making.

Centralization

- In centralized organizations, the importance of subordinates is reduced whilst the importance of senior executives is increased.

- Centralized structures were favoured by management theorists such as F.W. Taylor and H. Fayol due to faster decision making and better control.

- It is associated with a paternalistic or autocratic style of leadership (see Unit 2.3).

- Rapid decision making can result in fewer conflicts due to consistent policies coming from the top few highly experienced managers.

- Costs are also reduced as there is less of a need for hiring more specialists or departmental managers.

- However, centralized structures are highly inflexible, put added pressure on senior managers and can be demotivating for employees.

Keyword definition

Levels of hierarchy refer to the management structure of an organization based on the number of layers of formal authority, usually presented in a diagram or chart.

Keyword definition

The **chain of command** is the formal line of authority through which orders and decisions are passed down from senior management at the top to operational workers at the bottom of the hierarchy.

Keyword definition

Bureaucracy refers to the administrative systems of a business, such as the set of rules and procedures and formal hierarchical structures in an organization.

Keyword definition

Centralization refers to organizational structures where the majority of decision making is in the hands of a very small number of people at the top of the hierarchical structure.

Decentralization

- Decentralization involves passing responsibility and authority away from the Board of Directors and senior executives to individual departments.

- In decentralized structures, there is shared decision-making authority and responsibilities.

- Decentralization is associated with fewer tiers (flatter structures) in an organizational structure and wider spans of control.

- Unlike centralized structures which have a 'top-down' approach to management and decision making, decentralized structures are seen as 'bottom-up' and democratic.

- The larger the business, the more decentralized its organizational structure tends to be.

- Decentralized structures are often found in organizations with an informal corporate culture.

- Delegation and empowerment, vital aspects of decentralization, can result in better motivation for employees.

- It also results in quicker and more flexible decision making.

- However, decentralized structures can result in poor decision making due to the lack of experience and expertise of less senior staff.

- The decision to have a more centralized or decentralized organizational structure is influenced by several factors, such as the corporate culture, the size of the organization, and the nature of the decisions to be made (whether they are strategic or routine decisions).

> **Keyword definition**
> **Decentralization** refers to organizational structures which include the delegation of decision-making authority throughout an organization, away from a central authority.

> **Expert tip**
> Evaluation skills require candidates to demonstrate 'thinking' skills. Make sure you apply your understanding to the context of the business in question, e.g. bureaucracy is not suitable for creative industries that require autonomy. By contrast, the emergency services (fire, police and ambulance services) would require centralized structures and strict chains of command to ensure that the services are carried out properly without endangering the safety of the general public.

De-layering

- De-layering results in flatter structures and managers having wider spans of control.

- Reasons for de-layering include improving communications in the organization, having shorter chains of command, and cutting costs as there are fewer levels of management.

- The biggest disadvantage of de-layering is the potential stress and anxiety of subordinates due to the added workload.

- Firms may choose to downsize or de-layer because it improves or speeds up communication and is cheaper due to fewer layers of management.

- The move towards flexible working practices (see Unit 2.1) means less of a need for traditional hierarchical structures.

> **Keyword definition**
> **De-layering** is the process of removing one or more layers in the organizational hierarchy to make the structure flatter.

Types of organization charts (AO2, AO4)

Revised

Flat/horizontal

- A flat (or horizontal) organization has few layers of management (see Figure 2.3).

- Line managers have a wide span of control in flat hierarchical structures. This gives the manager a lot of authority over decision making but also places added pressure on his or her level of responsibility.

- Organizations with flat structures are suitable when employees are multi-skilled and can organize their own work effectively.

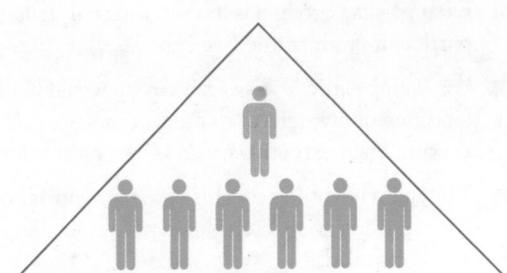

Figure 2.3 A flat organizational chart

- Flatter structures have shorter chains of command, which improves communication in the organization.

- The culture of relationships in flat structures is often open and informal. This is partly because there is minimal control over individual employees, which allows employees to take responsibility for their own work.

- With a large and wide span of control in horizontal structures, it can prove difficult to have tight control and close supervision of workers. This is because managers in a flat organizational structure with a wide span of control directly supervise a large number of people.

Tall/vertical

- There are many layers in a tall (or vertical) hierarchical organizational structure (see Figure 2.4). Roles, responsibilities and departments tend to be highly specialized.

- Generally, taller hierarchical structures are characterized by a narrow span of control, with each manager being responsible for fewer subordinates.

- Vertical structures are hierarchical, with clear chains of command. Rules, policies and procedures are written and formalized. This reduces the chances of making mistakes.

- Such structures can be motivational for junior staff as there are prospects for promotion and moving up the hierarchical structure.

- A drawback of vertical structures is the potential for miscommunication problems due to the large number of layers in the organization. Decision making can be slow due to formal, inflexible and bureaucratic structures.

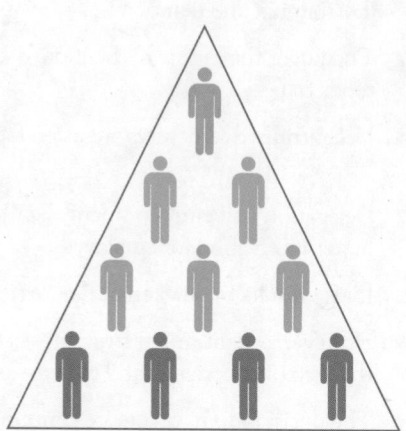

Figure 2.4 A tall organizational structure

Hierarchical

- Hierarchical structures are tall with many levels of responsibility. Such structures place people within an organization in terms of their rank.

- They are suitable when job roles are straightforward and routine as output can be easily measured and checked and because there are clear lines of accountability.

- The person directly above an employee on the next hierarchical level is known as the **line manager**. The line manager supervises and manages the subordinates on a day-to-day basis.

- Hierarchical structures are rigid and bureaucratic so responding to changes in the internal or external business environment (see Unit 1.5) can be slow.

- They tend to be overly administrative and bureaucratic so employees feel rather distanced due to the impersonal nature of the hierarchical structure.

Organization by product

- Organization by product is suitable for large businesses that have a broad product line of goods or services as this requires specialized expertise in marketing and operations.

- Each product group has its own internal structure related specifically to that particular product line (see Figure 2.5).

- For example, the Volkswagen Group would have different executives responsible for different divisions of its product range, e.g. Volkswagen, Audi, Porsche and Bugatti. Each executive would be responsible for all products under that division.

- The main advantage of this type of organizational structure is that products created using completely different and separate processes are better managed and controlled.

> **Keyword definition**
>
> **Organization by product** occurs when an organization groups its human resources based on the distinct goods or services it sells.

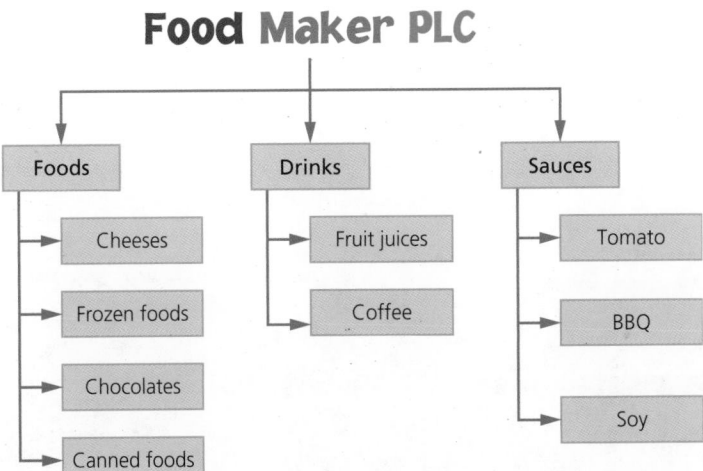

Figure 2.5 Example of a product organizational chart for Food Maker PLC

■ Organization by function

■ Functional organizational structures arrange individuals by specific functions performed, e.g. human resources, finance, operations management and marketing (see Figure 2.6).

■ It is the most common form of organizational structure.

■ Managers of different functional areas report to the respective director or vice president who holds overall responsibility for the department or division, e.g. marketing managers must report to the marketing director.

■ The advantage of this type of structure is that functions are separated by expertise but the challenges come when different functional areas turn into silos that focus only on their area of responsibility and don't support the function of other departments.

> **Keyword definition**
> **Organization by function** involves establishing the organizational structure according to business functions such as marketing, production, and finance.

Figure 2.6 Organization by function

■ Organization by region

■ Organization by region is suitable for businesses that are located in several different geographic regions within a country or around the world (see Figure 2.7).

■ Typically, operations are managed and overseen by a regional director.

■ There are efficiency gains and operational benefits of organizing people by different regions, e.g. to better support and meet the needs of customers in different locations.

■ It can support logistical demands and differences in different geographical locations.

> **Keyword definition**
> **Organization by region** refers to establishing the organizational structure according to different geographical areas.

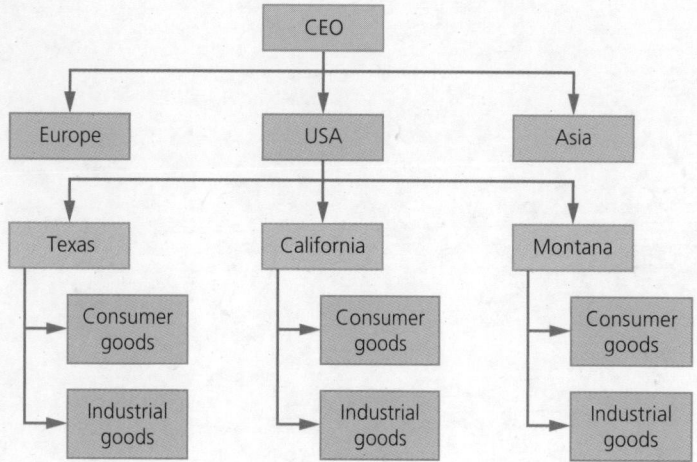

Figure 2.7 Organization by region

Changes in organizational structures (AO2)

Revised

In reality, organizational structures are not static. Changes in the internal and external business environments mean that organizational structures need to be more flexible and adaptable. Examples include: project-based organization and the Shamrock organization.

■ Project-based organization

- Using flexible project teams involves the temporary use of the most suitable employees from different departments for a particular project.

- Often referred to as a **matrix structure**, such a flexible organizational structure is conducive to a democratic leadership style (see Unit 2.3) as it encourages the generation of new and creative ideas from team members.

- Matrix structures are a popular way of organizing highly skilled and experienced staff. They help to utilize the synergies created from interactions amongst staff in the matrix.

- Project-based organization can create problems for the business because staff may have some uncertainties about prioritizing tasks when they have more than one line manager.

- Similarly, there can be difficulties in controlling team members from various departments in the project who have conflicting interests and priorities.

- Project-based organizational structures create opportunities for job enlargement and job enrichment (see Unit 2.4), thus boost morale and motivation. However, they can cause some staff to become demoralized due to the added workload and pressures of working on different projects.

- Additional resources and finance will be needed to facilitate the running of the projects.

■ Handy's Shamrock Organization

- Irish scholar Charles Handy's Shamrock Organization theory (1991) suggests that organizations face continual change so need to adapt accordingly.

- The changing organization comprises of three 'leafs' (types) of workers: core workers, peripheral workers and outsourced workers (see Figure 2.8).

  □ The **professional core** consists of full-time, experienced and essential staff needed for the organization's operations and survival. With improvements in technology and the trend for downsizing and delayering, there is less of a need for so many core staff in an organization.

> **Keyword definition**
> **Project-based organization** refers to the organization of human resources around specific projects that need to be completed.

- ☐ The **contingent workforce** refers to peripheral workers, i.e. the temporary, portfolio and flexitime workers employed by organizations on a short-term basis. However, this often causes job insecurity and low staff morale.

- ☐ **Outsourced vendors** are individuals or businesses hired on a contract basis to do specific tasks such as an advertising campaign. They are specialists in their field so can be expensive to employ.

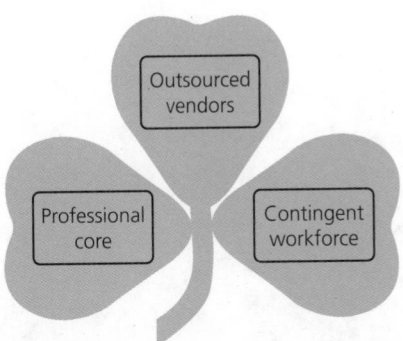

Figure 2.8 The Shamrock Organization

- ■ The model emphasizes the growing practice of outsourcing non-essential activities as well as the recognition of flexible working practices (see Unit 2.1).

- ■ The model presents cost savings and greater flexibility for organizations, e.g. labour costs are cheaper because only the core staff receive full employment perks (benefits), whereas peripheral and outsourced workers do not.

- ■ Handy's academic work on organizational structures has shaped the thinking behind present day organizational structures in many business organizations around the world.

How cultural differences and innovation in communications technologies may impact on communication in an organization (AO3)

- ■ **Communication** is the transfer of information from one party to another.

- ■ Managers spend a significant proportion of their time communicating with internal and external stakeholders. Effective communications enable managers and workers to have a better understanding and control of what they do.

- ■ Cultural differences can have a large impact on communications in an organization. Cultural ignorance can cause offence to others and can cause marketing messages to be misinterpreted or misunderstood by the wider community.

- ■ For multinational companies, an understanding of local cultures and traditions is a major competitive advantage when communicating with their target markets.

- ■ Innovations in communications technologies also impact on communications in organizations, e.g. internet technologies have reduced the costs of internal and external communication, both domestically and internationally.

- ■ Social networks and social media have become popular means of communication for many businesses around the globe.

- ■ However, innovations in mobile technologies have led to information overload from the overexposure of online marketing.

Expert tip

Whilst this section of the syllabus looks at the formal organizational structures, it is important for managers to be aware of and understand the informal structures that are likely to exist. Informal structures can help to promote a sense of belonging in the workplace. Knowledge and skills are unevenly spread out in an organization so informal networks can help to identify and exploit different sources of knowledge and skills.

CUEGIS CONCEPTS

Investigate how change and culture have impacted on the organizational structure for an organization of your choice.

2.3 Leadership and management

Revised ☐

The key functions of management (AO2)

Revised ☐

- According to French engineer and management theoretician, Henri Fayol, management is about: planning, organizing, commanding, coordinating and controlling. These management activities are task-oriented, rather than people-oriented.

- According to Irish management guru, Professor Charles Handy, management is about addressing and solving problems, in the same way as a general practitioner (doctor) would do. Managers identify the problems (symptoms), investigate the causes, decide on a course of action and then implement the plan.

- According to American management consultant and author, Peter F. Drucker, management is about setting strategic objectives in order to manage the organization and its people to establish the future direction of the business.

- Other functions of management include developing and motivating employees, measuring and evaluating performance against organizational objectives, establishing personal contacts and nurturing professional networks.

- Essentially, the functions of management concern the effective and efficient use of an organization's resources.

Management versus leadership (AO2)

Revised ☐

Table 2.4 Management versus leadership

Management	Leadership
Follow the culture of the organization	Set the culture of the organization
Manage others	Inspire others
Planning, organizing, controlling, commanding, coordinating, and setting objectives	Cope with and promote change, with a more emotional dimension to inspire and align people
Work within the parameters of organizational policies and procedures	Focus on the future
Focus on the present	Instigators of change, setting the strategic direction of the organization
Focus on operational objectives	Focus on vision and mission statements
Mainly concerned with processes	Mainly concerned with people
Tactical decision making	Strategic decision making
Deal with individual needs of staff	Focus on common needs
Policy makers and decision makers	Risk-takers and decision makers
More involved with administrative aspects of the organization	Are optimistic, innovative, inspirational, entrepreneurial and creative
Confirmative capacity (learning to do)	Adaptive capacity (learning to learn)

Leadership styles (AO3)

Revised ☐

Leadership style refers to the way in which managers and leaders provide direction, implement organizational plans, and motivate people.

■ Autocratic

- Autocratic leaders are authoritative, i.e. there are formal systems of command and control.

- They avoid discussions as employees are not involved in decision making.

- Delegation and consultation are non-existent.

- Communication is top-down and one way, i.e. managers order and instruct their subordinates.

Expert tip

Although distinctions are made between management and leadership, in reality, the terms are often used interchangeably and a distinction is somewhat unimportant as there are clear overlaps. A good leader has the capacity to manage and a good manager has the capacity to lead.

- It is most likely to be used when employees are unskilled, inexperienced, lack initiative and/or cannot be trusted.

- An autocratic approach may also be suitable or necessary when critical decisions must be made, e.g. the emergency services (police, fire and ambulance services) or in the military and navy.

- The success of the organization very much relies on the ability of the leader.

Table 2.5 Advantages and disadvantages of autocratic leadership

Advantages of autocratic leadership	Disadvantages of autocratic leadership
• Ensures there is control and close oversight within the organization	• Stifles initiative and creativity as employees are not involved in decision making
• Quick decision making takes place	• Demotivates workers as their ideas are not valued
• Employees have a clear sense of direction	• Does not nurture future leaders among employees so can damage competitiveness in the long term
• Effective when deadlines are imminent or major decisions need to be made	• Subordinates are usually ineffective if the leader is absent from work

Paternalistic

- Paternalistic leaders see the workforce as an extension of the family so make decisions that they perceive to be in the interest of their employees.

- It is often effective in family-run businesses.

- It is used in organizations where the leader is highly experienced and genuinely values the workers.

- There is close supervision of employees and their work (comparable to a parent's traditional control over their children).

Table 2.6 Advantages and disadvantages of paternalistic leadership

Advantages of paternalistic leadership	Disadvantages of paternalistic leadership
• A softer form of autocratic leadership which often results in improved staff motivation and lower staff turnover	• Employees can become dissatisfied as their viewpoints are often ignored (decisions are made by top management) so it does not help to develop their careers
• Feedback is invited, so this can improve relationships at work as employees' social needs are emphasized	• Communication is mostly downward
• There is often commitment and loyalty to leaders who workers perceive will take care of their well-being	• Paternalistic leaders can become too dictatorial and make poor decisions (does the parent or leader always know what is best?)

Democratic

- Democratic leaders involve workers in the decision-making process, i.e. consultation and collaboration are considered to be important to the organization.

- Leaders encourage discussion and employee participation, although they have the final say.

- Leaders delegate authority and empower their staff.

- It is likely to be effective when used with skilled, experienced and creative employees.

Table 2.7 Advantages and disadvantages of democratic leadership

Advantages of democratic leadership	Disadvantages of democratic leadership
• Can be motivational as workers feel their opinions and input are valued, thus creating a greater sense of belonging and staff loyalty	• Decision making is slower as employees have greater involvement in the process
• The collaborative environment often results in better informed solutions to challenges and problems	• Reaching a consensus over decisions can be time consuming and costly
• There is two-way communication, so this encourages the sharing of ideas in the workplace	• The possibility of disagreement among internal stakeholders during the discussion process can negatively affect day-to-day operations
	• Inappropriate for urgent decisions needed during challenging times faced by the business

■ Laissez-faire

■ Laissez-faire leaders delegate responsibility and authority to their staff, enabling them to complete tasks in their own way (although the leader sets broad goals and clear parameters within which the employees must operate).

■ At polar opposite to autocratic leaders, the success of laissez-faire leadership primarily depends upon the aptitude and attitude of the employees.

■ Staff are given the freedom to work without supervision from the management as there is a deliberate attempt to delegate power and authority.

■ It is suitable for mundane and routine tasks which do not require managerial supervision.

■ It is also suitable when staff can be trusted, are highly talented and self-motivated, and are willing and able to take on responsibility, e.g. Google and Facebook.

Expert tip

It is common in IB exams for students to claim that democratic leaders are better than autocratic ones, stating that the former are 'nicer' than the latter. This suggests a lack of critical thinking as the most effective leadership style depends on the context of the organization, its workers and the task at hand. Leaders do not exist to be popular, but to get things done.

Table 2.8 Advantages and disadvantages of laissez-faire leadership

Advantages of laissez-faire leadership	Disadvantages of laissez-faire leadership
• The freedom given to employees can allow them to excel in what they do best, without any constraints imposed by the management	• Individual goal setting could conflict with organizational objectives, especially as there is an absence of management control
• Provides opportunities for staff with vision and intrapreneurial skills (see Unit 1.1)	• Often criticized for the poor definition of the role/purpose of management
• Autonomy in decision making can have positive impacts on staff motivation, productivity and staff retention levels.	• As management take a 'hands-off' approach, monitoring and control of the organization's operations become very challenging.

■ Situational leadership

■ Situational leaders adapt their style of leadership according to differences in circumstances.

■ It is assumed that there is no single best leadership style but rather different styles are suitable depending on the context or situation.

■ Relationships at work have a key role in the success of situational leadership.

■ It relies on the skills and level of experience of the leader.

Table 2.9 Advantages and disadvantages of situational leadership

Advantages of situational leadership	Disadvantages of situational leadership
• It recognizes the need for leaders to be flexible in their style, given the dynamic nature of business management	• Most managers and leaders have a preferred or natural style, so expecting them to change their style according to different situations can be difficult
• It is practical and applies across a range of industries and business problems	• Employees may have grown accustomed to a particular leadership style in the workplace, so staff may become disoriented and unsettled were the leader to change his/her style
• Workers can benefit from the mix of support from leaders when appropriate, and directive activities at other times	• The inconsistent approach can mean the leader loses credibility with the employees.

Expert tip

Several factors affect the leadership style adopted in an organization, including the:

• nature of the task, e.g. whether it is routine or strategic

• time and cost required to complete the task

• type of labour, e.g. skilled or inexperienced

• personality and preference (natural style) of the leader

• organizational culture.

How ethical considerations and cultural differences may influence leadership and management styles in an organization (AO3)

Revised ☐

- Leadership is generally vital to the operational success of a business. It has implications across all areas of the organization and shapes its culture.

- Whilst leadership is important, a business can succeed in the absence of effective leadership if the staff are highly talented and self-driven.

- Management guru, Warren Bennis, claims that the success of an organization is 15% due to leadership, so other factors must make up the remaining 85%, e.g. the organizational culture.

- Irrespective of cultural differences, it is important that those who run organizations have leadership ability in order to inspire their staff towards a shared vision.

- Ethical considerations can have a large impact on leadership style, e.g. it might be innate for a dominant individual to lead in an autocratic way. For others, who naturally prefer to listen to the opinions of their staff, ethical considerations might lead to a more democratic style.

- Whilst charisma is important to inspire others, ethical leadership might be perceived to be more honest so is more likely to be accepted by employees.

- Organizational cultural differences also shape the leadership style adopted, e.g. a paternalistic style might be preferred in smaller, family-run businesses whereas a more democratic style may be preferred in larger organizations.

- Although the leader shapes the organizational culture, the way in which a business functions and the context in which it operates can also affect the leadership style, e.g. Chinese workers in the manufacturing sector are more receptive of autocratic leadership than their European counterparts, where labour laws and trade union activity are more prominent.

CUEGIS CONCEPTS

Investigate how ethical considerations and cultural differences may have influenced the leadership style in an organization of your choice.

Figure 2.9 Ethical leadership has a large impact on staff morale

2.4 Motivation

Motivation theories (AO3)

An important role of management is to motivate the workforce to ensure that they are efficient and productive. **Motivation** exists when people do something because they *want* to do it, not because they *have* to do it. Motivation is therefore the desire to achieve something. It influences people to behave in a certain way and has a direct impact on the outcomes of that behaviour.

■ Taylor

- Frederick Winslow Taylor (1856–1917) was an American engineer and management consultant who sought to improve efficiency and productivity.

- In his book, *The Principles of Scientific Management* (1911), Taylor argued that, 'We do not want any initiative. All we want of them [workers] is to obey the orders we give them, do what we say, and do it quick.' His approach to management was based on three factors:

  - ☐ *measurement* of what can be done better and how

  - ☐ *monitoring* to ensure targets are met, and

  - ☐ *control* by using rigorous analysis of the firm's inputs, outputs and costs.

- He argued that people work for only one reason: money. By motivating workers to become more efficient and productive, the business would generate more profit, thus enabling employees to be paid higher wages.

- Taylor advocated payment systems that reward those who meet or exceed output targets, and penalize those who don't. Such a payment scheme became known as piece rate. Taylor claimed that, 'what the workmen want from employers beyond anything else is higher wages'.

- He introduced rest breaks to the working day so that workers could recover from tiredness and hence a loss of productivity.

- Taylor argued that employers must reward the behaviour they seek and punish the behaviour they discourage in order to raise productivity.

- Henry Ford (founder of Ford Motor Company) used Taylor's theory by introducing scientific management in his factories, e.g. the division of labour and use of purpose-built machinery, such as conveyor belts for mass production, to increase efficiency and productivity. Today, many firms offer 'zero-hours contracts', i.e. no work equals no pay.

- Despite being criticized for being authoritarian and treating people as though they were robots or machines, Taylor believed his scientific management of human resources was in the best interest of his staff.

- Limitations of Taylor's theory include the following:

  - ☐ Not all workers today are motivated in the same way and the most efficient way of working for one person can be inefficient for another.

  - ☐ Taylor's approach does not acknowledge the complications of human behaviour, such as personal preferences and interpersonal difficulties.

  - ☐ Working harder due to scientific management practices can still mean staff are dissatisfied with the work environment.

■ Maslow

- Abraham Maslow (1908–70) was an American social psychologist who wrote about a **hierarchy of needs**, i.e. people are motivated by a series of needs (see Figure 2.10 and Table 2.10).

  - ☐ *Physiological needs* (also known as *basic needs* for human survival) are those thought to be the most important, so must be met first e.g. food and shelter.

  - ☐ *Safety needs* are vital to a person's well-being. They refer to the factors that make people feel secure, e.g. personal and financial security.

> **Expert tip**
>
> One of the difficulties with this topic is the sheer number of key terms that you will come across. Use revision strategies that will help you to remember the definitions of the key terms in this unit, e.g. the use of flash cards, crosswords, glossaries and online tools such as Quizlet.

> **Keyword definition**
>
> **Piece rate** is a payment system, advocated by F. W. Taylor, which rewards workers based on their level of output (productivity), e.g. $1 per batch produced or 5% per product sold. Piece rate is used to motivate and reward workers who are more productive.

□ *Love and belonging needs* are about being accepted by others. Hence, this refers to the social needs of people.

□ *Esteem needs* are about people feeling respected and having self-respect. Self-esteem exists when a person feels good about himself/herself and feels valued by others.

□ In his book, *Motivation and Personality* (1954), Maslow defined *self-actualization* needs as 'to become everything that one is capable of becoming' and 'what a man can be, he must be'. The highest level in Maslow's hierarchy of needs refers to the realization of a person's full potential.

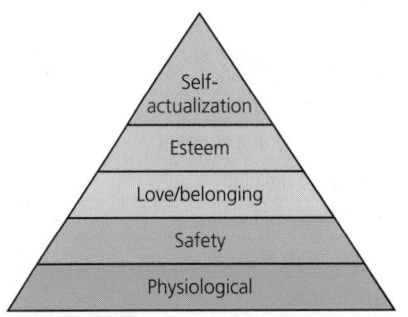

Figure 2.10 Maslow's hierarchy of needs

Table 2.10 Examples and business implications of Maslow's hierarchy of needs

Levels of human needs	Examples	Business implications
Physiological needs (basic needs)	Food, clothing, water, warmth and shelter	Pay award systems and decent working conditions
Safety needs	Physical security, financial security, economic stability, health and well-being	Job security, grievance procedures, insurance policies and clear job description
Love and belonging needs	Friendship, intimacy, social contact and social acceptance	Team working, co-workers, mentors and social facilities
Esteem needs	Status, recognition, competence, self-respect and independence	Status (job titles), power, trust, and recognition of achievements
Self-actualization	Self-fulfilment, mastery, and life accomplishment	Job opportunities to develop new skills and meet new challenges

■ Maslow argued that it is important for employers to understand that when one level of need is satisfied then it no longer motivates. Hence, they need to devise strategies to satisfy the higher level needs of their staff.

■ Lower order needs consist of physiological, security and love and belonging needs. Higher order needs consist of self-esteem and self-actualization. Nevertheless, Maslow argued that the different levels in the hierarchy are interrelated rather than separated.

■ However, criticisms of Maslow's theory include:

□ Debate about whether all humans have the same needs.

□ People place different levels of importance on different needs, e.g. not everyone is motivated by job promotional opportunities.

□ It is not realistic for most workers to reach self-actualization, i.e. can people's motivational needs be fully satisfied?

■ Herzberg (motivation–hygiene theory)

■ Frederick Herzberg (1923–2000) was an American psychologist and highly influential person in the field of business management.

■ Professor Herzberg defined motivation as, '*the will to work due to enjoyment of the work itself*'.

■ In his book, *Work and Nature of Man* (1966), Herzberg argued that removing factors that cause dissatisfaction in the workplace was a pre-requisite to positively increasing motivation.

■ Contrary to the findings of F. W. Taylor, Herzberg found that employee satisfaction did not stem from extrinsic factors (such as salary) as these are easily forgotten and become an expectation.

■ Influenced by the work of Maslow, Herzberg suggested that humans have two levels of needs, which employers should seek to satisfy at work:

□ Lower level needs, to meet people's physical needs in order to avoid pain and deprivation. Herzberg called these needs *hygiene factors*.

□ Higher level needs, to meet people's psychological needs and to enable them to grow psychologically. Herzberg called these needs *motivators*.

Table 2.11 Herzberg's two factor theory

Hygiene factors	Motivators
Company policy	Advancement
Conditions of employment	Nature of the job
Inability to develop	Opportunities to improve
Pay (wages and salaries)	Personal growth
Relationship with colleagues	Promotional opportunities
Relationship with management	Recognition (of achievement)
Treatment at work	Responsibility

- Herzberg suggested that as people work better due to the work being intrinsically interesting, the work provides the workers with opportunities for psychological growth.

- Herzberg introduced the concepts of job enrichment, job enlargement and job rotation to improve employee performance (see section below on types of financial rewards).

- Critics are doubtful about the role of wages and salaries being a hygiene factor, which could perhaps appear to be in both sets of needs. Indeed, many people seek promotional opportunities due to the higher financial rewards. Herzberg argued that pay is only a short-term, not a long-term, motivator.

Adams (equity theory)

- John Stacey Adams, a behavioural psychologist, put forward the equity theory (1963).

- Adams suggested that people seek a fair balance between their inputs (effort put into a job) and output (what they get out of it). Equity suggests people place emphasis on what is perceived to be fair and reasonable, e.g. demotivated students may not think it is worth putting in the effort to study if they believe the output (grades) will be low.

- Examples of *inputs* include employee effort, loyalty, adaptability and commitment.

- Examples of *outputs* include financial remuneration, recognition, praise, credibility (reputation) and promotional opportunities.

- Equity theory helps to explain why wages and salaries alone do not determine motivation as workers compare their input to output ratio with that of others in order to establish their own interpretation of equity (fairness) in the workplace.

- If workers feel that their inputs are fairly and adequately rewarded by outputs, then motivation will be high. By contrast, if workers perceive their inputs outweigh the outputs, then demotivation occurs. Adams argued that the extent of demotivation is generally proportional to the perceived inequity.

- Critics of the model argue that perceptions of equity are highly subjective, i.e. equity is a matter of opinion. Measuring equity in the workplace is therefore a fruitless, and perhaps pointless, task.

Pink

- Daniel H. Pink (1964–) is an American author who challenges twentieth century thinking about the effectiveness of traditional rewards to motivate people in the twenty-first century. Pink argues that such traditional rewards hinder the essential skill of creativity, required from today's workforce.

- In his book, *Drive: The Surprising Truth About What Motivates Us* (2009), Pink argues that human motivation is largely intrinsic. He argues that extrinsic factors no longer work because humans are not the same as horses, so you can't get people to move 'by dangling a crunchier carrot or wielding a sharper stick'.

- His theory is based on three intrinsic factors that drive (or motivate) people at work, school and in their personal lives: autonomy, mastery and purpose (see Figure 2.11). In his words: '*Carrots (rewards) and Sticks (punishments) are so last century. Drive says for twenty-first century work, we need to upgrade to autonomy, mastery and purpose*'.

- **Intrinsic motivation** comes from within a person, i.e. personal satisfaction from self-initiated achievement of a task. By contrast, **extrinsic motivation** involves engaging in an activity in order to earn external rewards or avoid an adverse outcome, such as punishments.

- **Autonomy** enables people to have control over their work but it does not mean abandoning accountability; employees must still be held accountable for their work, e.g. flexitime, portfolio working, and freelance work.

- **Mastery** allows people to become better skilled at something that matters to them as individuals, whether they are athletes, authors or astronomers. It is important because people generally want to improve at their work as it makes them feel better.

- **Purpose** gives context to autonomy and mastery. Students often become demotivated when they don't understand the purpose – they may ask, 'Why do I need to learn this?' Pink argues that employees who understand how their individual roles contribute to the purpose (vision) of their organization are far more likely to be satisfied in their work.

- Critics of Pink's theory are not convinced it applies across professions, national borders and cultures, e.g. do top professional footballers (soccer players) switch clubs (employers) primarily because of intrinsic values such as being able to play for a more prestigious club or to play in the first team each week (as Pink would argue) or mainly because of the financial rewards offered by the larger football clubs?

- Nevertheless, Pink's model does span across people's lives, not just in the workplace, including friendship groups, schooling and life itself. Put simply, motivation occurs when people strive to have more autonomy, mastery and purpose in their lives.

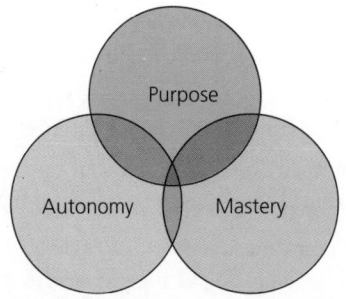

Figure 2.11 Pink's intrinsic motivators

> **Expert tip**
>
> It is important that you remember the names of the five motivational theorists and their theories from the IB syllabus:
>
> - Taylor – Scientific management
> - Maslow – Hierarchy of needs
> - Herzberg – Two-factor theory (hygiene and motivators)
> - Adams – Equity theory
> - Pink – Drive (intrinsic motivators)

EXAM PRACTICE

2   Sir Richard Branson, founder of Virgin Group, announced in 2015 that his staff would receive parental leave on full pay for up to one year after the birth or adoption of a child. However, the offer only applies to staff at Virgin Management, the company's investment and brand licensing division. Staff must also have spent at least four years at Virgin Management to qualify for full pay during their parental leave. Vodafone also introduced a global policy on maternity benefits of at least 16 weeks full paid leave for expectant mothers, even in countries where employment laws do not require them to do so. Maternity leave rules vary significantly across the world, e.g. 10 weeks of paid leave in Hong Kong, 12 weeks of unpaid leave in the USA and up to 39 weeks of partial payment in the UK.

   a   Explain one advantage and one disadvantage of providing fringe benefits beyond what is stipulated in employment laws.   [4]

   b   Using appropriate motivation theory, examine the likely effects on employee motivation of the changes to employment benefits at Virgin Management and Vodafone.   [6]

Types of financial rewards (AO2)

Revised ☐

Financial rewards are the combination of an organization's pay structure for its employees. These have to be carefully designed in order to:

- have the ability to recruit staff in a competitive labour market
- motivate employees to improve their performance
- retain workers/prevent staff from leaving for rival firms.

■ Salary

A salary is an annual sum of compensation (usually paid monthly) for doing a job, however long this might take. Salaried staff do not receive payments for any overtime. Salaries are therefore a fixed cost for businesses. For example, full-time teachers are paid a fixed monthly salary, irrespective of the number of lessons they teach in a particular month or the amount of homework they have to mark. Salaries are often part of the appraisal process (see Unit 2.1) and reflect any changes to a worker's job description.

■ Wages (time and piece rates)

- Wages are a type of financial payment that rewards workers based on time or output. Wages can be paid using time rate or piece rate.

- **Time rate** is a method of paying wages based on the number of hours worked, e.g. $8 per hour at a restaurant.

- **Piece rate** is a method of paying wages based on the number of products made or items sold, e.g. $1.50 per kilo of fruits packed in a farm.

- Wages therefore represent a variable cost for businesses.

Table 2.12 Advantages and disadvantages of piece rate payment systems

Advantages of piece rate	Disadvantages of piece rate
• Workers are paid purely on results so this should reduce slack (waste) in the workplace	• Quality control can become an issue as employees rush their work
• It can increase staff motivation (encourages staff to work harder)	• Can create unnecessary internal competition between workers
• Reduces perceived inequalities – more productive staff are better rewarded	• There is less stability for workers, often due to external factors beyond their control
• It can improve cash flow as less wages are paid if there is a decline in sales	• It becomes more difficult for the firm to monitor and control its (variable) costs

■ Commission

Commission is a form of financial reward paid to workers each time they sell a good or service. It is typically paid as a percentage of the value of the good or service sold, thereby encouraging staff to sell more products. It is a common payment system used for sales staff, such as real estate agents. Businesses usually pay employees a base salary plus commission.

Table 2.13 Advantages and disadvantages of commission

Advantages of commission	Disadvantages of commission
• Acts as an incentive for workers to produce or sell more	• Commission can be detrimental to team working if it encourages internal rivalry
• Customer service (customer satisfaction) is likely to improve in order to boost sales	• Customer service may decline if workers focus on the number of clients served
• It can help to identify staff who might need more training/skills development	• It can encourage a hostile culture and a lack of security, thus causing high labour turnover
• During times of low demand, commission can help firms to adjust their labour costs	• Commission may motivate workers in the short term, but may not do so in the long term

EXAM PRACTICE

3   A real-estate (property) agent earns a monthly salary of $2,500 plus 0.25% commission per transaction made. Calculate her total pay is she manages to sell $3.4m worth of real estate in a month. [2]

■ Profit-related pay

Profit-related pay is a financial reward system for employees based on the extent to which staff meet profit targets within a predetermined time period. It is paid in addition to the regular pay of employees. It can be applied to individuals, a team or the whole organization. Profit-related pay is common in the private sector, such as in the finance industry.

■ Performance-related pay (PRP)

Performance-related pay (PRP) is a financial reward system used to pay people whose work reaches or exceeds a required standard or target. Performance appraisals occur regularly, usually at least once per year, against agreed objectives and performance targets. PRP often comes in the form of cash bonuses and/or an increase in the wage rate or salary.

Expert tip

Whilst profit-related pay and performance-related pay (PRP) sound very similar, the firm's profit is very unlikely to be attributable to an individual employee. Hence, the former tends to be used for rewarding teams. PRP is often used as part of the appraisal process to reward individuals.

Table 2.14 Advantages and disadvantages of profit-related pay and PRP

Advantages of profit-related pay and PRP	Disadvantages of profit-related pay and PRP
● Can motivate people to be more productive in order to reach profit or performance targets	● Profit and performance targets might be set too high, so this becomes a form of demotivation
● Can promote team work and team spirit to meet organizational objectives	● These reward systems can create competitive rivalry between colleagues if not managed well
● Can be regarded as ethical as employers redistribute some of the profits to employees	● The pay-out from the organization's profits may be minimal (insignificant)
● PRP can be useful for rewarding individuals, which reflects their personal circumstances	● Can be costly for the business as it needs to distribute a proportion of profits to the staff
	● There may be disagreements about how performance is measure objectively

■ Employee share ownership schemes

An employee share ownership scheme is a financial incentive that rewards employees with shares in the company they work for. This is usually in recognition of their value to the company, such as their performance, loyalty or trust. Share ownership can encourage employees to improve their performance even more because more profit means more dividend payments for them as shareholders. There is also the potential for capital gain if improved profitability causes the share price to increase. However, having more shareholders dilutes ownership in the company and can prolong the strategic decision-making process due to the likelihood of more disagreements emerging.

■ Fringe payments (perks)

Fringe benefits (or **perks**) are any type of remuneration awarded to employees in addition to their basic pay. Examples of common fringe benefits include: staff discounts on purchases, health insurance, education assistance, fitness (gym) membership, cafeteria services (free food and drink for restaurant staff, for example), and pension contributions.

Examples of fringe benefits offered by some famous companies include:

- Patagonia provides employees with company bikes and has on-site volleyball courts and yoga lessons.

- Starbucks in the USA pays full tuition fees for its staff following an online degree course from Arizona State University.

- Yahoo! offers 16 weeks of paid maternity leave and $500 cash for new parents.

- In many countries, McDonald's offers its store managers a company car.

- Google offers its employees free food, drinks, gym, bowling alleys, climbing walls, and electric scooters to get around the office.

Keyword definition

Remuneration refers to the entire package of financial rewards received by an employee, e.g. basic salary, commission, bonuses, share options, housing allowance and other fringe benefits.

Table 2.15 Advantages and disadvantages of fringe benefits

Advantages of providing fringe benefits	Disadvantages of providing fringe benefits
• Tax benefits, e.g. some fringe benefits are exempt from income tax	• Fringe benefits are essentially financial awards so represent expenses for the business
• Healthcare coverage ensures that employees stay healthy	• Administrative fees are also incurred, e.g. administration for health care provision
• Firms that offer a variety of fringe benefits can build a better corporate image as employers	• Fringe benefits may not apply to all workers, e.g. maternity leave or company cars

Types of non-financial rewards (AO2)

Non-financial rewards refer to the compensation given to employees which does not involve cash or monetary payments. Businesses with excellent non-financial rewards can attract, motivate and retain skilled employees. Examples of non-financial rewards include job enrichment, job rotation, job enlargement, empowerment, purpose (the opportunity to make a difference), and teamwork.

■ Job enrichment

■ Job enrichment involves improving and developing the experiences of employees through a wider variety of tasks, some of which carry greater responsibilities and/or complexities.

■ It enables workers to have the potential to manage their own workload and to build their competence. Thus, it can help to create a sense of achievement in the workplace and boost the morale of employees.

■ Employers benefit from having a more appreciative, motivated and loyal workforce.

■ However, job enrichment usually costs the business more money to implement, including the costs of training and professional development of its employees.

■ It is not suitable for smaller businesses such as sole traders because of the associated costs.

■ Job rotation

Job rotation is a management technique that assigns staff to various tasks and departments over a period of time. It widens the range of activities of workers who switch between different roles and assignments. This helps to increase their level of knowledge, interest and motivation in the workplace. Job rotation offers many advantages:

■ Reduces the monotony (repetitiveness or boredom) of a routine job.

■ Helps with succession planning so that knowledge and skills are not lost if workers leave the organization.

■ Develops a wider range of expertise within the organization.

■ Enables workers to be more flexible (adaptable and multi-skilled).

■ Makes it easier to cover for absent colleagues, who may be sick or attending off-the-job training (see Unit 2.1).

The main disadvantage of job rotation is that it can reduce labour productivity if workers are expected to do too many tasks, especially in the short term when they are initially unfamiliar with the new tasks. Another disadvantage is the greater need for training, which costs money and takes time, of course.

Revised

Expert tip

In today's world, non-financial rewards can have an even more significant impact on staff motivation than traditional financial rewards. Recent research from Hay Group, a global management consulting firm, found that people value their work climate, career development and recognition as key reasons for employee satisfaction.

■ Job enlargement

Job enlargement involves broadening the work of employees by increasing the number of tasks, but not the depth of the tasks, i.e. it occurs at the same hierarchical level of responsibility and complexity. It enables workers to have a greater scope in their jobs, thereby reducing the monotony (boredom) of repetitive job tasks.

■ Empowerment

■ Empowerment is a form of non-financial reward that involves giving employees more responsibility and autonomy in their job.

■ It allows workers to make independent decisions without having to consult their line manager. This enables employees to develop a sense of ownership in their job roles and to take responsibility for the outcome of their work.

■ Empowerment shows that managers respect and trust their employees, thereby improving their level of motivation and job satisfaction.

■ It is suitable for laissez-faire management (see Unit 2.3) as it gives managers more time to concentrate on other operations of the organization and to focus on strategic decision making.

■ Purpose (the opportunity to make a difference)

Purpose as a non-financial reward refers to meaningful work. Working for a good cause can be motivating, e.g. health care workers, teachers and those in the emergency services do not necessarily work *because* of the pay. Instead, purpose reminds employees about *why* they are doing such a particular job, e.g. to look after others in society, to protect people's physical and emotional well-being, or to educate the next generation. They are intrinsically motivated by the social good that comes about from their efforts.

■ Teamwork

■ Teamwork is about the organization of human resources into groups or clusters, working in specific departments or working on a particular project.

■ Productivity should increase due to group dynamics, such as the various skills and expertise of different team members. It provides greater worker flexibility and co-operation.

■ Teamworking involves social interaction and support from team members. This helps to promote a sense of belonging in the workplace.

■ Teams are often empowered to set targets to achieve and make their own decisions. This can have positive impacts on staff motivation and self-esteem.

■ Teamwork also helps remove the drawbacks of internal rivalry between individuals because the performance of the team is more important than any individual's own accomplishments.

■ Nevertheless, teamworking can still create non-productive rivalry between team members and it does not necessarily suit everyone.

Figure 2.12 The benefits of teamwork

How financial and non-financial rewards may affect job satisfaction, motivation and productivity in different cultures (AO2)

Whilst employees may hold the same or similar values about their well-being, there is no universal approach to motivation in the workplace. It is important to acknowledge that what might motivate most people in your country might not necessarily be the case in other countries or cultures. For example:

- Empowering workers with decision-making power might help to boost motivation in some cultures where people value having more control over their working environment. However, not all cultures want or value such autonomy and prefer to be directed by senior management.

- Praise and recognition can be highly motivating for some people in some cultures where celebrating success is the norm. However, in other cultures, people prefer to be more reserved and humble so public praise may be more humiliating than motivating.

- Perceptions of fairness or equity differ throughout the world. In some cultures, it is the norm for workers to leave before their boss (after all, s/he is paid more so should work harder), whilst in other cultures it is regarded as rude and unprofessional to leave before the boss (after all, there is much work to be done).

- Similarly, in some cultures people work very hard and long hours, driven by the need for promotion and to get improved pay and benefits (so they perhaps 'live to work'). In other cultures, people are less entrepreneurial as they prefer more leisure time with their family and friends (so they 'work to live'). Average working hours in New Zealand, Hong Kong and Japan are higher than those in Spain, France and the UK.

- Organizational culture (see Unit 2.5) also has an impact on what motivates workers. In some cultures, autocratic leaders (see Unit 2.3) motivate workers to get jobs done efficiently, whereas democratic or paternalistic leaders are better suited in other organizations.

- Within an organization there can be different sub-cultures (see Unit 2.5). This means that not everyone within the same business organization is motivated by the same things.

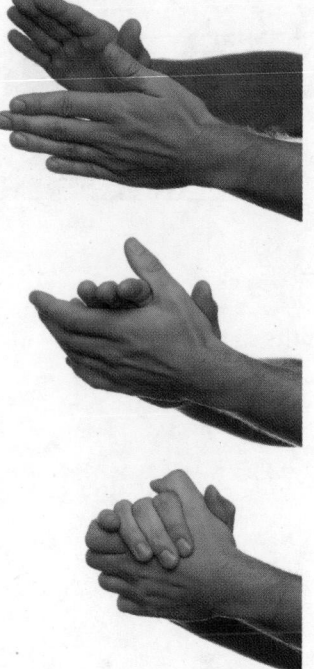

Figure 2.13 Praise is not welcome in some cultures

Expert tip

All the motivational theorists in the Business Management Guide (Taylor, Maslow, Herzberg, Adams and Pink) are from the USA. Do consider possible alternative perspectives, i.e. what motivates people in one part of the world does not necessarily motivate those in other regions.

CUEGIS CONCEPTS

Investigate the following for an organization of your choice:

- Change – How has change affected staff motivation?
- Culture – How does organizational culture impact on the level of staff motivation?
- Ethics – To what extent can the organization's rewards system be regarded as ethical?
- Strategy – Does strategy drive motivation or does motivation drive strategy?

2.5 Organizational (corporate) culture (*HL only*)

Revised ☐

Organizational culture (AO1)

Revised ☐

■ The term 'corporate culture' was coined by T. Deal and A. Kennedy (1982), referring to the set of values, attitudes, norms and beliefs in an organization.

■ It is influenced by the size of the organization, personalities and behaviour of senior managers, traditions in the organization, management attitudes towards risk-taking and societal cultural norms.

■ An organization's culture is formed over many years. However, external shocks such as a hostile takeover can change the organizational culture in a relatively short period of time.

■ Organizational culture underpins all operations and systems in the workplace, such as communication channels, organizational structures, reward systems, and workforce planning.

■ A strong and cohesive corporate culture creates a sense of belonging for both management and employees. It also minimizes potential misunderstandings and miscommunications in the workplace.

■ Similarly, corporate culture is directly associated with the corporate or brand image. Hence a positive corporate culture (e.g. Google) can create competitive advantages, thereby attracting customers and prospective employees.

Elements of organizational culture (AO2)

Revised ☐

■ The **cultural norm** of an organization is the dominant culture that exists within the organization.

■ **Cultural quotient** (CQ) refers to the ability and willingness of workers to understand other cultures in order to avoid cultural misunderstandings and close culture gaps.

■ A **culture gap** exists when there is a difference between the desired culture of an organization and the actual culture that exists.

■ Team norms are established by the people that make up the team and the leader or manager. Members of the team interact with one another based on the established cultural norm.

■ Irish academic and author Charles Handy (see Unit 2.2) suggests that there is a direct link between a firm's organizational structure and its corporate culture, e.g. tall structures tend to be more bureaucratic, whereas flatter structures are generally more democratic.

Types of organizational culture (AO2)

Revised ☐

■ Charles Handy's model of organizational culture (1999) shows four types of corporate cultures: power, role, task and person.

■ A **power culture** exists in centralized decision-making organizations (see Unit 2.2) where authority is concentrated in the hands of a few senior managers.

☐ It features centralized decision making from the senior leaders, with decisions made swiftly, without slow bureaucratic processes.

☐ A potential negative impact is the impact on staff esteem as they have no influence on decision making in the organization.

- Organizations with a **role culture** are based on rules and regulations.

  - ☐ Employees have clearly defined roles and operate within set rules and guidelines.

  - ☐ Official positions of responsibility and formal company policies are core to decision making.

  - ☐ This culture best suits bureaucratic organizations with tall hierarchical structures (see Unit 2.2), such as typical public sector organizations.

- A **task culture** exists when teams of individuals with a particular skills set and expertise are set up to tackle specific problems.

  - ☐ Individuals focus on achieving specific problems or projects.

  - ☐ Management need to ensure the team consists of the right mix of skills, personalities and leadership, often forming a matrix organizational structure (see Unit 2.2). This is important to ensure the team is productive in completing the set tasks or projects.

- A **person culture** exists when people see themselves or their skills being more important than the organization.

  - ☐ In such cultures, the organization only exists in order for people to work.

  - ☐ It is a collection of individuals with similar qualifications, training and expertise, all working in the same organization, e.g. accountants, lawyers and private doctors in a health clinic.

- An **entrepreneurial culture** is one that focuses on new product development and radical new ideas, which can turn into commercial successes. Staff are encouraged to take calculated risks and to pursue new business ventures.

- J. Kotter and J. Heskett (1992) suggested that organizations with an **inert culture** face resistance to change as workers hold negative perceptions about organizational change.

- By contrast, an **adaptive culture** entails a coherent and open-minded team with a high level of CQ. This helps to reduce the likelihood of culture clash, conflict and miscommunications.

> **Expert tip**
>
> Do not assume that only one type of corporate culture exists in an organization. Sub-cultures are likely to exist in different departments or areas of the organization.

The reasons for, and consequences of, cultural clashes within organizations when they grow, merge and when leadership styles change (AO3)

`Revised ☐`

- Culture clash might exist if the beliefs and values of employees differ from those of senior leaders.

- It often happens when there is a merger or takeover, resulting in a new senior management team or board of directors.

- An understanding and awareness of organizational culture is vital to managing change as a business grows and evolves.

- Different leadership styles within the organization can cause inconsistencies and confusion. Similarly, weak leadership is a cause of culture clash as workers lack direction and purpose.

- Radical change such as mergers and acquisitions (M&As) are likely to disrupt existing corporate cultures, creating uncertainties and causing anxiety for employees.

- Culture clashes are a major reason why many M&As fail.

- Miscommunications in the workplace are more likely to happen as a firm grows in size. Different languages being used by workers can create sub-cultures and cause further barriers to effective communication.

> **Keyword definition**
>
> **Culture clash** exists when there is a difference between the values and beliefs of individuals within an organization.

- As firms grow or evolve, a new vision and mission statement may be created but could be met with resistance to change from the workforce.

- Consequences of culture clashes include: lower staff morale, lower productivity, conflict in the workplace, higher labour turnover, and reduced profitability.

How individuals influence organizational culture and how organizational culture influences individuals (AO3)

Revised ☐

- As corporate culture is linked to the nature of organizational structures adopted in the firm, it has a direct impact on individuals.

- Organizational culture directly influences individuals, e.g. in a power culture, workers are suppressed because senior managers exercise strict command and control and hold all decision-making power. By contrast, firms with an innovative or person culture allow individuals to shape the culture of the organization.

- A strong and innovative culture can enable individuals to satisfy their higher order needs (see Unit 2.4), which influences their level of motivation and productivity. By contrast, a risk-averse culture results in individuals being less creative and innovative.

- The cultural norms influence individual behaviour, e.g. if the senior management team adopts an autocratic leadership style, then newly appointed managers who do not naturally use this approach may feel pressurized to adapt to the culture.

- Organizational cultures can and do change over time. As a firm grows or evolves, or as the external business environment changes, markets become more competitive which may necessitate managers to change the way in which things are done. To survive, it may be necessary to introduce new ideas and practices, ensuring people are able to adapt.

- Charles Handy argued that organizations with a person culture have individuals who see themselves as unique and superior to the organization. Such people can therefore exert major influence on organizational culture.

> **CUEGIS CONCEPTS**
>
> Investigate how a particular entrepreneur has changed or influenced the corporate culture for an organization of your choice.

2.6 Industrial/employee relations (*HL only*)

Revised ☐

The role and responsibility of employee and employer representatives (AO2)

Revised ☐

- **Employee representatives** are individuals or organizations (such as a trade union) who act as the collective voice of the workforce. They are usually elected by their colleagues (fellow employees).

  - ☐ Employee representatives are used as it is not practical for most businesses to negotiate with all their employees.

  - ☐ They have a duty to make the views of employees known to the management, e.g. training and development needs, better terms and conditions of employment, and improved pay.

  - ☐ They strive to build trust and improve relationships with employers.

  - ☐ They represent employees during times of legal disputes and conflict, e.g. cases of unfair dismissal or large-scale redundancies.

- ☐ Employers can benefit from recognizing employee representatives due to the inclusive style of management, which may improve the commitment and performance of the employees.

- **Employer representatives** are the individuals or organizations that represent the senior management team in the collective bargaining process. They negotiate on behalf of the employers in the process.

  - ☐ In some situations, the employer is legally obliged to consult or inform employees about developments in the business, e.g. relocation decisions, redundancies (job losses) or the threat of a hostile takeover from a rival firm.

  - ☐ Employers may typically use members of their senior management team in the process, although some may choose to use specialist management consultancy firms to represent their interests.

- The outcome of the negotiation and collective bargaining process depends on the methods used and the relative bargaining strengths of the employee and employer representatives.

Methods used by employees (AO3)

`Revised`

- **Industrial action** refers to the methods taken by employees to achieve their objectives. It is often associated with conflict between the interests of the employer and employees.

- Examples of such actions include: collective bargaining, slow-downs/go-slows, work-to-rule, overtime bans and strike action.

Collective bargaining

- Collective bargaining is the process by which employers' and employees' representatives negotiate on the terms and conditions of employment.

- Negotiations usually involve discussions regarding pay (wages and salaries), hours of work, and working conditions.

- Collective bargaining is important to individual workers as they have little, if any, negotiation power on an individual basis.

- Negotiations and collective bargaining allow employees to put some pressure on senior management to listen to their requests.

- The purpose of collective bargaining is to achieve a mutually beneficial outcome, thereby preventing conflicts from escalating beyond control.

Slow-downs/go-slows

- Go-slows are the act of working at the minimum allowable pace (under the rules of the workers' employment contract) in order to reduce productivity yet without the worker being sanctioned for breaching the terms and conditions of employment.

- Employees deliberately perform their duties with reduced efficiency and productivity, taking longer to complete each and every task.

- It is often used as an alternative to strike action which is a more extreme form of industrial action. Slow-downs mean that employees are still paid as they are at work, and are less risky and costly to workers and trade unions.

Work-to-rule

- Work-to-rule occurs when workers adhere to every single rule, policy and procedure of the organization with the intention of purposely disrupting production and reducing output.

- Employees strictly observe the rules and clauses of their employment contract, such as following all health and safety regulations very precisely. The intention is to get the employer to renegotiate rather than to serve the purpose of the rules and regulations of the organization.

- Workers withdraw any goodwill by refraining from tasks and activities which might be customary but not required by rule or in their job description, e.g. answering the telephone during a lunch break or leaving work slightly later than contracted in order to complete a task.

Overtime bans

- An overtime ban is a directive (command or order) from the employee representatives (such as a trade union) instructing its members to refuse working beyond their contracted hours.

- For most employees, overtime work is not part of an employee's employment contract.

- As workers do not engage in any extra work (overtime), this can limit the firm's productivity and profitability.

Strike action

- Strike action is an extreme method of industrial action as it involves employees refusing to work, which temporarily prevents the organization from continuing to operate.

- It is usually used as a last resort when the other methods of negotiation between employee representatives and employers have failed to resolve a conflict.

- However, those involved in strike action are not paid (as they refuse to work). Hence, strike action is usually only a temporary method used by employees.

- In many countries, there are legal issues surrounding the use of strike action, e.g. trade unions having to give advance warning to employers prior to taking such measures.

- Strike action is a potential cause of a crisis for businesses (see Unit 5.7).

Methods used by employers (AO3)

Revised

Collective bargaining

- Collective bargaining is the process by which pay and conditions of employment are settled by negotiations between representatives of employees and their employers.

- Negotiations and collective bargaining are important for the employer because they can help to prevent disruptive industrial action such as slow-downs or strikes.

- Industrial action would be detrimental for employers who would face lower staff goodwill and loyalty, lower productivity and reduced profitability.

Threat of redundancies

- In some circumstances, employer representatives might pressure or threaten employees with redundancies if industrial action continues.

- However, this does not mean that employers can simply abuse their power by dismissing their workers if they do not agree to the employer's demands. Workers are protected by employment laws that prevent such exploitation.

- The threat of redundancies, due to the loss of profits caused by industrial unrest, can be a legitimate reason for encouraging employees to renegotiate in order to prevent job losses.

■ Changes of contract

- As the threat of redundancies can cause negative media attention, employers may choose to change employment contracts for employees who cause industrial unrest.

- This needs to be completed legally, e.g. changing employment contracts when the time comes to renew contracts, such as changes to the terms and conditions of pay and working conditions.

- In extreme cases, the employer has the legal right not to renew the employment contracts of employees deemed to be counterproductive to the organization.

■ Closure and lock-outs

- Closure is an extreme method used by employers to deal with workers taking industrial action by stopping all business operations. This means there is no work for the staff, forcing them to renegotiate.

- Closure means that workers do not receive any pay. It can also result in job losses. Both consequences can weaken the bargaining strength of employees, driving them to compromise in the negotiation process.

- Lock-outs occur when the employer temporarily prevents employees from working during an industrial dispute. Typically, security guards are hired or locks are changed to prevent employees from entering the premises.

- Lock-outs eventually put financial pressure on workers as they are not paid during the period of being prevented from working.

- However, closures and lock-outs can be disadvantageous to the industry as such hostile actions can damage the organization's corporate image (see Unit 2.5).

Sources of conflict in the workplace (AO2)

Revised

- Conflict occurs when the needs and wants of employees are ignored or not met.

- Incompatible values within the organization (different perspectives or points of view) are a major source of conflict as this causes disagreements between different stakeholders.

- Miscommunications, misunderstandings and internal politics cause poor working conditions, lowering staff morale and productivity.

- Demoralized staff are likely to become less productive.

- **Grievance** exists when workers have a cause for complaint or conflict in the workplace, especially regarding unfair treatment. It is a perceived injustice which causes conflict.

- Unmanaged conflict can become a problem for businesses, resulting in lower morale, higher staff absenteeism, higher labour turnover, and industrial unrest.

- Conflict is not necessarily a negative thing as it raises and addresses real problems in the organization. Conflict itself is not necessarily the problem, but the way in which it arises and how it is managed can create problems.

Approaches to conflict resolution (AO3)

Revised

- Conflict not only damages working relationships but also the reputation of the organization. It acts as a barrier to effective communications and hinders productivity.

- Reducing or minimizing conflict in the workplace is in the best interests of all stakeholders in an organization.

- Methods of conflict resolution include: conciliation and arbitration, employee participation and industrial democracy, no-strike agreement and single-union agreement.

▪ Conciliation and arbitration

- ▪ Conciliation involves two parties in a dispute, such as employee and employer representatives, agreeing to use the services of an independent mediator (called the conciliator) to help in the negotiation process to help resolve their differences.

- ▪ Arbitration goes one step further as it involves an independent arbitrator deciding on an appropriate outcome. Both parties agree to be legally bound by the final decision of the autonomous arbitrator.

- ▪ During conciliation and arbitration, both parties are kept separate to avoid the tense moments which can further intensify conflict. The conciliator communicates back and forth between the two sides and steers the discussions towards a settlement that both parties can agree on.

- ▪ Conciliation avoids high legal fees as it can prevent the case being taken to court. It is a simpler process than arbitration. Indeed, the threat of high legal fees of a court trial means conciliation and arbitration have a high success rate.

- ▪ If one of the parties does not agree to the terms and conditions advised by the conciliator, it can take the case to arbitration.

- ▪ Both conciliation and arbitration can take up a lot of management time and financial resources.

▪ Employee participation and industrial democracy

- ▪ Industrial democracy is the practice of involving and empowering people in the workplace. This includes giving employees opportunities to share responsibilities and empowering them with decision-making authority.

- ▪ Industrial democracy occurs through employee participation, i.e. workers are involved in the decision-making process and are given responsibilities and autonomy to complete their jobs.

- ▪ Examples of employee participation include:

  - ☐ **Works council** – Employer and employee representatives that meet to discuss company-wide issues, e.g. health and safety at work or organizational change. Pay negotiations are left to trade unions, not works councils.

  - ☐ **Teamworking opportunities** – People tend to respond positively to working with others as this helps to satisfy their social needs or belonging needs (see Unit 2.4).

  - ☐ **Employee share ownership schemes** – Awarding employees with shares in the company is a common way to develop their sense of purpose and motivation.

- ▪ Motivation theorists such as Maslow and Herzberg (see Unit 2.4) argue that industrial democracy helps to increase productivity because workers are more involved, so feel valued.

- ▪ Employers also benefit from a more participative culture so are less likely to experience industrial unrest. Employers benefit from lower rates of absenteeism and labour turnover.

▪ No-strike agreement

- ▪ A no-strike agreement is a contractual agreement whereby a trade union pledges not to use strike action as a form of industrial action, provided the employer keeps to their obligations in the agreement.

- ▪ If workers choose to strike during the period of the agreement, employers have the legal right to fire (dismiss) the employees.

■ Single-union agreement

- A **trade union** (or **labour union**) is established to protect the interests of its members, e.g. to negotiate with employers for improved pay and conditions at work. The unions are financed by the membership fees.

- Workers can belong to more than one trade union. Not all workers in the same organization have to belong to the same labour union.

- A single-union agreement means employers negotiate with just one labour union which represents all employees in the organization. This helps to simplify the collective bargaining process and to speed up decision making.

Reasons for resistance to change in the workplace (AO2)

Revised ☐

- **Self-interest** – The pursuit of self-interest often takes priority over organizational objectives. Workers are often more interested in or concerned with the implications of change for themselves rather than how it might benefit the organization. Hence, they may feel that change is unnecessary and requires too much effort unless it directly benefits them.

- **Low tolerance** – The lack of open-mindedness for change often happens because people fear or dislike disruptions and uncertainties. They might also fear failure in adapting to change, so naturally resist it.

- **Misinformation** – Lack of understanding causes resistance to change when the purpose of change has not been communicated effectively. Employees often feel that change is not necessary, especially when things are going well for the organization.

- **Interpretation of circumstances** – Management and employees may disagree on the purpose and benefits of change. Different interpretations of a particular situation can cause conflict and hence resistance to change.

Human resource strategies for reducing the impact of change and resistance to change (AO3)

Revised ☐

- **Getting agreement/ownership** – Allowing workers to be involved in the decision-making process and giving them ownership of their work can help to prevent misunderstandings and misinterpretations of the purpose of change.

- **Planning and timing the change** – Rapid change is often poorly communicated and executed. Effective change management needs careful planning, including considerations regarding the timing of change. Training needs should be considered to facilitate the impact of change in the organization.

- **Communicating the change** – Effective communication of the purpose and rationale of change is vital to get support from staff. This helps to educate employees about the need for and benefits of change.

How innovation, ethical considerations and cultural differences may influence employer–employee relations in an organization (AO3)

Revised ☐

■ Innovation

- The extent to which innovation is part of the organizational culture impacts on employer–employee relations. Firms that allow employees to share ideas and pursue their interests can benefit from improved employer–employee relations.

- Innovations can bring about improved communications, thereby improving relationships in the workplace.

- Advances in technology can make it easier for firms to operate with a smaller workforce. This can have a large impact on industrial relations, at least in the short term.

- Innovation and change can increase stress levels of employees so this needs to be managed carefully.

Ethical considerations

- Unethical practices result in poor employer–employee relations, e.g. ignoring health and safety issues at work. By contrast, working for an ethical company that considers its social responsibilities can help to improve relationships at work.

- Staff morale is higher when working for an ethical organization; people tend to be more cooperative and productive when their needs are met, so intrinsic motivation is improved.

- Having a clear and agreed code of ethical conduct reduces the likelihood of conflict in the workplace.

Cultural differences

- The organizational culture shapes the behavioural norms in the workplace. This can either improve or hinder working relations, e.g. an open, blame-free culture can help to promote creativity and innovation.

- Cultural differences of multicultural employees mean that workers are motivated by different rewards, be they financial, non-financial, extrinsic or intrinsic.

- Sub-cultures within an organization (see Unit 2.5) can cause culture clashes and conflict. Similarly, new employees might have some difficulties adjusting to the cultural norms when joining an organization.

> **CUEGIS CONCEPTS**
>
> Investigate how the concepts of ethics, innovation and culture have impacted on the employer–employee relations for an organization of your choice.

Figure 2.14 Cultural differences can shape behavioural norms

Unit 3 Finance and accounts

3.1 Sources of finance

Revised ▢

Role of finance for businesses (AO2)

Revised ▢

- Finance is needed for starting up a new business or to fund an existing firm's expansion, e.g. the purchase or rent of premises, machinery, capital equipment and vehicles.

- Businesses need to finance on-going costs, e.g. the purchase of raw materials, components and stock (inventory). They need to pay wages to their employees and utility bills such as water, gas, telephone and electricity.

- Established businesses may seek additional sources of finance to grow.

- The need for finance can be categorized as capital expenditure and revenue expenditure.

> **Keyword definitions**
>
> **Capital expenditure** is the spending on fixed assets and capital equipment of a business. Examples include expenditure on buildings, equipment, tools and vehicles. Capital expenditure is commonly known as **investment expenditure**.
>
> **Revenue expenditure** refers to the need for businesses to finance their daily and routine operations. Examples include finance to pay for the purchase of raw materials, paying utility bills and remunerating employees.

Internal sources of finance (AO2)

Revised ▢

- The term 'sources of finance' refers to where a business gets its money from.

- Internal sources of finance come from within the business using its own resources, e.g. personal funds, retained profit and the sale of assets.

■ Personal funds (for sole traders)

- Sole traders and partners are likely to have their own personal funds from their savings in order to fund the start-up of their business.

- Sole traders and partners who do not invest (or risk) any of their personal funds are highly unlikely to secure finance from banks and other financiers.

■ Retained profit

- Retained profit refers to the surplus funds reinvested in the business rather than being distributed to shareholders in the form of dividends. This is shown at the bottom of the firm's profit and loss account (see Unit 3.4).

- It acts as an internal source of finance for the business as the funds belong to the owners of the organization.

- It is recorded on a firm's balance sheet as part of its equity (see Unit 3.4).

■ Sale of assets

- Businesses can sell some of their fixed assets to raise finance.

- It provides the business with an opportunity to dispose of fixed assets that are no longer needed (perhaps because they are old or obsolete), e.g. a supermarket chain might sell its fleet of old delivery vehicles in order to purchase newer ones.

- However, the sale of assets can compromise the firm's ability to raise working capital (see Unit 3.7) if there are insufficient resources for production.

External sources of finance (AO2)

- External finance comes from outside of the organization, i.e. via external stakeholders (see Unit 1.4).

- It is used when a business is unable to generate sufficient finance from its internal sources (the cheaper of the two categories of sources of finance).

- There are two main kinds of external sources of finance: share capital and loan capital.

◼ Share capital

- Share capital is a long-term, external source of finance for a limited liability company (see Unit 1.2) obtained by selling shares of the company to individual and institutional investors.

- An **initial public offer** (IPO) occurs when shares in a limited liability company are sold for the very first time.

- The value of share capital is based on the value of the shares when they were first sold, not the current market price of the shares.

- As an alternative to loan capital (which involves debt and incurs interest repayments), a limited liability company can raise finance by selling additional share capital. This does, however, dilute ownership and control for existing shareholders.

- If shares are sold, this is done via a stock exchange without the company being directly involved – the original share capital is not affected; only the share ownership changes hand between the seller of the shares and the buyer (the new share owner).

- Only public limited companies (see Unit 1.2) are allowed to trade their shares on a stock exchange.

> **Keyword definition**
>
> A **stock market** (or **stock exchange**) is a place for buying and selling shares in public limited companies. It oversees the IPO of new companies and subsequent share issues of existing companies. It is also the marketplace for buying and selling second-hand shares.

Figure 3.1 The New York Stock Exchange

◼ Loan capital

- Loan capital refers to borrowing funds from a financier (lender) such as a commercial bank.

- Examples include mortgages, bank loans and overdrafts (see below).

- A loan agreement is set for a period of time, such as one, five or twenty years. It is usually repaid in instalments over time or at the end of the loan agreement period.

- The lender charges interest on the loan amount. The interest rate can be fixed or variable.

■ A **mortgage** is a long-term source of loan capital which involves the financier demanding the borrower has **collateral** (a fixed asset such as property that provides financial security in case the borrower fails to repay the loan).

■ A **debenture** (or corporate bond) is a source of long-term loan capital, secured against a specific asset. Debenture holders do not have any ownership rights but usually get some interest on their investment and are paid dividends (if awarded) before shareholders receive any dividends.

Overdrafts

■ An overdraft is a financial service that enables a business to withdraw more money than exists in its bank account. It is, essentially, a type of short-term loan.

■ The loan period is negotiable, but tends to be short-term because the interest charges on overdrafts are usually very high.

■ Overdrafts enable a business to have emergency access to finance during times of short-term liquidity problems (see Unit 3.7) when cash flow is poor.

■ It is a very common type of borrowing for small businesses.

Trade credit

■ Trade credit is a very common source of external finance that enables a business to obtain goods or services from a supplier without having to pay for these immediately.

■ The usual trade credit period is between one and two months. Some suppliers offer a price discount for customers who pay their invoices earlier.

■ Examples of trade credit include the use of credit card and store cards which provide interest-free credit if the outstanding balance (the amount owed) is paid on time.

■ Hire purchase is another example. This involves paying for fixed assets (such as vehicles and expensive equipment) in regular instalments over a predetermined period. The finance company (lender) retains ownership of the fixed asset until the business pays the final instalment, thereby legally becoming the owner of the asset.

Figure 3.2 The use of credit and store cards is a popular form of trade credit

Grants

■ Grants are a form of financial assistance from the government, given to qualifying businesses to aid their operations, e.g. business start-ups and R&D (research and development).

■ Grants are often provided to reduce production costs for businesses and/or to encourage employment opportunities in less economically prosperous regions.

■ Grants are not widely available as a source of finance and are often only available to small businesses.

Subsidies

- Subsidies are provided in order to encourage output, e.g. public transport operators are subsidized in many countries to reduce their operational costs and hence prices. This helps to encourage people not to drive private vehicles.

- They help to stimulate investment that would otherwise be too expensive for businesses to pursue.

- Large businesses can qualify for subsidies, and this can cause controversy. For example, farmers and film (cinema) producers are subsidized in China and France to help these industries compete with foreign rivals.

Debt factoring

- A business might struggle to get payment from its debtors (individuals and firms that owe the business money). A **debt factor** is a business, such as a bank, that takes over the debtors of a business. Debtors are customers who have bought on credit.

- The debt factoring service provider will usually charge around 20% of the value of debtors as their fee.

- The provider takes its commission, before passing on the remaining amount to the business. This gives the business most of the value of debtors to improve its cash flow position without having to personally chase the payment from its customers.

Leasing

- Leasing is a common way for businesses to finance fixed assets without the necessary capital expenditure.

- A leasing contract commits the business to pay a monthly fee for a fixed period of time.

- The fixed asset is not the property of the business, and it is the leasing company that takes responsibility to maintain it.

- For example, schools might lease computers and laptops for teachers and students instead of buying them outright (which would be very expensive).

Venture capital

- Venture capital comes from external firms that invest in business start-ups and/or expanding small businesses with significant growth potential.

- Venture capital represents a combination of loans and share capital.

- To compensate for the high risks, venture capitalists often require rights to partial ownership and control of the company. Therefore, this dilutes the owner's control but does bring in much needed knowledge, experience and expertise.

- Venture capital can be useful for businesses that are unable to raise finance through the stock market or bank loans.

Business angels

- Business angels are wealthy individuals who invest in high-risk business projects with high profit potential.

- Business angels take huge risks because they invest their own personal funds, so if the project fails, they lose every dollar invested.

- They can provide a vital source of finance for small businesses that do not have access to conventional providers of finance such as banks.

Expert tip

Students often confuse grants with subsidies. Whilst both serve a common purpose, they are different. Grants are awarded for a specific purpose or project and can help to finance expenditure entirely, e.g. grants to fund higher education or to purchase computer equipment. Subsidies help to partially pay for the cost of something in order to encourage production (output).

Expert tip

Make sure you can explain the difference between hire purchase (HP) and leasing. With HP, ownership of the asset is transferred to the business after its final instalment is paid at the end of the credit period. With leasing (or hiring), ownership is not transferred throughout the entire leasing contract.

Expert tip

Students often incorrectly use 'business angels' and 'venture capitalist' interchangeably. Business angels are wealthy individuals who risk their own personal money in a project. Venture capitalists are institutional investors and risk the money of the investing organization.

Short-, medium- and long-term finance (AO1)

Revised ☐

- Businesses need sufficient access to sources of finance to meet current and future needs. Definitions of short-, medium- and long-term finance vary from country to country, but generally:

  - ☐ short term means up to one year, e.g. overdrafts, trade credit and debtors

  - ☐ medium term means up to five years, e.g. bank loans, subsidies and leasing

  - ☐ long term means more than five years, e.g. shareholders' funds, mortgages and debentures.

- The important thing for businesses is to match the type of finance to its use, e.g. short-term finance such as overdrafts should be used to provide finance for daily operations and to cope with fluctuations in cash flow (see Unit 3.7). By contrast, long-term finance is used to fund growth and expansion.

The appropriateness, advantages and disadvantages of sources of finance for a given situation (AO3)

Revised ☐

The appropriateness of different sources of finance depends on the situation faced by a business. For example:

- The sale of assets would be appropriate if a business is upgrading obsolete (outdated) fixed assets or if it is facing a major liquidity issue.

- The sale of shares is only available (suitable) for limited liability companies, i.e. it is not appropriate for sole traders and partnerships.

- If the owners of a business are unwilling to allow others to have a significant stake in their business, then venture capital and business angels are not appropriate.

- Loan capital is less appropriate for businesses with liquidity problems or with a very high gearing ratio (see Unit 3.6), i.e. firms that are already heavily indebted with external sources of finance.

- Debt factoring is suitable if the business needs quick access to cash and/or feels it is no longer able to secure the money owed by its debtors.

Table 3.1 Summary of the advantages and disadvantages of internal sources of finance

Source of finance	Advantages	Disadvantages
Personal funds	• There are no interest or administrative charges imposed	• These are unlikely to be sufficient to fund business operations
Retained profit	• It can be used to pay for goods outright, without the need to borrow	• There is unlikely to be sufficient funds to allow the business to grow sufficiently
	• Unlike bank loans, retained profits do not have to be repaid	• Shareholders might demand higher dividend pay-outs
Sale of assets	• Gets rid of outdated fixed assets	• May not fetch much money due to assets being second hand
	• Can provide much needed finance during liquidity crises	• The business may still need to replace the fixed assets

Table 3.2 Summary of the advantages and disadvantages of external sources of finance

Source of finance	Advantages	Disadvantages
Share capital	• Share capital reduces or removes the need to pay high interest on loans (debt) • A large amount of finance can be raised by selling shares	• Converting to a limited liability company can be complex, time consuming and costly • Dilution of ownership exposes a business to takeover bids
Loan capital	• Helps to fund the purchase of fixed assets • Accessible to most businesses	• All forms of loan capital incur interest charges • Increases debts of the business
Overdraft	• Quick and common source for dealing with liquidity problems	• Very high interest rates are charged on the debts
Trade credit	• Enables firms to buy now and pay later • It is usually offered interest-free	• Giving trade credit can increase the chances of bad debts • It can encourage overtrading, causing high inventory costs
Grants	• Grants do not have to be repaid	• Not easily accessible for most businesses
Subsidies	• Subsidies do not have to be repaid • There are tax breaks (benefits) for subsidized businesses	• Most businesses do not qualify for financial assistance, so subsidies are difficult to secure
Debt factoring	• Gets immediate access to cash without having to chase debtors	• The debt factor charges a large commission (fee) for its services
Leasing	• Gives access to fixed assets without capital expenditure • The lessor is responsible for maintenance costs • Upgrades are easily arranged	• Leasing is more expensive in the long term • The lessor can impose quantitative limits, e.g. a limit on the mileage for leased vehicles
Venture capital and business angels	• Useful for smaller firms that cannot raise finance via the stock market or bank loans • Gain the expertise and advice of the investors	• Often involves dilution of control and ownership of the business • Not easily accessible funds for many businesses

CUEGIS CONCEPTS

Investigate the sources of finance for an organization of your choice and examine how these have impacted on its business strategy.

Keyword definition

Overtrading exists when a business expands too quickly without sufficient sources of finance to sustain its operations.

3.2 Costs and revenues

Revised ☐

Types of costs (AO2)

Revised ☐

- **Costs,** or costs of production, refer to the payments that a business must make as part of its operations.
- Examples include: rent for hiring premises, wages to employees, the purchase of raw materials, and utility bills for gas, electricity and telephone charges. The section below examines the different types of business costs.

■ Fixed costs

- Fixed costs are costs of production that do not change with the level of output, i.e. costs that have to be paid even if there is no output.
- Examples include rent on land, leasing costs of equipment and machinery and salaries to managers.
- Diagrammatically, total fixed costs (TFC) are drawn as a horizontal line, starting on the *y-axis* at the value of fixed costs (see Figure 3.3).

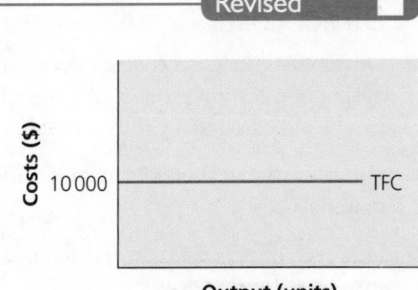

Figure 3.3 Fixed costs of $10 000 for a business

Expert tip

It is incorrect to assume that fixed costs do not change. For example, advertising costs can and do change over time, but not *because* of the organization's level of output.

◼ Variable costs

- ◼ Variable costs are costs of production that do change according to the level of output, i.e. costs that increase when there is a greater level of output or production.

- ◼ Examples include the costs of purchasing raw materials and the wages for employees.

- ◼ Diagrammatically, total variable costs (TVC) are drawn as an upwards sloping line, starting at the origin because no output means no variable costs to pay. (see Figure 3.4)

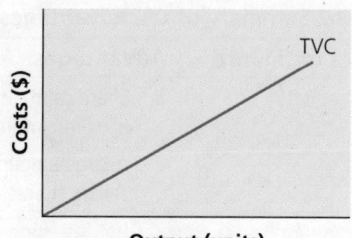

Figure 3.4 Variable costs of a business

> ### Expert tip
>
> What might be a variable cost for one business might not necessarily be so for another, e.g. the cost of fuel is a variable cost for taxi firms but not for a restaurant or cinema. It is important to consider costs in the context of the business being studied.

> ### Expert tip
>
> The total cost of production (TC) is made up of total fixed costs (TFC) and total variable costs (TVC), i.e. TC = TFC + TVC.

EXAM PRACTICE

1 Calculate the following costs to two decimal places (where appropriate) from the data in the table below:

   a   fixed costs of production.   [2]

   b   average fixed costs at 10 units and 15 units of output.   [2]

   c   average variable costs at 10 units and 15 units of output.   [2]

   d   average costs at 10 units and 15 units of output.   [2]

Output	Variable cost $	Total costs $
10	2000	4545
15	2850	5395

◼ Semi-variable costs

- ◼ Semi-variable costs have characteristics of both fixed and variable costs.

- ◼ For example, telecommunications service providers (for telephone and internet services) charge a minimum fixed monthly fee. This has to be paid irrespective of whether the service is used. However, the more the service is used the greater the cost becomes.

- ◼ Another example is electricity service providers. They might charge, for example, a minimum rate of $100 per month (the fixed component of the cost) and $0.15 per kilowatt hour (the variable component).

◼ Direct costs

- ◼ Direct costs are costs that can be clearly and specifically identified with the output of a certain product or project. For Higher Level students, direct costs can be allocated to a particular cost or profit centre (see Unit 3.9).

- ◼ Direct costs can therefore include variable costs of production, such as raw materials costs.

- ◼ However, direct costs can also include fixed costs, such as the cost of motor insurance for taxi drivers.

◼ Indirect/overhead costs

- ◼ Indirect costs (or overheads) are recurring costs that cannot be clearly identified with the production or sale of a particular good or service. For Higher Level students, indirect costs cannot be easily or objectively allocated to a particular cost or profit centre (see Unit 3.9).

- ◼ Examples include: rent, legal fees, salaries of administrative staff, accounting fees, telephone bills, insurance and electricity costs, which can be linked to all departments within a business.

Total revenue and revenue streams (AO2)

■ Total revenue

- **Sales revenue** or **sales turnover** refers to the income from the sale of goods and services.

- Total revenue (TR) is calculated by multiplying the quantity sold by the unit price.

    Total sales revenue = Price × Quantity sold

    or

    $TR = P \times Q$

Hence, if a cinema sells 1200 tickets for a movie, at an average price of $11, then its total revenue is $11 × 1200 = $13 200.

■ Revenue streams

Most businesses have more than one source of revenue. These various sources of income are known as revenue streams. Table 3.3 below shows examples of various revenue streams for different businesses.

Table 3.3 Examples of revenue streams for selected businesses

McDonald's	Apple	Virgin Group
Fast food sales	Computers	Virgin Atlantic (airline carrier)
Franchise license fees	Computer accessories	Virgin Money (finance)
Royalties from franchisees	Smartphones	Virgin Megastores (retail)
Rents paid by franchisees	iTunes	Virgin Radio (entertainment)

> **Expert tip**
>
> Do not confuse revenue with profit. Profit is the positive difference between total revenue and total costs, i.e. Profit = TR – TC. Only after all costs of production have been paid from a firm's revenues can it declare a profit or loss.

> **CUEGIS CONCEPTS**
>
> Examine how change has impacted on the costs and revenues for an organization of your choice.

> **EXAM PRACTICE**
>
> 2 Complete the cost, revenue and profit data in the table below. All figures are in US dollars ($). [4]
>
> | | October | November | December | January |
> |---|---|---|---|---|
> | Sales revenue | 5800 | 6000 | 8800 | |
> | Variable costs | 3480 | | 5280 | 2580 |
> | Fixed costs | 1500 | 1500 | | 1500 |
> | Total costs | | 5100 | 6780 | |
> | Profit | | | | 220 |
>
> 3 The table below refers to the costs and revenues of YT Toys Ltd when operating at 5 000 units of output per month:
>
> | Item | Cost/Revenue |
> |---|---|
> | Price | $20 |
> | Raw materials per unit | $8 |
> | Rent | $7000 |
> | Salaries | $8000 |
>
> a Calculate the total cost of producing 5000 units. [2]
>
> b Calculate the profit made by YT Toys Ltd if all its output is sold. [2]

3.3 Break-even analysis

Total contribution versus contribution per unit (AO2, AO4)

■ **Break-even** exists when a business sells enough goods and/or services in order to cover all its costs of production, i.e. the output level where the business does not make a profit or a loss.

■ For example, suppose an entrepreneur sells hot dogs and we are given the following information:

    ☐ The price of each hot dog is $6.

    ☐ The variable costs of each hot dog are $2.

    ☐ The rent is $400 per week.

■ If he only sells one hot dog, he earns $4 after paying his direct costs, i.e. $6 − $2 = $4. This is not profit, but contribution per unit. After all, he has to pay fixed costs (his rent on the hot dog stall) before declaring any profit. As fixed costs are $400, it means he has to sell 100 hot dogs to break even, i.e. $4 × 100 hot dogs = $400.

■ Hence, to work out the break-even quantity (BEQ), the following formula is used:

$$\text{Break even} = \frac{\text{Fixed costs}}{(\text{Selling price} - \text{variable cost per unit})}$$

■ This means that a firm breaks even when its total contribution equals its total fixed costs.

■ By contrast, contribution per unit only considers the difference between the sales price of one unit and the variable costs needed to make that unit of production.

> ### Keyword definitions
>
> **Contribution per unit** refers to the amount of money a business earns from selling each unit of output.
>
>   Contribution per unit = P − AVC
>
> The surplus is used to contribute towards the payment of fixed costs.
>
> **Total contribution** is used to work out profit or loss. It is calculated by multiplying the unit contribution by the quantity sold.
>
>   Total contribution = (P − AVC) × Q
>
> Profit or loss can then be worked out by taking away fixed costs from total contribution.

Aspects of break-even analysis (A02, A04)

The following points refer to Figure 3.5.

■ Costs and revenues are measured on the *y*-axis, expressed in a given currency.

■ The level of sales or output is shown on the *x*-axis, with an appropriate unit of measurement.

■ The total fixed costs (TFC) line is drawn as a horizontal line because the costs do not change when the level of output or sales changes.

■ The break-even point (BEP) occurs where total sales revenue (TR) equals total costs of production (TC).

■ The break-even quantity (BEQ) is labelled on the *x*-axis indicating the sales volume needed for the business to break even.

■ Similarly, the break-even revenue is shown on the *y*-axis, representing the value of the output needed to break even.

■ When the firm sells less than the BEQ, it makes a **loss**. When it sells more than the BEQ, the business earns **profit**.

■ The difference between the firm's sales volume and the BEQ is called the **margin of safety** (MOS). So, if the firm sells 280 hot dogs in a week but only needs to sell 100 to break even, its MOS is 180 hot dogs.

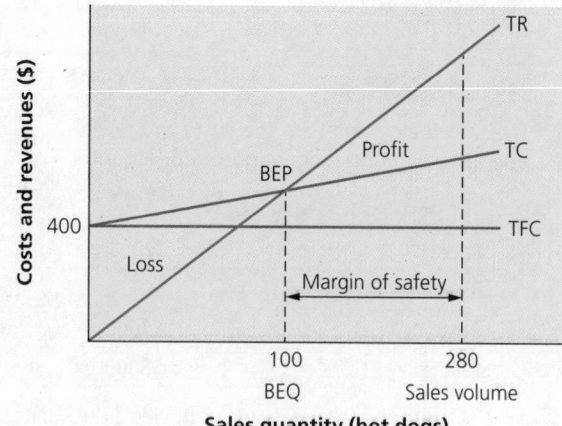

Figure 3.5 Break-even chart

Break-even quantity/point

Keyword definitions

The **break-even point** (BEP) is where the total costs of production equal the total revenue. The **break-even quantity** (BEQ) refers to the quantity of sales or output required to break even.

Profit or loss

Keyword definitions

Profit is the positive difference between a firm's total sales revenue (TR) and its total costs (TC). It is the reward for successful risk-taking in a business. Profit can be calculated in two ways:

Profit = TR − TC

Profit = Total contribution − TFC

A **loss** occurs if total costs exceed total revenues.

EXAM PRACTICE

4   BHS Cupcakes has variable costs of $0.25 per cupcake and sells these for $1.50 each. Its fixed costs are $10 000 per month. It sells an average of 9 500 cupcakes per month.

a   Calculate the contribution per unit for BHS Cupcakes. [2]

b   Calculate how many cupcakes BHS Cupcakes must sell each month in order to break even. [2]

c   Calculate the margin of safety for BHS Cupcakes. [2]

d   Illustrate the above answers on an accurately plotted break-even chart. [5]

Target profit output

Keyword definition

Target profit output (or **target profit quantity**) refers to the sales volume (quantity) needed in order to reach the target profit.

$$\text{Target profit quantity} = \frac{\text{Fixed cost} + \text{Target profit}}{\text{Price} - \text{Variable cost per unit}}$$

Target profit

Keyword definition

Target profit is the desired or expected profit from a business, i.e. how much profit it aims to earn. It can be easily determined from a break-even chart by comparing the total cost and total revenue curves at each level of output.

Target price

Keyword definition

Target price is the amount charged to customers in order to reach break-even (or any desired target profit). The target price for break-even is found using the formula:

Target price = Average Fixed Cost + Average Variable Cost

or

Target price = (Total Fixed Cost ÷ Output) + Average Variable Cost

Expert tip

The *y*-axis should be correctly labelled as 'Costs and revenue ($)', i.e. it should include an appropriate currency. The *x*-axis should be appropriately labelled too, and include the correct unit of measurement (such as tonnes, kilos, number of customers, or even hot dogs, depending on the context of the question). This is a common area for error that students often lose marks on.

Expert tip

The margin of safety (MOS) is measured along the *x*-axis. This means the correct unit of measurement for the MOS is the units of output. Too often, students incorrectly express the MOS using the *y*-axis in terms of a currency.

5 Calculate the total contribution required for Anson Miu & Co. based on the following data: Fixed costs = $10 000 per month and target profit = $35 000 per month. [2]

6 Suppose Li & Tse Jewellers has a target profit of $200 000 per year, earns a unit contribution of $500, and incurs fixed costs of $50 000. Calculate the target profit output for the firm. [2]

7 Suppose Bhardwaj Watches has fixed costs of $3500 per month, direct costs of $120 per watch, a sales target of 60 watches per month and a target profit of $2500. Calculate the target price for Bhardwaj Watches. [2]

8 Paine & Nguyen Consultancy charge $500 per person for their training courses, with unit variable costs of $420. Their fixed costs are $12 000 per month.

   a Calculate how many people must pay for training with the firm each month in order for the firm to break even. [2]

   b If the firm has a target profit of $20 000, calculate how many people are required to pay for training courses each month. [2]

The effects of changes in price or cost on the break-even quantity, profit and margin of safety, using graphical and quantitative methods (AO2, AO4)

■ A higher price will reduce the break-even quantity. Diagrammatically, the total revenue (TR) line will be steeper due to the higher price, so break-even occurs at a lower level of output. The opposite is true for a reduction in price, i.e. the firm would have to sell more in order to break even.

■ This means that a higher price will reduce the margin of safety (because the firm breaks even earlier). However, this assumes that the sales volume does not fall following the increase in price.

■ Higher costs of production (fixed and/or variable costs) will increase the break-even quantity. Diagrammatically, the total cost line would be steeper if only variable costs increase or shift upwards if there is an increase in fixed costs.

9 Study the data below for Alyssa Stephen's Hot Dog Stall and answer the questions that follow.

   • The price of each hot dog is $6.
   • The variable costs of each hot dog is $2.
   • Her rent is $400 per week.
   • Sales quantity = 280 hot dogs per week.

   a Suppose Alyssa Stephen's Hot Dog Stall raises its price to $7. Construct a fully labelled diagram to show the old and new break-even following the firm's decision to raise its price. [6]

   b Assuming there is no change in the demand for hot dogs at Alyssa Stephen's Hot Dog Stall, calculate the new margin of safety. [2]

The benefits of break-even analysis (AO3)

- It is a visual tool which enables managers to easily interpret the relationship between fixed costs, variable costs, price, revenues and profits.

- It is a strategic decision-making tool, e.g. if the analysis shows a very high BEQ with a very low MOS, the decision might be to refrain from implementing such a high-risk decision.

- The model works well for the analysis of single-product firms.

- It is useful for analysing and predicting the impacts of changes in the price on the profitability of the business.

- Similarly, it is useful for predicting the effects on profitability if the business changes its costs.

The limitations of break-even analysis (AO3)

- The model assumes that costs and revenues are static, i.e. it assumes unchanging conditions in the market. In reality, variables such as inflation and interest rates (see Unit 1.5) will affect the forecasts.

- Prices and costs are assumed to be constant, so the TR and TC lines are linear. In reality, firms are likely to experience economies of scale (or diseconomies of scale) as their output levels increase. Businesses are also likely to offer price discounts to people who buy in bulk.

- It is not always easy to classify certain costs as being only fixed or only variable, e.g. electricity charges might be considered as semi-variable costs (see Unit 3.2). Hence, this can prove problematic for the construction of break-even charts.

- As most businesses sell a range of products, this might require fixed costs to be allocated to different cost and profit centres (see Unit 3.9). Therefore, break-even analysis might not be suitable for multi-product businesses.

- The effectiveness of the model depends on the accuracy of the data used. Prices and costs are only estimates (forecasts) which the business might not have computed accurately, thus limiting the usefulness of the predictions.

- The model also assumes that only one product is produced and sold by the business. For example, hotels have different prices for different types of rooms, as well as other related services such as laundry and catering services.

- As a quantitative tool, break-even analysis ignores qualitative issues in decision making, e.g. the impact of working at higher levels of output may cause huge amounts of stress and demotivation for the workforce.

CUEGIS CONCEPTS

Examine the extent to which break-even analysis is a useful management tool for an organization of your choice. Consider the concepts of change and strategy in your answer.

Figure 3.6 The Burj Al Arab Hotel in Dubai charges a range of prices for different types of accomodation

3.4 Final accounts (*some HL only*)

The purpose of accounts to different stakeholders (AO3)

- **Final accounts** comprise of the profit and loss account, the balance sheet, and cash flow statements (see Unit 3.7).

- They are important because they show directors, owners (or shareholders) and other stakeholder groups the financial performance of the business during the accounting period.

- The final accounts enable managers to have the necessary quantitative data to support decision making.

- For external stakeholders, the purpose of accounts is to help them to make rational judgements about the business, e.g. banks and other lenders can assess the extent to which the business can afford debt (borrowing).

- It is important for shareholders to hold directors accountable for their use of the company's funds and to assess how safe their investment is, e.g. the final accounts indicate the firm's ability to survive in the short term.

- Potential shareholders and investors will be interested in a firm's final accounts as this may affect their willingness to invest in the company, e.g. they will use the accounts to measure the firm's liquidity position.

The principles and ethics of accounting practice (AO3)

- **Integrity** – Accountants need to be open and honest in all aspects of their professional conduct, e.g. final accounts should be reported accurately and truthfully with the tax authorities and all other interested stakeholders.

- **Objectivity** – The reporting of final accounts should not contain bias or undue influence of other parties. Accounting practices should be free from any conflict of interest between the business and its various stakeholder groups.

- **Professional competence and due care** – This means accountants have a professional duty to continue their professional knowledge and act diligently. They should stay up to date with developments in the industry, including changes in legislation and accounting practices.

- **Confidentiality** – Accountants must respect the confidentiality of financial data and information acquired as a result of their profession. They must not disclose any of this to third parties unless there is a legal or professional duty to do so. The data must not be used for personal gain of the accountant or third parties. This is both a legal and ethical obligation.

- **Professional behaviour** – Accountants must avoid any action that could bring their profession into disrepute, e.g. they must comply with relevant laws and regulations regarding accounting practices.

Final accounts (AO2, AO4)

■ Profit and loss account

- The profit and loss account shows the net profit (or loss) after all costs have been deducted from the organization's revenues, per time period (see Figure 3.7).

- **Sales revenue** refers to the money a business earns from selling its goods and services.

- **Cost of goods sold** (COGS) refers to the direct costs of production. COGS can include raw materials, components, packaging and direct labour costs.
  The formula is COGS = Opening stock + Purchases – Closing stock.

- **Gross profit** is the amount of profit from ordinary trading activities. It is calculated by taking away the value of COGS from the sales revenue.

- **Expenses** are the indirect costs of production, such as rent, insurance and management salaries. Interest and tax are not included in this section because they are expenses that are beyond the control of the business, making historical benchmarking difficult or meaningless.

- **Net profit before interest and tax** shows the value of profit before deducting interest repayments on loans (the rate being determined by the central bank) and taxation on profits (the rate being determined by the central government).

- **Net profit after interest and tax** shows the actual amount of profit the business has at its disposal after all costs are deducted (including interest and tax payments). The net profit can then be distributed between the shareholders and/or retained in the business.

- **Dividends** are the payments that a company pays to its shareholders from its net profit after interest and tax. The amount distributed to shareholders is determined by the board of directors.

- **Retained profit** is the amount of net profit remaining after all costs are paid and shareholders have been compensated. It is an important internal source of finance (see Unit 3.1) that can be used for maintenance, investments, financing growth or kept as reserve finance.

> **Expert tip**
>
> Dividends do not have to be paid out to shareholders every year if the company declares a profit. Instead, the directors may choose to use the funds (retained profits) as an internal source of finance.

Profit and loss account for (*Company name*), for the year ended (*Date*)

	$m
Sales revenue	700
Minus Cost of goods sold	350
Gross profit	350
Minus Expenses	200
Net profit before interest and tax	150
Minus Interest	10
Net profit before tax	140
Minus Tax	25
Net profit after interest and tax	115
Dividends	35
Retained profit	80

Figure 3.7 Format of the profit and loss account

Source: *IB Diploma Business Management Guide*

EXAM PRACTICE

10 Malanow Ski Company has an opening stock of $45 000, a closing stock of $35 000, and has purchased stock during the year costing $65 000. Calculate the firm's cost of goods sold (COGS). [2]

11 Construct the profit and loss account from the data for Axner Insurance Company for the year ending March 2016. [4]

	$
Cost of goods sold	430 000
Dividends	65 000
Expenses	80 000
Gross profit	270 000
Interest and tax	55 000
Net profit	190 000
Net profit after interest and tax	135 000
Retained profit	70 000
Sales turnover	700 000

■ Balance sheet

■ The balance sheet shows the value of an organization's assets and liabilities at a particular point in time (see Figure 3.8). Assets are the items of value that a business owns, e.g. buildings, equipment, stock and cash. Liabilities are the debts the business owes to others, e.g. money owed to banks or suppliers.

■ **Fixed assets** are long-term assets (lasting more than 12 months) used to produce goods and services, e.g. land, buildings, vehicles, equipment, tools, and machinery. The value of most fixed assets depreciates over time (their value drops) so deducting accumulated depreciation gives the net value of fixed assets.

■ **Current assets** are short-term, liquid assets of the business that are intended to be used up within the year, i.e. cash, debtors and stock:

  □ **Cash** – This is the money a business has at its premises and in bank accounts, making it easily accessible.

  □ **Debtors** – These are customers who have received goods or services, but have yet to pay for them. The typical credit period given to customers is between 30 and 60 days.

  □ **Stock** – Inventory of goods for sale within a short period of time.

■ **Current liabilities** are short-term debts that need to be repaid within 12 months of the balance sheet date, i.e. overdrafts, creditors and short-term loans:

  □ **Overdrafts** – An overdraft is a banking service that enables customers to overdraw on their bank account, i.e. to take out more money than exists in the account. They are used for very short-term purposes and typically repaid within a few months in order to avoid high interest charges.

  □ **Creditors** – Suppliers may give trade credit (the option to buy now but pay later), which needs to be repaid, typically within 30 to 60 days.

  □ **Short-term loans** – Advances (loans) from a financial lender, such as a bank, that need to be repaid within 12 months.

■ **Working capital** is the amount of money available for the day-to-day running of a business. It is needed to fund business activity and trade, e.g. to pay for wages, raw materials, and utility bills. It is calculated by the difference between current assets and current liabilities. Hence, working capital is also known as **net current assets**.

■ **Net assets** are the overall value of a firm's assets after all liabilities are accounted for. Hence, net assets = Total assets − Total liabilities.

■ The value of net assets on a balance sheet must balance with the value of **equity**. This is the firm's internal sources of finance, made up of share capital and retained profit.

Expert tip

SL students do not need to calculate depreciation but may need to include the figure for accumulated depreciation when constructing a balance sheet in the final exams.

- **Share capital** is the value of equity in a company funded by shareholders. The value can increase over time if the business issues (sells) more shares as a source of finance.

- **Retained profit** is the amount of money remaining after all costs have been paid (including interest and tax) and allocating a proportion of the profits to shareholders (in the form of dividends). It is recorded in both the profit and loss account and the balance sheet (as a source of equity).

Balance sheet for (*Company name*) as of (*Date*)

	$m	$m
Fixed assets		
Fixed assets	500	
Minus Accumulated depreciation	20	
Net fixed assets		480
Current assets		
Cash	10	
Debtors	12	
Stocks	35	
Total current assets	57	
Current liabilities		
Overdraft	5	
Creditors	15	
Short-term loans	22	
Total current liabilities	42	
Net current assets (working capital)		15
Total assets less current liabilities		495
Minus **Long-term liabilities** (debt)	300	
Net assets		195
Financed by:		
Share capital	110	
Retained profit	85	
Equity		195

Figure 3.8 Format of the balance sheet

Source: *IB Diploma Business Management Guide*

EXAM PRACTICE

12 Construct a balance sheet for Lietz Watch Company from the data below presented on 31 March 2016. [4]

	$
Retained profits	100 000
Net current assets	150 000
Long-term liabilities	200 000
Share capital	300 000
Net assets	400 000
Fixed assets	450 000

Different types of intangible assets (AO1)

- An intangible asset is a non-physical asset that adds value to an organization, e.g. customer goodwill and intellectual property rights (patents, copyrights and trademarks).

- **Goodwill** refers to the established reputation and networks of a business, enabling it to be worth more than the market value of its quantifiable assets. It helps to attract and retain workers and to establish new investors. The value of goodwill is only realized when the business is actually sold.

- A **patent** is the exclusive right granted to an organization by the government to make use of an invention or process for a particular period of time. It gives the inventor an incentive to invest time and money to conduct research and development. Patents give the business a unique selling point (USP) for a given time period.

- **Copyright** as a form of intellectual property right gives the owner legal rights to a creative piece of work, e.g. book, music or movie. It provides legal protection against competitors using its published works.

- **Trademarks** are the legal protection for an organization's registered symbol (logo), word (brand), or phrase (slogan). Some large multinational companies such as Apple, Coca-Cola and Toyota have brand values worth billions of dollars.

Expert tip

It will prove useful to learn and understand the formulae used to construct the final accounts:

Key term	Formula
Cost of goods sold (COGS)	Opening stock + Purchases – Closing stock
Depreciation: straight line method (per year)	(Purchase cost – residual value) ÷ Lifespan of asset
Depreciation: reducing balance method (per year)	Purchase cost × Depreciation rate
Expenses	Net profit – Gross profit
Gross profit	Sales revenue – Cost of goods sold
Net assets	Fixed assets + Working capital – long-term liabilities
Net profit	Gross profit – Expenses
Equity (or Owners' equity)	Total assets – Total liabilities
Retained profit	Net profit after interest and tax – Dividends

Methods of depreciation (AO2, AO4) and the strengths and weaknesses of each method (AO2) *(HL only)*

- Although depreciation reduces the value of fixed assets, there is no actual cash outflow from the business. Instead, it is recorded on the profit and loss account as an expense, thereby reducing profit for the year.

- It is important to calculate depreciation as managers, shareholders, lenders, the government and potential investors all want to know how much the business is actually worth. If it is not considered, profits become overstated until the time comes for the fixed assets to be replaced.

- Wear and tear is the major cause of the fall in the value of fixed assets, such as vehicles and machinery. As the asset is continually used, it does not perform as well. Used items fetch a lower market value.

> **Keyword definition**
>
> **Depreciation** is the decline in the value of a fixed asset over time, mainly due to usage (wear and tear) and newer models or better technologies being available.

- In many cases, the asset has a **residual value** (or **scrap value**) when being replaced. However, the scrap value at the end of the asset's useful life is difficult to forecast accurately.

- Fixed assets can also become obsolete (outdated) as newer models and better technologies become available over time. In such cases, the scrap value of the asset could be zero.

Straight line method

- The straight line method of calculating depreciation reduces the value of fixed assets by equal amounts each year (see Figure 3.9).

- It is calculated using the formula:

$$\text{Annual depreciation} = \frac{\text{Purchase cost} - \text{Residual value}}{\text{Lifespan}}$$

- The main advantage of straight line depreciation is the simplicity of the method to calculate depreciation.

- The main weakness is that most fixed assets, such as vehicles or computer hardware, depreciate significantly more in the early part of their life. Writing off the same amount of money each year can create misleading figures for the book value of the fixed assets.

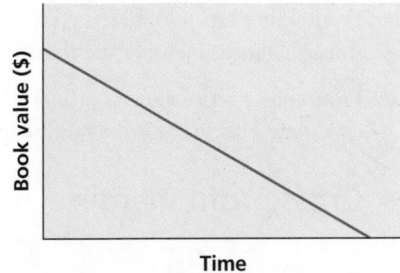

Figure 3.9 The straight line depreciation method

EXAM PRACTICE

13 Tse and Li Solicitors recently purchased a new computer system for $120 000. It has an estimated useful life of four years with an estimated residual value of $20 000. Calculate the amount of annual depreciation for the firm. [2]

Reducing/declining balance method

- The declining balance method of depreciation reduces the value of a fixed asset by a predetermined percentage each year. This results in a larger amount of depreciation during the earlier stages of the asset's useful life (see Figure 3.10).

- For *each* year, the depreciation is calculated using the formula:

Net book value × Depreciation rate

- Thus, the firm's tax liability will be lower in the earlier years compared with the straight line method. However, the value of the firm's net assets will also be lower.

- The main advantage of the declining balance method of calculating depreciation is that it is more realistic (accurate) in measuring the market value of fixed assets compared to using the straight line method.

- However, the main drawback is that it is more difficult (time consuming) to calculate.

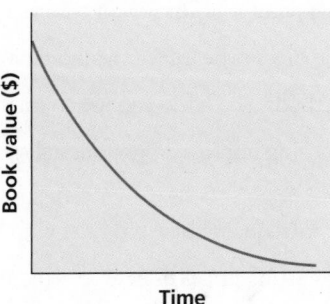

Figure 3.10 The reducing balance depreciation method

EXAM PRACTICE

14 Harlow and Wang Stationers purchase a printing machine for $100 000 with an expected useful life of five years. The firm uses a depreciation rate of 30%. Calculate the residual value of the asset after five years. [3]

15 Marc Morris purchases a manufacturing machine for $20 000. It has a useful life of five years and a residual value at the end of this period of $3000. He estimates a depreciation rate of 25% if the reducing balance method is used. Calculate and compare the results of the straight line and reducing balance methods. [6]

3.5 Profitability and liquidity ratio analysis

Revised ☐

Profitability and efficiency ratios (AO2, AO4) and possible strategies to improve these ratios (AO3)

Revised ☐

- Ratio analysis is a financial management tool for analysing and judging the performance of a business.

- It allows for historical comparisons of a business in different time periods.

- Profitability ratios look at the level and value of a firm's profits and enable stakeholders to measure the return on their investments.

- Profitability ratios express profits as a percentage of sales revenue. They can be calculated using the gross profit margin or net profit margin.

■ Gross profit margin

- Gross profit is the difference between a firm's sales revenue and its cost of goods sold (COGS).

- The formula for calculating the gross profit margin is:

$$\text{Gross profit margin} = \frac{\text{Gross profit}}{\text{Sales revenue}} \times 100$$

- So, if sales revenue equals $10 million, COGS equals $6m, the gross profit = $10m − $6m = $4m. Hence, GPM = $4m ÷ $10m = 40%.

- The higher the GPM, the more profitable the firm has been.

- Methods a business can use to improve its GPM include:

  ☐ using improved promotional strategies to persuade more customers to buy its products

  ☐ introducing new products with higher gross profit margins

  ☐ cutting prices of products sold in highly competitive markets in order to attract more customers

  ☐ sourcing suppliers with cheaper raw material prices, resulting in lower COGS.

> **Keyword definition**
>
> **Gross profit margin** (GPM) is a profitability ratio that shows a firm's gross profit expressed as a percentage of its sales revenue.

■ Net profit margin

- Net profit is the surplus remaining after all production costs, including expenses, have been fully paid.

- The net profit margin (NPM) shows the percentage of sales revenue that is turned into net profit. It is calculated using the formula:

$$\text{Net profit margin} = \frac{\text{Net profit before interest and tax}}{\text{Sales revenue}} \times 100$$

- So, if sales revenue equals $10 million, COGS equal $6 million and expenses equal $3 million, then net profit = $10m − $6m − $3m = $1m. Hence, the NPM = $1m ÷ $10m = 10%.

- The higher the NPM, the greater the financial return as a percentage of the firm's sales revenue. It also indicates greater efficiency in managing the firm's expenses.

- To improve the NPM, managers can strive to reduce excessive and unnecessary day-to-day expenses. In the long run, it could even consider relocating to areas with lower rent charges.

> **Keyword definition**
>
> **Net profit margin** (NPM) measures a firm's overall profit (after all costs have been deducted) as a percentage of its sales revenue.

16 Joe Heaton's Kitchen has a gross profit of $3.5 million, sales revenue of $5.5 million and expenses of $1.5 million. Calculate the firm's gross profit margin and net profit margin. [4]

ROCE

■ Capital employed is the sum of all assets less current liabilities, i.e. fixed assets + working capital. On the balance sheet, it is also found by the formula: Equity + Long-term liabilities.

■ ROCE is an important ratio that measures the financial performance of an organization compared to the amount of capital invested in the business.

■ It is calculated using the formula:

Return on capital employed (ROCE) = $\dfrac{\text{Net profit before interest and tax}}{\text{Capital employed}} \times 100$

■ The ROCE ratio can be improved by using strategies that:

☐ Increase the level of a firm's sales revenues, e.g. promotional offers, reduced prices to entice customers, wider distribution networks or improved products.

☐ Reduce costs of production, e.g. better stock control systems (see Unit 5.5), improved quality management systems (see Unit 5.3), or taking greater advantage of economies of scale (see Unit 1.6).

☐ Sell unproductive assets in order to have better liquidity. A reduction in such assets results in a better cash position for the firm.

> **Keyword definition**
>
> The **return on capital employed** (ROCE) ratio measures a firm's efficiency and profitability in relation to its size (as measured by the firm's capital employed).

> **Expert tip**
>
> Many students seem to think that profitability ratios are used to see how much profit a business earns. This can be done simply by looking at a profit and loss account. Ratios require the comparison of two numbers, such as comparing net profit against sales revenues.

17 Andre Pannu and Partners have a gross profit of $100m, expenses of $10m and capital employed of $300m. Calculate the firm's return on capital employed. [2]

Liquidity ratios (AO2, AO4) and possible strategies to improve these ratios (AO3)

Revised ☐

■ Liquidity ratios calculate the extent to which a business can pay off its short-term debts with its current assets.

■ Managing liquidity is important to prevent a liquidity crisis (when a business is unable to pay its short-term debts).

■ The two categories of liquidity ratios are the current ratio and the acid test ratio.

Current ratio

■ The current ratio measures the value of a firm's liquid assets (cash, stocks and debtors) compared to its short-term liabilities (overdrafts, creditors and short-term loans).

■ It is calculated using the formula:

Current ratio = $\dfrac{\text{Current assets}}{\text{Current liabilities}}$

■ So, if a firm's current assets equal $15.6 million and current liabilities equal $11.2 million, then its current ratio = $15.6 million ÷ $11.2 million = 1.39:1. This figure means that for every $1 of current liabilities, the firm has $1.39 in liquid assets.

■ As an absolute minimum, the current ratio must be 1:1, i.e. the firm has enough liquid assets to pay off its short-term liabilities. Ideally, the ratio should be around 2:1 for most industries.

> **Keyword definition**
>
> **Liquidity ratios** are the financial ratios that look at a firm's ability to pay its debts.

> **Keyword definition**
>
> The **current ratio** is a short-term liquidity ratio which calculates the ability of a business to meet its debts within the next 12 months.

- To improve the current ratio, a business can:
  - ☐ attract more customers and encourage them to pay by cash
  - ☐ deposit cash that is not being used imminently into higher interest accounts
  - ☐ use its cash balance to pay off short-term debts
  - ☐ negotiate with suppliers for an extended credit period to improve its liquidity
  - ☐ fund short-term debt with long-term liabilities, which allows the firm to repay debts over a longer period of time.

> **Expert tip**
>
> A higher current ratio is not always a good thing. A business can have too much stock, which ties up working capital. It can hold too much cash, which should be used to fund business activity instead. It might also have too many debtors, which again harms working capital.

EXAM PRACTICE

18 Claire Hao Accessories has the following financial data: cash = $150 000, debtors = $65 000, overdrafts = $55 000, short-term loans = $25 000, stocks = $145 000, and trade creditors = $80 000. Calculate the firm's current ratio using this information. [3]

■ Acid test/quick ratio

- The acid test ratio (or quick ratio) is similar to the current ratio except that stock (inventory) is excluded from the calculation of current assets.

- It is a suitable measure of liquidity for businesses with stocks that are not always easily converted into cash or for products that have a long working capital cycle (see Unit 3.7).

- The quick ratio is calculated using the formula:

$$\text{Acid test (quick) ratio} = \frac{\text{Current asset} - \text{stock}}{\text{Current liabilities}}$$

- So, if current assets equal $15.6 million, current liabilities equal $11.2 million and stock equals $1.8 million, the acid test ratio = ($15.6 million − $1.8 million) ÷ $11.2 million = 1.23:1. This figure means the business has $1.23 of liquid assets (without having to sell any of its stock) for every $1 of current liabilities it incurs.

- An acid test ratio of less than 1:1 means the firm has a liquidity problem as there are insufficient funds from its current assets to pay off short-term debts.

- To improve the acid test ratio, a business can:
  - ☐ Use the same methods that improve the current ratio.
  - ☐ Improve its stock control management system (see Unit 5.5); when the value of a firm's stocks (inventories) falls, the acid test ratio increases.

> **Keyword definition**
>
> The **acid test ratio** is a liquidity ratio that measures a firm's ability to meet its short-term debts. It ignores stock because some inventories are difficult to turn into cash in a short time frame.

> **CUEGIS CONCEPTS**
>
> Discuss the role of final accounts and ratio analysis in formulating the corporate strategy for an organization of your choice.

3.6 Efficiency ratio analysis (*HL only*)

Revised ☐

Efficiency ratios (AO2, AO4) and possible strategies to improve these ratios (AO3)

Revised ☐

- Efficiency ratios are used to measure how well an organization uses its resources and available capital to generate income.

- Examples of efficiency ratios include: the stock turnover (or inventory turnover), debtor days, creditor days and gearing ratios.

- The ratios are used by management to help improve the organization, e.g. reducing the time taken to collect cash from customers or speeding up the time to convert stock into cash.

- There is a positive correlation between efficiency ratios and profitability ratios (see Unit 3.5), i.e. when businesses are efficient with their resources, they tend to be more profitable.

■ Inventory/stock turnover

■ The stock turnover ratio is used to calculate how many times a firm's inventory needs to be replaced in a given time period (typically a year) or how quickly its stock is sold and replaced.

■ It is calculated using one of two formulae:

$$\text{Stock turnover (number of times)} = \frac{\text{Cost of goods sold}}{\text{Average stock}}$$

or

$$\text{Stock turnover (number of days)} = \frac{\text{Average stock}}{\text{Cost of goods sold}} \times 365$$

■ Hence, a business with \$10 000 of average inventory and total cost of goods sold of \$100 000 has effectively sold its stock 10 times over. Alternatively, it takes an average of 36.5 days for the firm to sell its average inventory holding.

■ The average stock value is found by the formula: (Opening stock + Closing stock) ÷ 2.

■ Stock turnover varies for businesses operating in different industries, e.g. supermarkets will have a higher inventory turnover rate than high-end jewellers or manufacturers of luxury cars.

■ Businesses that sell perishable products rely on a short working capital cycle so need to have a high stock turnover rate. By contrast, those selling products that are durable and with a large profit margin can afford for the stock turnover to be lower.

■ Stock turnover is a less relevant financial ratio to service providers such as tuition colleges, insurance firms, tour operators and hairdressers because they hold few, if any, tangible products for sale.

■ Methods to improve the stock turnover ratio include:

☐ Disposing of obsolete stock to reduce the firm's level of stock.

☐ Offering a narrower range of products so there is better stock control and less stockpiling.

☐ Adopting a just-in-time stock control system (see Unit 5.5) as stocks of raw materials and components are ordered only when needed, i.e. there is no need to hold any amount of inventory.

> **Keyword definition**
> The **stock turnover ratio** measures the number of days it takes a business to sell its stock or the number of times the business replenishes its stock during a given period of time.

EXAM PRACTICE

19 Wenger Co. has cost of goods sold (COGS) valued at \$525 000. It started the year with stock worth \$250 000 and at the end of the year has closing stock valued at \$50 000. Calculate the company's stock turnover ratio. [2]

■ Debtor days

■ The debtor days ratio calculates the average debt collection period of a business, i.e. the time taken to collect money from its customers who have bought goods and services on credit.

■ It assesses how efficient an organization is at managing its credit control systems.

■ It is calculated using the formula:

$$\text{Debtor days ratio (number of days)} = \frac{\text{Debtors}}{\text{Total sales revenue}} \times 365$$

■ In general, the lower the debtor days ratio the better it is for the business. A higher ratio suggests that sales revenue has grown faster than cash receipts from customers, i.e. a higher proportion of customers pay using trade credit.

> **Keyword definition**
> The **debtor days ratio** measures the average number of days a business takes to collect debts from its customers who have bought goods and services on trade credit.

- Methods to improve the debtor days ratio include:
  - ☐ encouraging customers to pay by cash, e.g. offering a cash discount
  - ☐ reducing the credit period offered to clients
  - ☐ tighter credit control, i.e. offering credit only to customers with a good track record of paying their invoices on time.

EXAM PRACTICE

20 Skarkey Ltd sells 100 000 units of output at a price of $15 each. It has debtors to the value of $300 000. Calculate the firm's debtor days ratio. [2]

■ Creditor days

- The creditor days ratio calculates the length of time taken, on average, for a business to pay back its suppliers.

$$\text{Creditor days ratio (number of days)} = \frac{\text{Creditors}}{\text{Cost of goods sold}} \times 365$$

- In general, a business that delays paying its bills and short-term debts can maximize its cash flow (assuming there are no interest charges for late payment or loss of goodwill from suppliers).

- When the value of creditors rises, the ratio also rises. This suggests that more is being bought on trade credit or the timing of payments to suppliers has been delayed, i.e. it takes longer to pay creditors.

- For a business, the debt collection period (as calculated by the debtor days ratio) should ideally be shorter than the creditor payment period (creditor days ratio).

- Trade credit is typically offered for 30 to 45 days, so a creditor days ratio in this region is generally acceptable. However, this varies between industries and countries.

- Methods to improve the creditor days ratio include:
  - ☐ negotiate extended credit periods with suppliers
  - ☐ seek alternative suppliers that offer better trade credit terms and conditions
  - ☐ pay for stocks and other items of expenditure with cash, rather than using trade credit.

> **Keyword definition**
> **Creditor days ratio** measures the average number of days a business takes to repay its creditors.

EXAM PRACTICE

21 Harrington Inc. has sold stock valued at a cost of $202 000. It owes $24 900 to trade creditors. Calculate the firm's creditor days ratio. [2]

■ Gearing ratio

- The gearing ratio is a measure of efficiency and financial risk to help managers interpret the extent to which the firm's capital employed has been financed by borrowed funds.

- Gearing involves the use of loans and other external sources of finance (such as debentures and trade credit) to fund business activity and expansion.

- The gearing ratio is calculated using the formula:

$$\text{Gearing ratio} = \frac{\text{Loan capital}}{\text{Capital employed}} \times 100$$

- A highly geared firm is generally vulnerable to increases in the interest rate as the repayment on existing loans intensifies. It is also at greater risk during a recession as revenues decline rapidly yet repayment of its loans still exists.

- Firms with a high gearing ratio are highly dependent on borrowing and long-term debt, so are seen as being risky investments.

> **Keyword definition**
> The **gearing ratio** reveals the degree to which a business is financed by loan capital by comparing loan capital and the total capital employed.

- Conversely, firms with a lower gearing ratio have greater dependency on internal funding so are less exposed to fluctuations in interest rates. A low gearing ratio suggests that the firm is financially stable so there is a low risk of it facing liquidity issues.

- Methods to reduce a firm's gearing ratio include:

  ☐ paying off some long-term liabilities (loan capital), such as the repayment of a mortgage or debentures (see Unit 3.1)

  ☐ improving working capital (such as improved inventory control or faster collection of payment from debtors) to produce cash which can be used to pay off debts

  ☐ using more internal sources of finance, such as retained profits or share capital, to fund business growth and expansion.

> **Expert tip**
>
> High gearing does not necessarily mean unaffordable gearing, especially if interest rates are low and there is high market growth potential. A firm might have a high, but affordable, gearing ratio with the loans being used to fund its expansion. Hence, it can actually lead to long-term profits.

EXAM PRACTICE

22 Delgado Ltd has an existing bank loan of $10 million. It has share capital of $15 m and retained profit of $5 m. Calculate the firm's gearing ratio. [3]

23 Calculate the gearing ratio for the two firms below from the limited data. Outline which company represents higher risk for potential investors. [4]

	Ho Bakery Ltd	Chang Bakery Ltd
Capital employed	$250 000	$260 000
Long-term liabilities	$80 000	$90 000
Mortgage	$35 000	$27 000

> **Expert tip**
>
> Make sure you revise Unit 3.4 when revising the units on ratio analysis (Units 3.5 and 3.6). Quite often in the exams, students are asked to calculate ratios from the balance sheet and profit and loss accounts.

> **CUEGIS CONCEPTS**
>
> Discuss how organizational culture and innovation impact on the efficiency for an organization that you have studied.

3.7 Cash flow

Revised ☐

The difference between profit and cash flow (AO2)

Revised ☐

- Net cash flow is the difference between cash inflow (cash received from the sale of goods and services) and cash outflow (used to pay for the operational costs of the business).

- Net cash flow is an indication of how a business is doing in terms of whether it is able to pay its bills and other costs.

- Profit is the revenue remaining from the sale of goods and services after all costs are paid.

- Profit is usually earned when a sale in made, e.g. a business earns $460 profit from the sale of a product sold at $1000 for which the costs were $540. However, the cash is not necessarily received immediately as some customers might pay by trade credit (see Unit 3.1).

- It is possible for cash flow to be negative when a business earns a profit, whilst cash flow can be positive even if a business makes a loss.

- A profitable business can still go bankrupt if it has negative cash flow, i.e. it does not have the cash to pay for its operational costs. Cash flow is therefore of more importance for smaller businesses to focus on than profit.

- Businesses often borrow money (such as bank overdrafts and loans) to survive until sufficient cash flows in.

- In the short term, a business must have sufficient cash to run its operations whether it is profitable or not. In the long term, a business must be profitable whilst managing its cash flow.

The working capital cycle (AO2)

Revised

- Working capital is the money that a business has available for its operational activities, e.g. to buy raw materials, settle invoices, pay for its marketing or to pay wages to workers.

- Without working capital (or circulating capital), the business is unable to operate or trade.

- It is shown on a firm's balance sheet (see Unit 3.4) as net current assets, i.e. the difference between current assets and current liabilities.

- The working capital cycle refers to the time lag between a firm paying for its operational and production costs of a good or service and it actually receiving the cash from the sale of the product (see Figure 3.11).

- Businesses that receive cash regularly from the sale of goods and services have short working capital cycles, e.g. supermarkets and barbers. Those with long production schedules for which customers pay in instalments and/or by credit have longer working capital cycles.

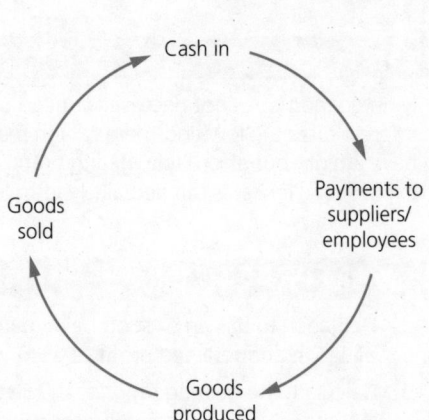

Figure 3.11 The working capital cycle

Cash flow forecasts (AO2, AO4)

Revised

- Cash flow is the movement of money in and out of an organization, based on actual movements of cash or based on forecasts.

- Monitoring a firm's cash flow is important to avoid liquidity problems (periods when there are cash shortages), so the business has enough money to continue its daily operations.

- Cash inflow mainly comes from the sale of goods and services.

- Cash outflow occurs when a business pays for its items of expenditure, e.g. raw materials, staff wages, utility bills, insurance and rent.

- **Net cash flow** is the difference between cash inflows and cash outflows.

  Net cash flow = Cash inflow − Cash outflow

- There is positive cash flow if the inflows exceed the outflows for a given time period. Negative net cash flow means outflows exceed the inflows.

- Cash flow problems can arise due to internal reasons (poor cash flow management) or external factors (such as seasonal demand).

- Being able to predict how cash will flow in and out of the business can help its financial management and decision making.

■ Calculating cash flow forecasts

■ Cash flow forecasting refers to the prediction of cash coming in and moving out of a business over a given period of time, e.g. the next six or twelve months.

■ The **closing balance** is the amount of cash at the end of a trading period, usually one month. This figure becomes the 'opening balance' in the subsequent time period.

■ The **opening balance** is the amount of cash at the beginning of a trading period, usually each month. It is equal to the value of the closing balance in the previous time period.

EXAM PRACTICE

24 Menelao Computers has the following financial information: opening balance = $70 000, cash outflows = $80 000, and cash inflows = $120 000. Calculate the closing balance for the firm.   [2]

25 Shield Sports Equipment has produced a cash flow forecast which predicts a closing year-end balance of $150 000. The company later discovers that payment of $17 000 was not processed from the sales figure and that an invoice for $13 000 is yet to be paid. Calculate the closing balance for the firm.   [2]

26 Study the following financial information and answer the questions that follow.

Kaergaard & Co. cash flow statement (excerpts):

Opening balance: $35 500
Cash inflow: $195 000
Cash outflow: $150 000

a   Calculate the net cash flow for Kaergaard & Co.   [2]
b   Calculate the closing balance for Kaergaard & Co.   [2]

> **Key formulae**
>
> **Cash flow forecasting formulae:**
>
> Net cash flow = Cash inflow − Cash outflow
>
> Closing balance = Opening balance + Net cash flow
>
> Opening balance = Closing balance in preceding month

The relationship between investment, profit and cash flow (AO2)

Revised ☐

■ Investment refers to the capital expenditure (see Unit 3.1) of a business, e.g. the spending on fixed assets such as premises, equipment and machinery.

■ Investment decisions are made on the assumption that profit will be generated in the future.

■ However, investment expenditure clearly leads to cash outflow, at least in the short term.

■ The benefits of an investment project are likely to be reaped over several years (see Unit 3.8).

■ Assets purchased for the investment project may be sold at the end of their useful life, minus their depreciated value (see Unit 3.4). This can generate much-needed cash inflow.

■ Survival and sustainability mean that entrepreneurs must invest in their business for their longer-term profitability. The lack of investment and inability to adapt to change has forced many businesses to collapse, e.g. HMV, Blockbuster and Kodak.

■ By contrast, successful investments lead to improved cash flow and profitability.

Strategies for dealing with cash flow problems (AO3)

- The strategies used to deal with cash flow problems depend on the causes of the problems, such as:

    - ☐ sales revenue are lower than expected

    - ☐ costs of production are higher than budgeted

    - ☐ unexpected costs arise

    - ☐ customers who buy on credit (see Unit 3.1) are slow to pay

    - ☐ some customers who buy on credit fail to pay (bad debts)

    - ☐ overstocking of items that do not sell well.

- Hence, to solve cash flow problems, a business can reduce its cash outflow, improve its cash inflow and/or look for additional finance.

■ Reducing cash outflow

- The business could seek to improve trade credit from its suppliers (see Unit 3.1), e.g. paying on credit rather than paying cash in advance.

- It could reduce the duration of credit offered to its customers (although this might reduce demand from some customers).

- Offer price discounts to customers who make early payment of invoices.

- Reduce delivery costs by negotiating a bulk-buying deal with suppliers (although this could lead to higher costs of stock control).

- Lease rather than buy assets such as equipment, machinery and buildings, e.g. the firm might sell its head office, but immediately lease it back on a long-term basis.

- Holding lower levels of stock (inventory).

- Renegotiate rents or even consider relocation to cheaper premises.

- Negotiate with suppliers for longer trade credit periods or look for cheaper local suppliers.

■ Improving cash inflows

- The business could strive to improve its marketing in order to increase brand awareness, sales and customer loyalty.

- It could consider raising the prices of products that have a high degree of brand loyalty.

- Alternatively, it could lower the prices of products that face fierce competition.

- It could improve its product portfolio management (see Unit 4.5) by stocking more of the best-selling products and reducing or removing stocks of products that don't sell well.

■ Looking for additional finance

- Use a bank overdraft or bank loan (see Unit 3.1) during times of negative cash flow or when the closing balance is negative. However, this would incur interest repayments.

- Seek growth opportunities, e.g. a sole trader might form a partnership to benefit from an additional source of finance and shared skills and responsibilities with the partner(s).

- Selling fixed assets to raise income, e.g. unused or obsolete equipment, furniture and machinery. In extreme cases of liquidity crises, the business might even sell vehicles, premises or subsidiary companies.

> **Expert tip**
>
> When tackling cash flow forecasts, be sure to look out for negative cash flow figures and/or negative closing balances. Business management is about decision making and problem solving – if there aren't any problems for the business in question, then cash flow forecasts wouldn't be required.

EXAM PRACTICE

27 a Complete the three-month cash flow forecast for Axner & Co. [4]

 b Explain two causes of cash flow problems. [4]

 c Explain two ways that Axner & Co. might resolve its cash flow problems. [4]

	July ($)	August ($)	September ($)
Sales revenue	1500		1900
Bank overdraft	0	100	
Cash inflow		1700	1900
Materials	350	400	450
Wages	200	200	
Rent	900	900	900
Utility bills	100	150	200
Cash outflow			1870
Net cash flow			
Opening balance	0	−50	0
Closing balance	−50		

CUEGIS CONCEPTS

Investigate the impact of change and ethics on the management of cash for an organization of your choice.

3.8 Investment appraisal (*some HL only*)

Revised ☐

Investment opportunities using payback period (AO3, AO4)

Revised ☐

- **Investment** is business expenditure on fixed assets with the potential to generate future financial benefits, e.g. the purchase of a new building or upgrading of computer systems.

- **Investment appraisal** is a quantitative decision-making tool used to assess and justify the capital expenditure of a firm in terms of whether it will be financially worthwhile.

- The payback period (PBP) method of investment appraisal measures the time it takes for an investment project to earn enough profit to recover the initial cost of the investment.

- The PBP allows a firm to see whether it will recover the cost of a fixed asset (such as a commercial vehicle, photocopier machine or computer) before it needs to be replaced.

- Where annual net cash flows from the investment project are known, the formula used to calculate the payback period is:

$$\text{Payback period} = \frac{\text{Cost of the investment}}{\text{Annual net cash flow}}$$

- The larger the annual contribution (or annual net cash flow), the faster the payback period.

- An investment project is generally accepted or considered desirable if the PBP is relatively short (which depends on industry norms and the management's maximum desired PBP).

> **Keyword definition**
> The **payback period** (PBP) is the amount of time it takes for a business to recover the initial cost of an investment project.

- The PBP method is suitable for firms that:
  - ☐ focus on time as a priority for investment decisions
  - ☐ regard liquidity to be of more importance than profitability
  - ☐ pursue a quick return on their investment.

Table 3.4 Advantages and disadvantages of payback period

Advantages of payback period	Disadvantages of payback period
● It is the simplest and quickest method of investment appraisal to calculate	● It ignores the timing of the net cash flows, despite the future value of cash being lower
● It is easy for managers to understand the results	● It is not generally suitable for long-term projects, i.e. those with a long PBP
● The depreciation of fixed assets do not directly affect the PBP but can be easily included in the calculation	● Time, rather than profitability, is the focus of attention, which could be unrealistic for most private firms
● Helps managers choose projects with a short PBP to reduce investment risks	● It does not consider the useful life of the asset after its payback period

EXAM PRACTICE

28 Nimes Construction Co. is considering investing €1 155 000 in new machinery. The annual net cash flows arising from the investment are €330 000. Calculate the project's payback period. [2]

29 Brownsword Books is considering an investment of $220 000 in new printing equipment that is expected to generate the following cash flows over the next five years:

Year	Net cash flow
1	$30 000
2	$40 000
3	$60 000
4	$70 000
5	$60 000

The management at Brownsword Books wants a quick recovery of the investment expenditure due to the competitive nature of the industry.

a   Define the term payback period. [2]

b   Calculate the payback period for Brownsword Books and comment on your findings. [4]

Investment opportunities using average rate of return (ARR)

Revised ☐

- The average rate of return (ARR) measures the predicted annual profit generated from an investment project expressed as a percentage of the investment cost.

- The ARR is compared to the firm's desired rate of return to determine whether to accept or reject an investment proposal. This is often based on the prevailing interest rate in banks and/or the predicted ARR for other proposed investment projects.

- It is calculated using the formula:

$$ARR = \frac{\text{Average annual profit}}{\text{Initial investment}}$$

- The higher the value of the ARR, the more financially attractive an investment project tends to be.

- The higher the interest rate, the less attractive the ARR tends to be as it is safer to just leave cash in the bank instead of being burdened with risks, especially for firms that need to borrow money to fund their investment projects.

> **Keyword definition**
>
> The **average rate of return** (ARR) is an investment appraisal technique that calculates the average annual profit of an investment project expressed as a percentage of the initial amount invested in the project.

Table 3.5 Advantages and disadvantages of average rate of return

Advantages of ARR	Disadvantages of ARR
• The ARR is simple to understand and straightforward to calculate • Unlike the payback period, the ARR focuses on profitability rather than time • The firm can use the ARR to evaluate its performance • As the ARR is expressed as a percentage, it can be useful to compare the attractiveness of a range of different investment projects	• Unlike the net present value method, the ARR ignores the timings of cash flow • Unlike the PBP, the ARR focuses on profits rather than cash flow in order to break even quickly and to generate cash to invest in other projects • The figures are predictions only, so tend to be less accurate the longer the investment project is under consideration

EXAM PRACTICE

30 The management at Chandelier World is investigating the feasibility of replacing its old precision-cutting machinery. The new machinery would cost $460 000. It would increase the firm's annual revenue by $150 000 but raise operational costs by $60 000 a year. The estimated useful life of the new machinery is 12 years with no scrap (second-hand) value. The management wants an average rate of return (ARR) of 15% on all its capital investments.

   a Calculate the average rate of return (ARR) of the new machinery for Chandelier World. [2]

   b Comment on whether Chandelier World should purchase the new machinery. [2]

31 Villano Watch Company is deciding whether to upgrade its computerized invoicing system for $155 000. The expected gains (or total contributions) from doing so over the system's expected useful life cycle of five years is shown below.

Year	Total contribution
1	$30 000
2	$40 000
3	$50 000
4	$40 000
5	$30 000

Calculate the average rate of return and comment on whether Villano Watch Company should invest in the computerized invoicing system. [4]

Investment opportunities using net present value (NPV) (AO3, AO4) (*HL only*)

Revised ☐

■ Net present value (NPV) is the difference between the total present values of future net cash flow and the initial cost of the investment project.

■ It is calculated by taking away the cost of the investment project from the sum of the present values for the duration of the project.

■ If the interest rate is 10% per annum, then the present value of receiving $1000 in one year's time is $909.10. This means $909.10 invested today, earning 10% would be valued at $1000 in a year's time. The discount rate is therefore 0.9091.

■ The NPV shows the monetary value of the total financial return on an investment project expressed in today's value.

■ The NPV looks at the opportunity cost of money as cash received in the future is worth less than it is worth presently.

■ In general, the higher the interest rate, the lower the present (current) value of money that is received in the future.

> ### Keyword definitions
>
> **Net present value** (NPV) is an investment appraisal technique that calculates the real value of an investment project by discounting the value of future cash flows. Once the initial cost of the investment project is deducted from the total discounted cash flow, the NPV is found.
>
> A **discount rate** is a number used to reduce the value of a sum of money received in the future in order to determine its present value.

- If the NPV figure is positive, then the investment project is feasible on financial grounds. The higher the NPV, the more attractive the investment project.

- The longer the investment project under consideration, the longer it takes for net cash flows to materialize, so the lower the future value (net worth) of the project tends to be.

- The higher the discount rate, the lower the NPV because of the higher opportunity cost of receiving cash in the distant future.

Expert tip

Discount tables will be provided to HL students in the final exams when required – see page 89 of the *Business Management Guide*.

Table 3.6 Advantages and disadvantages of net present value

Advantages of NPV	Disadvantages of NPV
• It considers future net cash flows (earnings) expressed in today's value, making the calculations more realistic	• It is difficult to forecast net cash flows in the distant future
• It is more accurate than the ARR as the NPV discounts the future values of net cash flows (money is worth less in the future)	• The NPV can be tedious to calculate, especially as so many variables can alter the final net cash flow figures
• Managers can compare the effects of different discount rates on their investments	• It can be difficult to decide on an accurate discount rate if the inflation and interest rate fluctuate considerably

EXAM PRACTICE

32 Kucharek Parlour is considering the purchase of five industrial massage chairs for a total purchase price of $65000. The estimated net cash flows during the useful life cycle of five years from the investment are shown below, along with the discount rates at 4% for the duration of the investment.

Year	Net cash flow	Discount rate
1	$15000	0.9615
2	$20000	0.9246
3	$30000	0.8890
4	$20000	0.8548
5	$20000	0.8219

a Calculate the payback period of the investment project. [2]

b Calculate the average rate of return from the investment project. [2]

c Explain why the net present value method of investment appraisal discounts future net cash flows. [2]

d Calculate the net present value of the investment project. [3]

e Explain whether the purchase of the industrial massage chairs represents a feasible investment for Kucharek Parlour. [4]

Expert tip

This unit only considers some of the quantitative tools used in investment appraisal. In reality, non-quantitative techniques should also be used to judge whether an investment project is worthwhile, e.g. whether the investment decision is well suited to the organization's aims and objectives, its corporate culture and external factors such as the state of the economy.

CUEGIS CONCEPTS

Investigate how globalization and strategy have impacted on the investment decisions for an organization of your choice.

3.9 Budgets *(HL only)*

Revised ☐

The importance of budgets for organizations (AO2)

Revised ☐

A budget is a plan of the costs and revenues with the purpose of achieving the objectives of a business in a given time period, usually one year. A budget usually includes all the activities of a business and its predicted level of sales revenue. Budgets are important to organizations for several reasons:

- **Planning** – The budgeting process helps decision makers to plan their operations based on the amount of money they have been allocated in the budget per time period.

- **Cash flow forecasting** – Helps to plan the timing of business expenditure based on the planned revenue streams.

- **Prioritizing** – Forces budget holders to prioritize their activities, e.g. which members of staff to send on training and which courses to send them on.

- **Controlling** – Enables managers to identify and analyse differences in planned and actual revenues and expenditure. This helps them to better understand possible financial problems and to devise corrective actions.

- **Target setting** – Budgets help departments within a business to set financial goals, thereby preventing costs spiralling out of control.

- **Accountability** – Budgets make people accountable for their actions and spending. Formally monitoring this through budgetary control is important, especially in organizations with an informal management style (see Unit 2.3).

- **Benchmarking** – Budgets provide a basis for measuring the degree of success or failure (see section on variance analysis below). Managers can see if cost and/or revenue targets are met and to take corrective action if need be.

- **Motivating** – Empowering budget holders can act as a form of motivation (see Unit 2.4), especially if there are financial rewards linked to the attainment of financial targets such as sales revenue.

However, there are some limitations of budgets:

- Preparing, setting and updating budgets may be expensive and time-consuming.

- If budgets are inflexible and unrealistic, regardless of changes in circumstances, staff may become highly demotivated.

- Similarly, setting realistic budgets may be difficult in a dynamic business exposed to the constant forces of change. Hence, budgets could be a waste of time and resources.

- The culture of many organizations is that budgets are often related more to power and status, than to the needs of the business. Department budget holders may exaggerate budgets to elevate their position in the organization.

- Budgeting is only based on forecast costs and revenues, so may turn out to be rather inaccurate.

- In organizations that do not allow budgets to be carried over to the next financial year (to prevent overspending), budget holders may feel the need to spend towards the end of the financial year rather than having the money taken away by the master budget holder.

CUEGIS CONCEPTS

The budgeting process may be detrimental to organizational culture. It may limit cooperation and cohesion between departments as they compete to improve their own budgets (to enhance their own status and protect their own self-interest) at the expense of other departments. Therefore, such an internally competitive culture is harmful to the overall success of the business.

The difference between cost and profit centres (AO1)

Revised ☐

- A **cost centre** is a department or division within an organization that is responsible and held accountable for its own costs. The cost centre does not generate any direct revenue but adds to the cost of running the business.

- Examples include the following departments: personnel (human resources), research and development (R&D), marketing, technical support, and customer service.

- A **profit centre** is a department or division within an organization that is responsible and held accountable for both its own costs *and* revenues, and hence the resulting profits.

- An example is multiple chain businesses, with each branch or store of the organization responsible for its own profits or losses.

The roles of cost and profit centres (AO2)

Revised ☐

- **Monitoring and control** – Cost and profit centres help businesses to control each aspect of their operations. This is particularly the case for large and expanding businesses. Thus it becomes easier and more accurate to monitor the organization's performance by using variance analysis of each centre.

- **Enhancing decision making** – The speed and the quality of decision making improves because managers of cost and profit centres are empowered to make autonomous decisions.

- **Motivational** – Empowering, entrusting and delegation of responsibility to cost and profit centres can be highly motivating for employees.

- **Accountability** – Using cost and profit centres helps to make managers accountable for their specific responsibilities, including the ability to control costs and/or revenues.

However, there are some limitations of establishing cost and profit centres:

- Centres can create unhealthy and destructive competition between the various departments, hindering the organization's ability to reach its targets.

- Distributing the firm's fixed costs to cost and profit centres is a somewhat subjective and arbitrary task, and so can lead to arguments between employees. For example, how should rents and utility bills be split between the various centres?

Variances (AO2, AO4)

Revised ☐

- A variance exists when the actual outcome differs from the budgeted figure, e.g. a variance would occur if sales were planned to be 5000 units but actual sales were only 4500 units.

- Variances are usually measured each month, by comparing the actual result with the budgeted figure.

- Variances are classified as either **favourable variances** (if they cause higher than expected profits) or **adverse variances** (if they result in a fall in profits).

Table 3.7 Examples of variances for Joyce Tong Garments Co.

Variable	Budget	Actual	Variance
Sales of product A (units)	1 000	1 110	110 units favourable
Sales of product B (kgs)	50 000	45 000	5 000 kgs adverse
Raw material costs ($)	45 000	51 000	$6 000 adverse
Wages ($)	110 000	107 000	$3 000 favourable

> **Keyword definitions**
>
> A **favourable variance** exists when the difference between the actual and budgeted figure is beneficial to the business, i.e. sales revenues are higher than planned and/or costs are lower than planned.
>
> An **adverse variance** exists when the difference between the actual and budgeted figure is disadvantageous to the business, e.g. actual sales revenues are lower than planned or wages are higher than budgeted.

■ Regular variance analysis helps to provide an early warning sign to managers. For example, if sales for a particular product are below budget, managers can respond by reducing output or increasing marketing expenditure in an attempt to boost sales.

■ Budgetary control is important but variance analysis also allows businesses to examine whether budgets and targets are being adhered to. Hence, variance analysis acts as an additional control mechanism.

■ The budgeting process and variance analysis help to ensure that no department or individual budget holder spends more than the business expects, thus preventing unpleasant surprises.

EXAM PRACTICE

33 Calculate the variance for the following items for Anita Mata Caterers:
  a Cost of materials: budgeted = $10000 but actual = $11500   [1]
  b Cost of labour: budgeted = $3700 but actual = $3200   [1]
  c Sales of cakes: budgeted = $26000 but actual = $24800   [1]

34 Stefan Hagan runs a successful hair salon business. His latest monthly budget is shown in the table below.
  a Explain why Stefan Hagan uses budgeting.   [2]
  b Complete the missing figures for Stefan Hagan Hair Salon.   [4]
  c Explain why a favourable variance might be investigated by Stefan Hagan. [2]

Variable	Budgeted ($)	Actual outcome ($)	Variance ($)
Wages		4400	400 adverse
Salaries	6500	6500	0
Stock	1700	1800	
Revenue	16550		340 favourable
Direct costs	3600	3450	

The role of budgets and variances in strategic planning (AO2)

Revised ☐

■ Budgets are vital in strategic planning because they ensure that the financial implications of business decisions are fully considered.

■ By empowering budget holders, such as heads of departments, budgets allow senior management to concentrate on core business issues (strategic planning) and only to get involved if significant variances occur.

■ Budgets enable a business to turn its strategy into practice. This is because all business operations need to be funded by the money available from various budgets of the organization.

■ The process helps to provide a benchmark against which a manager's success (or lack of) can be measured and rewarded, e.g. a sales manager who exceeds an agreed sales budget might receive an annual bonus or qualify for the company's share ownership scheme (see Unit 2.4).

■ The effectiveness and appropriateness of leadership becomes questionable if budgets are ignored or not adhered to.

■ Budgets and variance analysis enable senior managers and other key stakeholders to measure the degree of success or failure of the firm's business strategy.

4.1 The role of marketing

Marketing and its relationship with other business functions (AO1)

■ Marketing is the process of anticipating, identifying and satisfying the needs and desires of customers in a profitable way.

■ The marketing department of an organization aims to provide the right products, suitably priced, distributed conveniently for customers to purchase, and promoted effectively to attract customers.

■ The marketing department of a business has close ties with the production department, as sales forecasts (see Unit 4.3) produced by marketers help in preparing production schedules.

■ It also has links with the human resources department as market research can help to predict the level of customer demand, thus determining the number of workers needed.

■ Marketing is also connected to the financial function of businesses. For example, marketing helps the finance and accounts department to set appropriate budgets for research and development, or promotion and advertising. The finance department will also work with the marketers to determine suitable prices for the various goods and services being sold.

The differences between marketing of goods and marketing of services (AO2)

■ Services are unique from goods in four ways:

☐ **Intangible** – Unlike goods, services are not physical in their nature.

☐ **Inseparable** – The service received is attached to the people who deliver the service.

☐ **Perishable** – Services do not last but are usually consumed at the time of purchase.

☐ **Variable** – services are heterogeneous, i.e. each customer experience is unique.

■ Hence, the marketing of services is characterized by the emphasis on product differentiation due to the unique experiences that customers have.

■ The marketing of services builds upon the marketing of products so includes the same elements (the 4Ps in the marketing mix): product, price, promotion and place.

■ The marketing of services includes three additional elements (called the **extended marketing mix**): people, process and physical evidence (see Unit 4.6):

☐ *People* refers to the customer service element of a service.

☐ *Process* refers to the way a service is provided, e.g. waiting times, payment methods, after-sales care and delivery methods.

☐ *Physical evidence* refers to visible and tangible aspects of a service, e.g. staff uniform, lighting and ambience, and the cleanliness of the building.

■ Due to the difficulties in ensuring a consistent standard of output, the marketing of a service is generally more challenging than the marketing of a tangible product.

Market orientation versus product orientation (AO2)

Revised

■ Product orientation

■ Product orientation is an inward-looking marketing approach that focuses on making products that a business knows how to make or has been making for a long time, rather than focusing on needs and wants of potential customers.

■ It is the approach used by technologically advanced and highly innovative manufacturers of high-tech goods.

■ Product-oriented businesses invent and innovate, which can give them a unique selling proposition.

■ Product-oriented businesses are more focused on issues relating to internal production. This can lead to a business losing its market if competitors are instead highly focused on customer needs, e.g. Apple missed out on two years of sales in the large smartphones (phablets) market due to its product-oriented approach, allowing Samsung to dominate the market.

■ Product orientation can succeed when businesses have a strong market reputation, such as Google or Apple, or where the pace of change is very slow.

■ Market orientation

■ By contrast, market orientation is an outward-looking marketing approach that focuses on meeting the specific wants and needs of customers and potential customers, i.e. firms focus on marketing products they can sell rather than what they can make well.

■ Market-oriented businesses research what the customers want, then focus their energies on making the right products, and improve these in line with customer feedback.

■ Businesses that take this approach use promotions and advertising to keep customers informed of changes and developments in the products on offer.

■ It forces businesses to be more flexible (by focusing on changing consumer needs and wants), thereby lowering the risks of failure.

■ As market-oriented firms are able to align their products with the expectations and demands of customers, there is a higher likelihood of success.

■ Whether a business opts for market or product orientation depends on several factors:

  ☐ The nature of the product, e.g. market orientation is used for mass-produced goods but product orientation is more suitable for innovative and high-end quality products.

  ☐ Organizational culture, e.g. pioneering firms such as Apple and 3M focus on product orientation whereas retailers such as Walmart focus on meeting the needs and wants of their customers.

  ☐ The number of competitors, e.g. an industry with few competitors means a product-oriented approach could be suitable.

The difference between commercial marketing and social marketing (AO2)

- Commercial marketing focuses on the marketing of goods and services that people want and need.

- Successful commercial marketing helps businesses to increase their sales and profits.

- It does not focus on the ethics of marketing, e.g. the marketing of alcoholic drinks or fast food would be considered in the same way as the marketing of any other product.

- It focuses on providing the right products, at the right prices and places, and promoted to the right customers in order to maximize sales.

- Social marketing is about influencing and changing the social behaviour of people in order to benefit society over the long term, e.g. environmental protection, anti-smoking campaigns, or promoting healthy eating.

- Social marketing uses commercial marketing strategies to achieve the desired social change, e.g. anti-drink-driving campaigns.

- A social marketing campaign is deemed to be successful if it achieves the desired social change.

- It is often used by not-for-profit organizations, such as charities or co-operatives, governments or by businesses with a strong culture of being socially responsible (see Unit 1.3).

- Social marketing can give businesses a significant competitive edge over their rivals as it can attract customers who perceive the business as ethical and driven by moral values.

> **Keyword definitions**
>
> **Commercial marketing** is the use of marketing strategies to meet the needs and wants of customers in a profitable way for the benefit of the owners of the business.
>
> **Social marketing** refers to marketing activities designed to influence the behaviour of the general public in order to benefit the wider community.

Characteristics of the market in which an organization operates (AO1)

- A market is traditionally made up of buyers and sellers coming together to exchange goods and services at a mutually agreed price. This can happen physically or online (see Unit 4.8).

- Marketers often conduct market research and produce market analyses in order to better understand their customers and the markets in which they operate, such as:

  ☐ the **market size** – the value of sales revenue in the industry

  ☐ a **competitor analysis** – to identify the nature and degree of intensity of competition in the industry

  ☐ the **market growth** potential – the probable increase in the size of the market in the foreseeable future.

- Markets can cater for private individuals (selling **consumer products**) or other businesses (selling **producer products**).

- Consumer goods can be perishable (such as fresh flowers and food products) or durable (such as furniture, televisions, smartphones and motor vehicles).

- Markets can provide **homogeneous products**, i.e. physically identical products such as potatoes, oranges or oil. Firms are unable to charge premium prices for such products unless there is some form of **product differentiation** (see Unit 4.2) such as branding.

- Some businesses operate in **mass markets**, catering for a broad range of customers. Other products are marketed in **niche markets**, catering for a small and select market segment.

■ The competitiveness of a particular industry depends on the nature of barriers to entry in the industry, e.g. aircraft manufacturing is dominated by Boeing and Airbus due to the high costs of entry, prohibiting competition.

Market share (AO4)

Revised ☐

■ Market share is a measure of a firm's relative size. It is sales revenue of a particular business expressed as a percentage of the total market size.

■ Market share is calculated by using the formula:

$$\frac{\text{Total sales of a particular business}}{\text{Total sales of the market}} \times 100$$

■ It allows a business to compare itself to the size of its competitors in terms of sales revenue or sales volume.

■ Market share data helps to reveal the extent to which a market is competitive by adding the market share of the largest few firms in the industry.

■ As a common marketing objective, businesses strive to increase their market share.

> **Keyword definition**
> **Market share** refers to a firm's portion of the total value of sales revenue in a particular industry.

EXAM PRACTICE

1 Kowloon Pots has a 16.4% market share of the garden pots market in Hong Kong. The market is worth $14 million per year. Calculate the annual sales of Kowloon Pots. [2]

The importance of market share and market leadership (AO3)

Revised ☐

■ Being able to compare the relative size of businesses enables managers to take appropriate actions to remain competitive.

■ Having a large market share can give a business competitive advantages, e.g. brand loyalty, economies of scale (due to larger scale operations) and higher profits as customers are less sensitive to higher prices being charged.

■ Economies of scale, customer loyalty and price leadership in an industry are all forms of competitive advantage for market leaders and so act as barriers to entry for firms wanting to compete in the industry.

■ Market leaders also enjoy a good corporate reputation, which can help to attract more investors and better quality employees. In addition, retailers and distributors are more likely to stock the products of market leaders, further helping to improve their sales and profits.

■ However, changes in the external business environment (see Unit 1.5) can change the fortunes of a firm without much warning, including those which are market leaders. Unit 5.7 outlines examples of crises that can threaten the survival of even large and well established firms. Still, it is the larger firms that have the best chance of survival in these instances.

> **Keyword definition**
> **Market leaders** are firms with the largest market share in a given industry.

The marketing objectives of for-profit organizations and non-profit organizations (AO3)

Revised ☐

■ Marketing objectives will differ depending on the type of organization under consideration. A for-profit business is likely to strive for improved profitability whereas a non-governmental organization might choose to focus on social marketing to promote its social cause.

- The marketing objectives of a non-profit organization (NPO) focus on the work it does or the cause it supports, rather than focusing on marketing a physical product.

- The major difference between the marketing of for-profit organizations and NPOs is the fulfilment of customer needs. The for-profit organization's marketing objectives focuses on meeting the customer's needs for his or her own benefit. For NPOs, the focus is about recognizing and meeting the need of others.

- Marketing objectives provide a clear purpose and framework for a firm's marketing activities.

- Marketing objectives tend to be SMART – specific, measurable, achievable, realistic and time constrained, e.g. to increase market share by 2.5% by 2023. Examples of marketing objectives include:

  - ☐ *Increased market share* – A firm strives to account for a greater proportion of the industry's sales revenue.

  - ☐ *Target new customers* – In an attempt to sell more goods and services, a business may target its products at new customer markets, both domestically and overseas.

  - ☐ *Enhance customer relationships* – Developing customer relations helps to improve customer satisfaction and loyalty, thereby giving the business a competitive advantage.

  - ☐ *Improved product and brand awareness* – Marketing activities aim to improve customer recognition of the product and brand in order to increase sales and market share.

  - ☐ *New product development* – Producing new products that appeal to new and existing markets can help to improve a firm's sales and competitiveness.

  - ☐ *Brand management* – This involves using marketing to remind customers about a brand, rather than to promote a particular good or service.

  - ☐ *Increased profitability for a business* – Achieving the above marketing objectives helps to achieve the main aim of most organizations, i.e. to increase profits.

  - ☐ *Increased awareness of social issues* – In addition to some of the above marketing objectives, NPOs will also aim to raise awareness of their social cause.

> **Keyword definition**
> **Marketing objectives** are the specific goals of the marketing department in order to help achieve the overall objectives of the organization. They are included in a marketing plan and help to formulate appropriate marketing strategies.

How marketing strategies evolve as a response to changes in customer preferences (AO3)

`Revised ☐`

- Consumer tastes change over time. Successful businesses change their marketing strategies in response to changes in customer preferences.

- The growing popularity of mobile devices and internet technologies mean that an increasing number of organizations now rely on e-commerce (see Unit 4.8) and social media (see Unit 4.5) as part of their marketing strategy.

- Marketing objectives and strategies may need to change as a good or service enters different phases of its product life cycle (see Unit 4.5), e.g. extension strategies might prevent sales from declining when the industry becomes saturated.

- The growing trend and social expectations of firms behaving in a socially responsible way directly impacts on their marketing strategies. Indeed, having a reputation for being socially responsible can improve an organization's competitiveness.

- Globalization has had a huge impact on altering consumer demand. Firms need to adapt their marketing strategies to suit different local preferences and cultural norms in overseas markets.

How innovation, ethical considerations and cultural differences may influence marketing practices and strategies in an organization (AO3)

Revised

■ Innovation

- Innovations in internet technologies have an increasingly large impact on the marketing practices and strategies of all businesses, be they large or small, for-profit or non-profit organizations, e.g. e-commerce (see Unit 4.8) enables firms to promote their cause in a cost-effective way.

- Information communications technology (ICT) facilitates market practices and strategies, e.g. online subscriptions and newsletters.

- E-commerce has also provided an extra channel of distribution, creating huge marketing opportunities for firms such as e-Bay, Amazon.com and iTunes.

- The growing popularity of guerrilla marketing (see Unit 4.5) has meant that firms need to be ever-more creative in their marketing strategies in order to grab the attention of the general public. Innovative guerrilla marketing techniques can help a firm to stand out in a world of advertising clutter.

■ Ethical considerations

- Marketing ethics are the moral aspects of a firm's marketing practices and strategies. Unethical marketing happens when moral codes of practice are ignored or when marketing activities (such as market research or advertising campaigns) cause offence to the public.

- Marketing practices and strategies that ignore ethical considerations are likely to result in negative consequences for a business, e.g. customer complaints, damaged corporate image and a public relations disaster.

- The use of unethical marketing, deliberate or unintentional, is a high-risk strategy that can backfire. With the widespread use of social media and social networks, bad publicity is not necessarily better than no publicity for a business.

- Examples of unethical marketing practices and strategies include the following:

  - *Bait and switch* – Marketing methods aimed at luring customers by using advertising deals that are just too good to be true (the bait) who become hooked but find that the product is no longer available so end up buying a more expensive alternative (the switch).

  - *Ambiguous advertising claims* – Using unproven or untested claims that can mislead and deceive the public, e.g. promoting health benefits and medical cures from the consumption of certain uncertified products.

  - *Product misrepresentation* – Giving misleading and ambiguous information to customers in order to persuade them to pay for certain goods or services, e.g. inaccurate product descriptions.

  - *Pester power* – Using children to pressurize their parents to buy certain products, e.g. toys, sweets (candy), fast food, sportswear and mobile apps.

■ Cultural differences

- Cultural differences can have a significant impact on marketing practices and strategies, especially for multinational businesses using international marketing techniques (see Unit 4.7).

- The marketing practices and strategies of successful firms in the domestic market do not necessarily work in international markets due to societal and cultural differences.

- Cultural factors have a large and direct impact on the demand for certain goods and services in different parts of the world, e.g. KFC includes rice products on its menu in China, whilst there are no beef products sold in McDonald's restaurants in India.

- Hence, marketing is only successful if international marketers truly understand and cater for differences in cultural values.

> **CUEGIS CONCEPTS**
>
> Examine how the concepts of change and ethics have impacted on the marketing strategies for an organization of your choice.

4.2 Marketing planning (including introduction to the 4 Ps)

Revised ☐

The elements of a marketing plan (AO1)

Revised ☐

- It is usually preceded by a marketing audit – a review may address issues such as the intensity of competition in the market, the firm's product portfolio as well as an assessment of the effectiveness of its past marketing efforts.

- The main components of a marketing plan typically include: the executive summary, market research, target market(s), the product, the existing competition, marketing objectives, marketing strategies and the associated budget(s).

- The marketing plan should include a situational analysis, examining all the internal and external aspects that may impact sales of the business.

- There is likely to be a review of the firm's current marketing mix in terms of its strengths, opportunities, weakness and threats

- **Marketing strategies** refer to the approaches taken by an organization to achieve its marketing objectives.

- Marketing plans and marketing strategies cannot work effectively without all four elements of the traditional marketing mix.

> **Keyword definition**
>
> A **marketing plan** is a document that outlines a firm's marketing objectives and strategy for a stated period of time.

The role of marketing planning (AO2)

Revised ☐

- Marketing planning is the systematic process of conducting a marketing audit, setting marketing objectives and devising marketing strategies in terms of the marketing mix to achieve those objectives.

- The main role of marketing planning is to identify and meet the needs of customers. Thus, the plan allows marketing managers to make more informed decisions about their marketing strategies.

- The plan allows marketers to have a sense of purpose and direction, i.e. the marketing plan provides a written guide for a business to follow in marketing its goods and services.

- As the marketing plan is one part of the organization's overall business plan, managers can align marketing plans and strategies with the overall aims and objectives of the organization.

- The operations department uses these sales forecasts (see Unit 4.3) to create a production schedule. The finance department uses the forecasts to create budgets (see Unit 3.9). The human resources department uses sales forecasts for workforce planning (see Unit 2.1).

- It also acts as a forecasting tool because it requires managers to estimate sales resulting from market research.

- It enables the business to engage in meaningful marketing communications, e.g. advertising, promotional, and public relations campaigns.

The four Ps of the marketing mix (AO2)

Revised ☐

- The **marketing mix** is a term coined by Jerome McCarthy (1964) used to describe the four key components of marketing: product, price, promotion and place (see Unit 4.5).

- Also known as the **4 Ps**, the marketing mix is a business tool used within a marketing plan to refer to the set of actions that an organization uses to market its products or brands: product, price, promotion and place.

  - ☐ **Product** refers to what the business is selling. The term refers to both goods and services.

  - ☐ **Price** refers to how much the business is selling its products for.

  - ☐ **Promotion** refers to the methods used to ensure customers know about a firm's products.

  - ☐ **Place** refers to the methods of distributing products to customers, e.g. using wholesalers, retailers, e-commerce, mail order or vending machines.

An appropriate marketing mix for a particular product or business (AO2, AO4)

Revised ☐

- The marketing mix for a particular product or business will depend on several factors, such as:

  - ☐ Whether it is a good or service (see Unit 4.1).

  - ☐ The size of the business, e.g. sole trader or multinational company.

  - ☐ The size of the market, e.g. the market for horse saddles or the market for bottled water.

  - ☐ The firm's market share – businesses with larger market share have greater customer loyalty and are able to charge higher prices.

  - ☐ The firm's marketing budget (see Unit 3.9) and available sources of finance to fund its marketing activities.

  - ☐ Consumer profiles, e.g. gender, age, educational attainment or income levels.

  - ☐ The countries or regions where the product is sold, because culture can have a significant impact on the marketing of certain goods or services.

- Businesses often conduct market research (see Unit 4.4) to determine the products desired by specific target markets, e.g. Tesla, the US electric vehicle maker, targets adults with a relatively high income who would typically buy high-end brands such as BMW, Audi, Porsche or Mercedes-Benz.

- Legal and ethical aspects of marketing will also affect the marketing mix used. For example:

  - ☐ The ethics of marketing should be considered when targeting children in the marketing of products such as toys, fast food and beauty products.

  - ☐ Promotional strategies must comply with advertising codes of conduct in different countries, e.g. adverts should be accurate, honest and truthful.

  - ☐ Legal restriction can apply to the marketing of some products, e.g. alcohol, cigarettes, fast food, soft drinks or medicines.

CUEGIS CONCEPTS

Investigate how the concepts of innovation and ethics have impacted on the marketing mix for a product, brand or business of your choice.

The effectiveness of a marketing mix in achieving marketing objectives (AO3)

- An effective marketing mix enables a firm to achieve its marketing objectives, e.g. increased market share, better product positioning and improved consumer satisfaction.

- Marketing strategies to achieve the firm's marketing objectives include product development, market development and diversification (see Unit 1.3).

- All elements in the marketing mix must be effective in order for the firm to succeed. An outstanding product that is not promoted well or set at the right price or widely distributed will fail to sell well.

- Many businesses use the AIDA model to judge the effectiveness of their marketing mix, i.e. it must grab the **a**ttention of customers, get them **i**nterested, create consumer **d**esire and generate **a**ction (spending).

- Other measures of the effectiveness of a marketing mix include the impact on sales revenues, brand recognition, customer loyalty, market share and profits.

The difference between target markets and market segments (AO2) and possible target markets and market segments in a given situation (AO4)

- A market segment is a sub-group within a larger market, made up of customers with similar characteristics, e.g. age, gender, income, ethnic group, or religion.

- As it can be expensive to create a different marketing mix for different market segments, firms often resort to targeting specific segments.

- Once a market is segmented, particular sub-groups can then be targeted using an appropriate marketing mix and strategies to achieve the firm's marketing objectives, e.g. Samsung's marketing aimed at young people in their 20s will be somewhat different to their strategies targeted at older customers in their 40s or 50s.

- Segmentation allows firms to gain greater knowledge about their customers. This knowledge is likely to create more cost-effective and successful marketing. Hence, without market segmentation, a firm's marketing mix might be inappropriate for its potential market.

- Market segmentation can be useful in identifying new business opportunities, e.g. finding an unfilled niche in the market.

- However, market segmentation only generates a limited number of groupings, with potential stereotyping of customers. Some customers may not fit neatly into these categories.

- Ultimately the purpose of market segmentation and targeting is to allow firms to generate greater sales and higher profits. Being more customer focused enables businesses to improve the cost effectiveness of their marketing whilst increasing sales, market share and profits.

> **Keyword definitions**
>
> A **market segment** is a distinct group of customers with similar characteristics and similar needs or wants.
>
> A **target market** is a particular market segment that a business aims to focus its marketing effort on.

The difference between niche market and mass market (AO2)

- Niche markets are small and focused, so there are opportunities for high profit margins because premium prices can be charged.

- A niche market is identified as a group of customers with a distinctive set of traits who have rather unique needs or desires, e.g. organic foods, customized products, eco-tourism, or the market for private tutors of beginner's Italian in Taiwan.

> **Keyword definition**
>
> **Niche marketing** is a corporate strategy based on identifying and serving a relatively small market segment.

- It enables small firms to operate profitably as large organizations do not often cater for these markets due to the limited opportunities to exploit economies of scale.

- There are few barriers to entry in most niche markets. However, this also means there is a high risk of new businesses entering the industry, which increases direct competition.

- Mass markets are those which provide goods and services that appeal to an extensive number of customers.

- In mass markets, producers sell standardized products to large consumer markets, so profit margins are lower on each unit sold.

- Mass marketing helps a firm to enjoy economies of scale by catering for a large number of customers, leading to larger profits from increased sales.

> **Keyword definition**
>
> **Mass marketing** is marketing strategy aimed at all consumers in a market without trying to differentiate them into separate market segments.

How organizations target and segment their market and create consumer profiles (AO2)

`Revised`

- Market segmentation acknowledges the fact that customers are different, such as demographic factors based on characteristics including religion, gender and marital status. Hence, in any market there will be several market segments.

- Organizations choose to segment their market in order to create distinct consumer profiles in several ways, based on demographic, geographic or psychographic factors.

- Segmentation enables businesses to gain a better understanding of consumer profiles in each segment. This is crucial to devising an effective marketing mix.

- Consumer profiles usually include the person's age, gender, marital status, education, occupation and income level, area of residence and spending patterns. Knowledge of consumer profiles is an important consideration when devising the marketing mix.

- *Socio-economic segmentation* seeks to classify consumers according to their income, profession or education. Businesses can then devise different marketing mixes targeted at each market segment.

- *Psychographic segmentation* focuses on personality traits, lifestyles and attitudes, e.g. customers who like to buy organic produce.

- *Demographic segmentation* focuses on population structures such as age, gender, ethnicity, marital status, language, family size and religion.

- *Geographic segmentation* is based on the physical location of the customer. This includes consideration of the natural environment and climate of the location. It is useful when target markets have different preferences based on where they are located.

- *Market segmentation* is followed by targeting. This enables an organization to devise an appropriate marketing mix for different market segments in the industry.

- Market segmentation allows a business to target its efforts and marketing strategy more effectively by devising an appropriate product, price, place and promotion mix for each segment. This offers prospects of higher sales and growth for the business.

- It can also be cost-effective if targeting leads to an efficient use of the organization's resources in conducting successful and justified marketing activities.

> **Keyword definitions**
>
> **Market segmentation** is the process of splitting a market into distinct consumer groups to better understand their needs.
>
> **Consumer profile** refers to the demographic and psychographic characteristics of consumers in different markets.
>
> **Targeting** is the practice of devising an appropriate marketing mix and marketing strategies for different market segments.

A product position map/perception map (AO2, AO4)

- A perception map helps a business to illustrate the position of its products in a market, relative to its rivals in the industry (see Figure 4.1).

- Having a clearer idea of customer perceptions helps a business to fine-tune its marketing strategies to enable it to increase sales and maximize profits.

- Different categories of products can be seen in a perception map that uses price and quality as the benchmark variables:

  □ A **premium product** on a perception map is perceived by customers as one that offers high quality at a high price, e.g. Cartier watches, Porsche cars or Häagen-Dazs ice cream.

  □ A **cowboy product** on a perception map is perceived as one that offers low quality but at a high price. This strategy can maximize sales in the short term but is unsustainable.

  □ A **bargain product** is perceived as one that offers high quality but at a low price. This short-term tactic can help to boost sales and gain brand awareness.

  □ An **economy brand** is one that offers low quality but at a low price, e.g. supermarket own-branded products such as toilet tissue, wines and canned foods.

- If a firm finds its position on a perception map to differ from what the firm envisaged, it needs to **reposition** the product or brand by appealing to a different market segment or by an improved marketing mix.

> **Keyword definition**
> A **product position map** is a visual representation of customers' perception of a product, relative to its competitors, e.g. its price and quality.

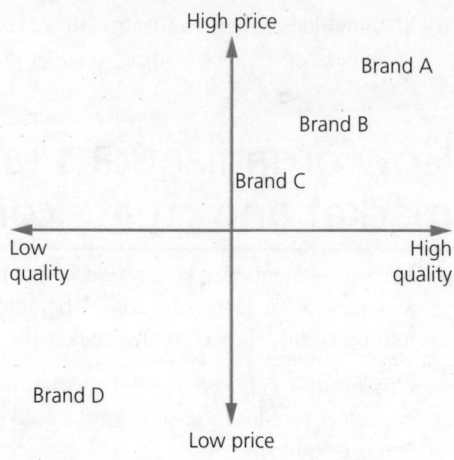

Figure 4.1 Example of a perception map

The importance of having a unique selling point/proposition (USP) (AO2)

- A unique selling proposition (or unique selling point) can be an important source of competitive advantage for a business, e.g. Apple's USP has been its distinctive and highly innovative products.

- Businesses with a USP focus on marketing the exclusive features and attributes of the product.

- Having a USP makes a business special and differentiates it from competitors. This helps to improve brand awareness (recognition) and brand loyalty, and so gives the business a competitive advantage over its rivals.

> **Keyword definition**
> A **unique selling point** (USP) is any aspect of a business, brand or product that makes it distinctive (stand out) from those offered by their competitors.

How organizations can differentiate themselves and their products from competitors (AO3)

- Product differentiation creates a perception amongst consumers that the firm's product is different or unique, and so creates better value relative to its competitors.

- Market research and market segmentation data enable a firm to differentiate its products.

- Firms try to differentiate their products by altering some or all aspects of the marketing mix. For example:

  □ **product** – adding new features, changing the colour, or introducing different sizes

  □ **price** – differentiated pricing for different market segments

  □ **place** – using e-commerce for the convenience of customers

  □ **promotion** – using logos, slogans and branding.

> **Keyword definition**
> **Differentiation** is the act of making a business or its products distinct from its rivals in the industry.

Table 4.1 Advantages and disadvantages of differentiation

Advantages of differentiation	Disadvantages of differentiation
• Allows the firm to charge a higher price due to the uniqueness of the product • Creates brand awareness, brand recognition and brand loyalty • Creates placement (or distribution) advantages as more retailers will want to have the product for sale	• It can be a very expensive strategy • Making products unique can mean that it is difficult to reap the benefits of economies of scale if the products were mass produced • It can create confusion in the minds of consumers through excessive differentiation and advertising clutter

4.3 Sales forecasting *(HL only)*

Revised ☐

Up to four-part moving average, sales trends and forecasting using given data (including seasonal, cyclical and random variation)(AO4)

Revised ☐

- Sales forecasting is necessary to help an organization with its business functions, such as:

  ☐ If sales are predicted to increase for the foreseeable future, the human resources department may recruit more workers.

  ☐ Cash flow forecasts will also rely on sales forecasting data. Profit forecasts will depend on the level of sales expected over a certain time period.

  ☐ Production schedules will be based on the expected level of sales. Stock (inventory) management will depend on the forecasted level of sales.

- Hence, sales forecasting drives many other aspects of strategic planning in a business. Managers want to understand the trend in the market and the underlying reasons for this.

- It is an important tool that enables a business to identify opportunities and threats in advance.

- Sales forecasts are generally based on recent sales trends, market analyses of the industry and the state of the economy (such as the expectation of a recession or economic boom).

- Forecasts are often presented in the form of time series data. This sales forecasting technique predicts sales revenue by using the underlying trends from a series of actual sales data recorded at regular times in the past.

- The moving average technique is the simplest method of sales forecasting. It enables managers to identify a trend from the data set, as well as changes in the trend, for a given period of time.

- There are two steps to calculating the moving average:

  ☐ Calculate a moving total, e.g. total sales for four months.

  ☐ Calculate the centred average of this data set, i.e. the average of the monthly figures.

  ☐ For example, suppose a firm's sales figures for the last four months are: $121 000, $123 000, $122 000 and $124 000. The firm's four-point moving average is $122 500 (i.e. the sum of the sales figures for the period of $490 000 divided by four months).

- It is a useful way to identify trends where there are strong seasonal influences on sales (see Table 4.2) or when sales are irregular for no obvious reason.

> **Keyword definition**
>
> **Sales forecasting** is a quantitative technique used to predict the level of sales revenue that a firm expects to earn over a certain period of time.

> **Keyword definition**
>
> The **moving average** is a quantitative method used to discover the underlying trend by levelling out variations in a data set. Such deviations are typically caused by seasonal, cyclical and random variations.

Table 4.2 Calculating the moving average using four-point averages

Month	Visitors	Four-point moving average
Jan	20 000	
Feb	20 500	
Mar	22 000	21 375
Apr	23 000	22 625
May	25 000	24 500
Jun	28 000	27 000
Jul	32 000	29 750
Aug	34 000	30 000
Sep	26 000	29 000
Oct	24 000	26 500
Nov	22 000	24 000
Dec	24 000	

■ The data in Table 4.2 shows the monthly visitor numbers to a campsite. This is shown diagrammatically in Figure 4.2, which suggests there are seasonal factors affecting the level of demand.

■ To calculate the four-point moving averages, in order to identify a trend line (see Figure 4.3), it is necessary to calculate the arithmetic mean of each data set consisting of four months. So, the average visitor numbers from February to May is 22 625 people, i.e. $\frac{(20\,500 + 22\,000 + 23\,000 + 25\,000)}{4} = 22\,625$.

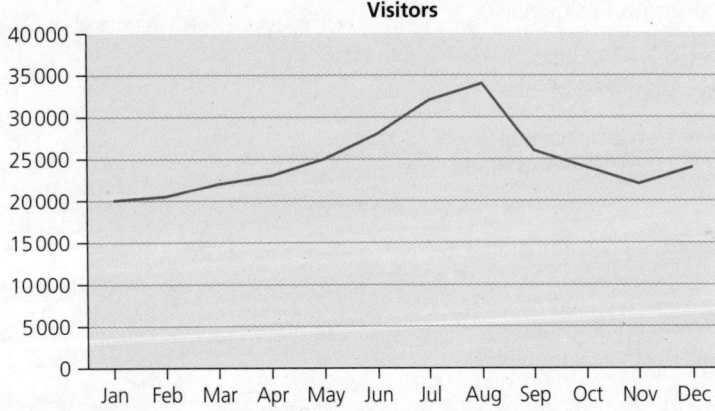

Figure 4.2 Raw data of number of visitors to campsite

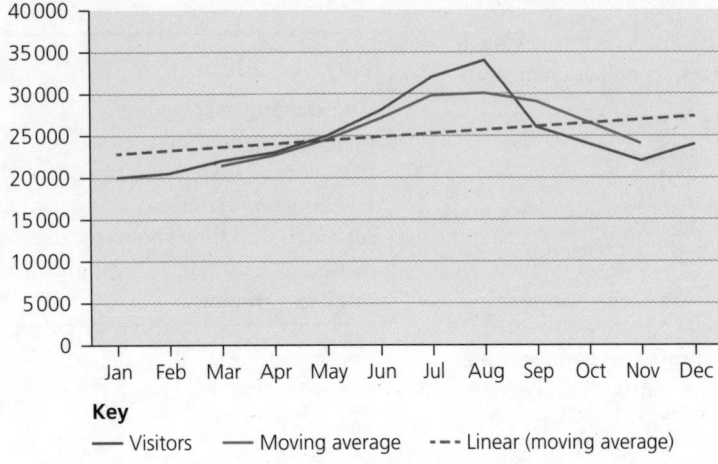

Key

— Visitors   — Moving average   - - - Linear (moving average)

Figure 4.3 Raw data and trend line of number of visitors to campsite

- The moving average line shows the four-point centred moving averages, which smooths out some of the seasonal variations in the visitor numbers.

- The linear (moving average) line shows the line of best fit, i.e. the trend.

- Sales forecasting enables managers to extrapolate the sales trend as part of their planning. Extrapolation assumes that sales patterns are stable in the near future.

- It identifies the trend by determining the line of best fit and then simply extending this line to make the predictions (see Figure 4.4).

> ### Keyword definition
> **Extrapolation** is a sales forecasting technique that makes future predictions of sales (in units or dollars) based on trends identified from using past data.

EXAM PRACTICE

2   Calculate the three-year moving averages for Alexis Corp. from the data below.   [4]

	Year 1	Year 2	Year 3	Year 4	Year 5
Sales ($)	200 000	250 000	240 000	270 000	280 000

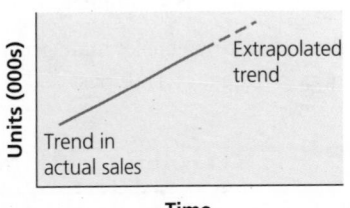

Figure 4.4 Extrapolation of sales data

Seasonal variations

- Seasonal variations are deviations in the values of sales data around the trend line, repeated on a regular basis.

- These variations are caused by environmental or cultural factors which cause different people to have different levels of demand at different times of the year.

- To calculate the seasonal variation, managers find the numerical difference between the observed data values and the values on the trend line. The variations can be expressed in absolute money terms or as a percentage of the deviation from the trend.

- Calculations of seasonal variations are used to adjust the predicted sales revenue from the trend over a one-year period in order to generate a more accurate prediction of quarterly sales.

- Many products face seasonal fluctuations in demand, e.g. umbrellas, ice cream, Easter eggs, Christmas trees, school uniform and IB examiners.

> ### Keyword definition
> **Seasonal variations** are expected periodic fluctuations in sales revenues over a given time period, e.g. peak periods during certain times in the year.

Cyclical variations

- Cyclical variations are generally attributed to fluctuations in the business cycle (see Unit 1.5), such as a booming economy (with high rates of economic growth) or a recession (when activity is low, causing mass-scale job losses in the economy).

- Unlike seasonal fluctuations, which occur at predictable intervals during the year, cyclical variations can last more than a year, e.g. many countries took more than five years to get over the global financial crisis of 2008.

- To make the predicted figures more accurate, the forecaster adjusts the sales figures by the average of the cyclical variations along the trend line.

> ### Keyword definition
> **Cyclical variations** refer to the recurrent fluctuations in sales revenues linked to the business cycle.

Random variations

- Random variations are caused by irregular, accidental and unforeseen factors, e.g. a natural disaster, prolonged periods of inclement weather, the outbreak of a war, an infectious epidemic, a corporate scandal, or a public relations disaster following a major product recall.

- As random variations are erratic and unpredictable, there is no specific formula that can be used to isolate and identify the deviations.

- Random variations can occur at any time, thus causing unusual and irregular sales revenue figures.

> ### Keyword definition
> **Random variations** are unpredictable and erratic fluctuations in sales revenues, caused by irregular factors.

The benefits of sales forecasting (AO3)

Revised

- Sales forecasting techniques such as moving averages help to identify trends by smoothing out seasonal, cyclical or random variations in the data set.

- It is a useful planning tool to help managers to reduce the uncertainties of the future.

- Identifying the trend enables the business to extrapolate or predict future sales revenues as a basis for strategic and financial planning.

- Sales forecasting enables managers to allocate various budgets for the different functional areas of a business.

The limitations of sales forecasting (AO3)

Revised

- Only sales forecasts for a short period of time are likely to be accurate so the usefulness of the tool can be questioned.

- The key assumption of sales forecasting techniques is that what happened in the past is likely to continue in the future. This can prove to be unrealistic so extrapolated results can be somewhat overly simplistic. It ignores the concept of change in the real business world.

- To be of value, forecast data must be based on reliable information and data, although these are not necessarily easy or cheap to collect.

- Sales forecasts can be accurate for predicting the sales of single items but tend to be less accurate for firms that sell a broad range of products.

- It is not always suitable for all types of businesses, e.g. product-oriented industries with very dynamic customer preferences such as the fashion and high-tech industries.

- Qualitative factors that affect sales revenues are not incorporated in sales forecasting techniques.

> **CUEGIS CONCEPTS**
>
> Investigate how sales forecasting changes (or influences) the decisions made in an organization of your choice.

> **CUEGIS CONCEPTS**
>
> For a business of your choice, discuss whether there are ethical dilemmas in the choice of data that are used and how this affects the forecasts.

4.4 Market research

Revised

Why and how organizations carry out market research (AO2)

Revised

Reasons why businesses conduct market research include the desire to:

- determine customer preferences about a product, e.g. design, colour, size, smell or taste

- discover the likelihood of customers buying their products

- assess customer sensitivity to different price levels

- discover and learn about new market trends

- reduce the risks of marketing activities such as new product launches and pricing decisions

- investigate various market demographics and their potentially different reactions, preferences and behavioural variations, e.g. age, gender, religion, marital status, location and income level

- explain sales patterns and variances (see Unit 3.9).

> **Keyword definition**
>
> **Market research** is the systematic process of collecting, collating, analysing and interpreting data and information about existing and potential consumers, competitors and markets. It is used by businesses to aid their marketing planning and marketing strategies.

In general terms, organizations can carry out market research in one of two ways.

■ Primary research is market research that does not already exist about a good or service. Features of primary research include the following:

☐ The collection of first-hand data for a specific purpose.

☐ It often represents a limited or skewed perspective.

☐ Hence, there is a need to select a sample that is representative and statistically significant to ensure the results are reliable.

☐ Often provides in-depth qualitative data and information.

☐ Primary sources are not always objective sources as they are often based on people's opinions and the judgement of the researchers.

☐ It is relatively expensive to gather the data and information compared with secondary market research.

■ Secondary research is the market research of data and information that already exists. Features of secondary research include the following:

☐ Reusing second-hand data and information already collected by someone else for a different purpose.

☐ Generally draws findings from large, representative samples.

☐ Some secondary sources involve a cost, e.g. subscription and association fees.

☐ The internet has revolutionized how secondary market research is obtained, by offering convenience, speed and an immense range of online sources.

> **Keyword definition**
>
> **Primary market research** (or **field research**) is the systematic process of collecting, recording, analysing and interpreting new data and information about a specific issue of direct interest to the business, e.g. questionnaires, interviews, focus groups and observations.

> **Keyword definition**
>
> **Secondary market research** (or **desk research**) is the collection, collation and interpretation of existing data and information from previously available sources, such as market analyses, academic journals, government publications and media articles.

Table 4.3 Advantages and disadvantages of primary market research

Advantages of primary research	Disadvantages of primary research
• It provides bespoke, specialist market research data, which is up-to-date and unique to the requirements of the business	• Relatively higher costs of conducting primary research compared with secondary market research
• It can give businesses a competitive edge by gathering new data and information about customer purchasing patterns and habits in order to anticipate changes in their spending behaviour	• The monotonous task of conducting primary research such as carrying out lengthy interviews or a tedious number of questionnaires
• It enables firms to focus on more effective and targeted marketing approaches, rather than an expensive and less effective mass marketing approach	• The time-consuming process of collecting, collating and interpreting primary data
• It can provide detailed and informative qualitative findings to inform a firm's marketing and corporate strategies	• Decision making can be delayed due to the lengthy time involved in designing, conducting, collating and interpreting primary research
• New technologies allow online surveys to be conducted faster, easier and more cheaply	• Imperfections in primary market research techniques (such as biased questions or a statistically invalid sample size) lead to unrepresentative and misleading research findings

Table 4.4 Advantages and disadvantages of secondary market research

Advantages of secondary research	Disadvantages of secondary research
• Relatively faster and cheaper to collect than primary research	• The data and information have to be adapted to the firm's particular needs
• Often available free of charge, e.g. company websites, government statistics and online news media sources	• The data and information can become out of date very quickly
• Ease of access to data sources, especially with online sources such as Wikipedia and online search engines such as Google	• Rival firms also have access to the same secondary data sources
• Allows access to a wide range of sources	• There may be biases in the data and research that is not apparent to the user

> **Expert tip**
>
> Organizations can use internal sources of secondary data, i.e. data previously published by the firm itself, such as company reports, historic sales figures and profit levels. This differs from external secondary market research data (published by other organizations, such as market analyses reports and academic journals), which is what students tend to write about.

Methods/techniques of primary market research (AO2)

Revised ☐

Primary market research can be conducted using several methods, including: surveys, interviews, focus groups and observations.

■ Surveys

- Surveys are a method of gathering both qualitative and quantitative information from a sample of individuals for market research purposes.

- They are the most popular method of primary research.

- There needs to be a large enough sample of consumers to provide statistically valid and representative data.

- They are often used to gain customer feedback from people who have recently bought a good or service, e.g. hotel guests, restaurant diners or car drivers.

- Questionnaires are used to ask consumers or potential consumers for their opinions and preferences about a particular good or service.

- A combination of closed questions (e.g. 'Yes/No', or 'Male/Female') or open-ended questions (e.g. 'Tell us about…' or 'What is your opinion concerning…') can be asked.

- Variations include postal surveys, personal surveys, self-completed surveys, telephone surveys and online surveys.

- They can be an expensive and time-consuming method of market research.

- They can suffer from selection or interviewer bias and/or poorly worded questions, thus generating unrepresentative results.

- Questions can be poorly worded, so the findings are misleading and inaccurate.

- Furthermore, many people are reluctant to fill out questionnaires or they do so in a hurry, without giving much thought to the questions or their responses.

■ Interviews

- Interviews are conducted by an interviewer who asks respondents (interviewees) a series of questions. Interviews tend to be more detailed than surveys.

- They can be face-to-face (e.g. interviewers ask people on the street or in shopping malls a series of questions) or interviews on the telephone.

- Like questionnaires, they can be specifically designed to meet the needs of the organization.

- They help to determine the interviewee's opinions and beliefs.

- Questions that are difficult to understand can be explained to interviewees. This can help to resolve the issue of cultural and linguistic bias that surveys can suffer from.

- As it involves only a small number of customers, the results might not reflect the views of the market in which the business is interested.

- There is also potential interviewer bias, which could distort the results or analysis of answers.

- Interviews are time-consuming and can be costly to conduct.

Focus groups

- Focus groups are small groups of customers and consumers who meet together with a researcher for market research purposes.

- They involve groups brought together on one or more occasions, where consumer panels are asked to answer and discuss questions about a specific good or service.

- They enable detailed investigation of the psychology of customers, e.g. their opinions and attitudes, and what motivates them as consumers of the product.

- As part of the target market, focus groups are used to identify the wants and needs of different market segments.

- Using focus groups can be costly as participants are usually provided with financial incentives such as gifts and free samples.

Observations

- Observations involve researchers watching and recording customer behaviour, e.g. identifying which supermarket aisles customers spend most of their time in.

- Unlike surveys and interviews, observations are not dependent on the willingness and ability of research subjects (those selected for market research) to respond accurately.

- The information collected from observations tend to be more objective and accurate as there is no interviewer bias.

- However, analysing the results from observations is very labour-intensive and time consuming.

Methods/techniques of secondary market research (AO2)

Revised

Secondary market research can be conducted using several methods, including: market analyses, academic journals, government publications and media articles.

Market analyses

- Market analyses refer to the collection of data and information about market characteristics of a particular good, service or industry, e.g. market size, market growth potential and information on competitors.

- It is a quick and relatively cheap way of examining and assessing the potential of a new good or service.

- New businesses often rely on market analyses reports to prepare their business plans.

- Valuable sources for conducting market analyses include: market research firms, annual company reports, websites of competitors and trade journals or publications.

- It is often included as part of a firm's SWOT analysis (see Unit 1.3).

Academic journals

- These are formal scholarly journals related to a specific academic discipline such as business management, psychology, natural science or economics.

- They are written by academics such as university lecturers and professors, and the content is often peer-reviewed.

- They are typically written in a standard format: abstract, methodology, results and findings, discussion, conclusions, bibliography and appendix. Citations and footnotes are also used.

- The intended audience is the research community, e.g. professionals and academics such as university students and professors.

- They often serve as a critique of existing market research or an introduction of new research presented for academic scrutiny.

- Academic journals are generally objective as they are not usually written for the benefit of any single business.

- Examples include: the *Academy of Management Journal*, the *Cambridge Journal of Economics*, and *Journal of International Management*.

Government publications

- Government publications refer to official documentation and information released by local, national, international governments or treaty organizations (such as the European Union or United Nations).

- These documents vary widely in purpose and content. Unlike academic journals, there is no standardized format with government publications.

- Governments produce a huge volume of publications on a broad variety of issues, thus providing researchers with a rich choice of data and information.

- Examples include: population statistics, unemployment figures, inflation rates (consumer price levels), economic growth rates, the annual government budget, and international trade data.

- Government publications are a major source of information in virtually every field of research.

- Most government publications are available to the general public and are usually accessible free of charge.

- However, many researchers under-use government publications because the documents tend to be difficult to find.

Media articles

- Media articles are documents or articles that appear in print or online media.

- Examples include the following:

  ☐ Newspapers, both in published format and online versions, providing a vast range of market research information, e.g. the *International Herald Tribune*, the *Times of India*, the *Wall Street Journal* and *USA Today*.

  ☐ News magazines, e.g. *TIME*, *Businessweek*, *The Economist* and *Fortune*.

  ☐ Trade journals, e.g. *Advertising Age* (marketing), *The Grocer* (supermarkets), *Autocar* (automobiles) and *Computer Weekly* (ICT).

- Access to media articles is usually straightforward with plenty of non-subscription websites available (e.g. bbc.co.uk) and the spread of news via social media and social networks (e.g. Twitter and Facebook).

- Users of media articles need to be conscious of potential bias from the authors of the articles.

Ethical considerations of market research (AO3)

Revised ▢

- Ethical considerations result in the expectation that market research is conducted objectively, using honest, unbiased and reasonable techniques.

- This includes the protection of research subjects (respondents) regarding the confidentiality of their personal data.

- There should be an absence of deliberate bias, stereotyping and prejudices of market researchers. Examples include:

  ☐ not telling respondents what the information collected is to be used for

  ☐ manipulating data to change the results

> **Expert tip**
>
> Many students confuse academic (or scholarly) journals with business magazines and other popular business media (e.g. *Bloomberg Businessweek* or *Forbes* and *Fortune* magazines). Remember, the authors of academic journals are academics rather than professional journalists.

- □ breaching confidentiality, i.e. unauthorized disclosure of customer information to third parties

- □ invasion of privacy, i.e. infringing people's right to privacy

- □ using market research data and information for personal gain.

- Such considerations are important for firms in order to avoid a public backlash if their market research practices are perceived as unprincipled and immoral.

- Unethical behaviour can negatively impact a firm's relationship with its key stakeholders.

The difference between qualitative and quantitative research (AO2)

Revised

Table 4.5 Features of qualitative and quantitative research

Qualitative research	Quantitative research
• Involves an in-depth investigation into the motivations and reasons behind consumer behaviour	• Relies on a large number of responses to get numerical results
• Based on opinions and perspectives	• Uses closed questions, categorical selections and/or scaled rankings for responses in order to gather and calculate results easily
• Often uses primary research to find out about consumers' tastes, opinions and buying behaviour	• Quicker and easier to collect, collate and interpret than qualitative responses
• Can be conducted using market research techniques such as focus groups, questionnaires and interviews	• Tries to establish correlations, i.e. whether there is a relationship between two or more variables
• Can provide a wealth of information despite the low number of respondents	• Quantitative analyses help to make decision making more objective
• Provides far more detailed and honest information regarding the motivation, attitudes or habits of consumers	• Quantitative analyses alone do not reveal the 'whole picture' without qualitative input

Keyword definitions

Qualitative research is based on opinions, feelings and perspectives, e.g. why they prefer a certain brand. It generates in-depth, non-numerical information. The results of qualitative research are usually descriptive rather than predictive.

Quantitative research is based on facts and figures, i.e. numerical patterns, correlations and results, such as how many people prefer a particular brand over its rivals. The results of quantitative research are usually predictive rather than descriptive.

Methods of sampling (AO2)

Revised

- 'Population' is a statistical term that refers to all potential customers of a particular market or all the people that fulfil a chosen criterion, for a market research exercise.

- 'Sampling' is the practice of selecting a small group of customers from the population of a certain market for the purpose of market research (see Figure 4.5).

- Sampling seeks to create a group of respondents for market research who are regarded to have representative views of the target market.

- Sampling is used as it is impractical, too expensive and unnecessary to include the entire market population for research purposes.

- Sampling methods include: quota, random, stratified, cluster, snowballing and convenience.

■ Quota sampling

- A quota refers to a pre-determined allocation of specific sub-groups of the population for sampling, e.g. 25 females and 35 males in a sample size of 60 people.

- It involves selecting a certain number of people from different market segments with shared characteristics, e.g. age, gender, religion, ethnicity or income levels.

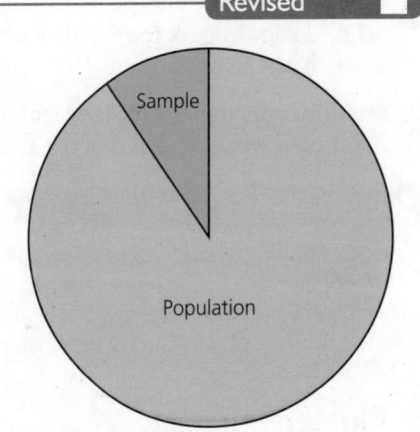

Figure 4.5 The difference between sample and population

- The assembled quota sample has the same proportions of individuals as the entire population (of the market for the product) regarding known characteristics.

- The purpose is to gather representative data from sub-groups to get around the issues of random sampling.

- It is suitable when researchers want to investigate a trait or a characteristic of a certain sub-group or to observe relationships between sub-groups.

- Researchers need to determine in advance the specific characteristics on which they will base the quota sample. This is vital to ensure representative results from the research.

- Quota sampling is often used with convenience sampling, so the researcher has control of who is included in the sample.

■ Random sampling

- This method involves selecting individuals in such a way that everyone in the total population has an equal chance of being chosen.

- Research subjects are often randomly chosen by a computer using information stored in a database.

- Hence, there is no bias in the selection of respondents for market research, so the outcome of the research is likely to be more accurate.

- Random sampling is a simple, quick and cheap method of sampling, especially as research subjects are readily available.

- However the convenience of random sampling also means there is a high probability that the selected sample is unrepresentative of the population.

■ Stratified sampling

- A stratified sample requires the proportions in the sample to reflect the proportions in the population as a whole, based on common strata (divisions or segments) such as age, gender and socio-economic status.

- A number of respondents proportional to the population from each segment is chosen randomly, e.g. if the target population consists of 40% male and 60% female, a 50-person sample would include 20 males (40%) and 30 females (60%).

- However, it is more difficult to organize such samples as they require fairly detailed knowledge of the population characteristics, so the cost of conducting research can be high.

- Stratified sampling is often used with random sampling so the researcher does not control who is included in the sample.

EXAM PRACTICE

3   OOI Pharmaceuticals wants to sample 80 members of staff to get feedback about its canteen facilities. The workforce consists of 75% full-time workers and 25% part-time staff. Stratify the sample in order to calculate the number of full- and part-time staff used for the sample.   [2]

■ Cluster

- Cluster sampling involves selecting several geographical areas and then randomly choosing people within these areas for market research purposes.

- It is suitable and cost-effective if travel costs between clusters are high.

- It can suffer from bias and sampling errors because respondents are selected from only a few areas (clusters) to make extrapolations about the population.

- Increasing the number of clusters would be one way of reducing the bias and improving the validity of the findings, but it would also increase the costs of market research.

■ Snowballing

- Snowball sampling involves the use of customer referrals to reach out to their friends, family or colleagues for market research purposes.

- The method requires minimal planning and is a cheap method of selecting subjects for sampling, especially as it can be operated through social media networking sites.

- It is useful when the researcher does not have access to a sufficient number of people with the desired characteristics.

- However, it can lead to biased samples as friends and family are often like-minded people, with similar habits and tastes.

- In addition, researchers using this sampling method have no idea of the true distribution or sub-groups of the population. The choice of the initial contacts is therefore of vital importance.

■ Convenience

- Samples are created using subjects who are easily accessible to the researcher, e.g. IB students often use other students or their teachers when conducting research for their HL Internal Assessment in Business Management.

- The selection of research subjects in convenience sampling is usually self-selected (because the research subjects are easily accessible) or unguided, e.g. volunteers who choose to respond.

- However, the findings could be skewed and unrepresentative of the wider population.

- Generalizations and inferences are difficult to make as the researchers are unlikely to use a sample that covers sufficient sub-groups within the population.

Results from data collection (AO2)

Revised ☐

> **Keyword definitions**
>
> **Sampling errors** are the mistakes that arise from sampling design, e.g. the sample size being too small, selecting an unrepresentative sample, the use of inappropriate sampling methods or having bias built into the research.
>
> **Non-sampling errors** are market research mistakes that are not attributed to human errors, e.g. untruthful answers by respondents which distort the findings.

- Results from data collection can contain both sampling and non-sampling errors.

- Results are often presented using different formats, including:

  ☐ Pie charts to show percentages, e.g. the percentage of respondents who selected a certain choice in a survey.

  ☐ Line graphs to show time-series data, e.g. a firm's profit figures over the past five years.

  ☐ Bar charts to show frequencies, e.g. comparative sales figures of different companies.

  ☐ Tables are also used to present numerical data in various formats.

- Qualitative results may be simplified by presenting the main findings in a summary.

Expert tip

When analysing results from data collection shown in graphs and charts, it is important to check the data axes carefully. Don't assume that the examiner knows what you understand.

CUEGIS CONCEPTS

Businesses are increasingly resorting to social media (e.g. Twitter, WhatsApp and Facebook) and websites (e.g. SurveyMonkey and Zoomerang) to collect and collate data faster, more cheaply and more frequently. Investigate how a business of your choice has used technology in an innovative way for market research purposes.

4.5a The 4 Ps: Product

The product life cycle (AO4)

- The product life cycle (PLC) refers to a marketing theory that illustrates the different stages a typical product goes through from its launch to its eventual withdrawal from the market.

- The PLC diagram (see Figure 4.6) shows sales revenue on the *y-axis* and the timeline on the *x-axis*.

- The five typical stages of the PLC are:

  □ *Research and development* – The first stage of the PLC which involves designing and developing a product before being launched for sale.

  □ *Introduction* – When the product is launched onto the market for sale. It usually requires significant investment in promotion and advertising to sustain sales.

  □ *Growth* – When sales increase rapidly with the product becoming well known to the market.

  □ *Maturity* – When sales revenue are at, or near, their maximum with minimal or no more scope for growth, i.e. sales become saturated.

  □ *Decline* – The last stage in a product's life cycle, when sales continually decline. The product is eventually withdrawn from the market.

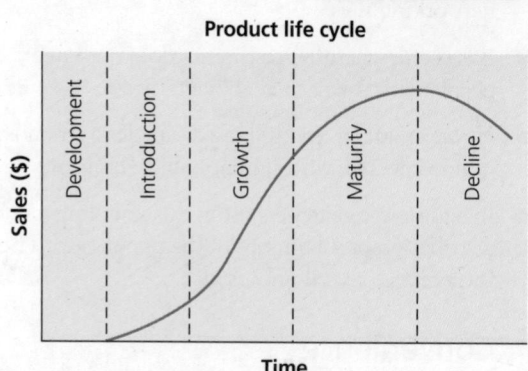

Figure 4.6 The product life cycle

CUEGIS CONCEPTS

Examine how changes (such as the forces of technology and fashion) have impacted on the product life cycle in an industry of your choice.

The relationship between the product life cycle and the marketing mix (AO2)

Managing the marketing mix for a product varies according to the stage of the product in its life cycle. Examples are shown in Table 4.6 below.

Table 4.6 PLC stage and the appropriate marketing mix

PLC stage	Marketing mix
R&D	• Expenditure on market research to refine the product • Pricing, distribution and promotion ideas are discussed prior to launch
Introduction	• Marketing efforts to raise brand and product awareness, e.g. sales promotion campaigns • Advertising expenditure is high in an attempt to boost sales • Limited distribution channels so sales are generally low • Possibly high prices if there is limited competition and to recoup R&D costs, or low prices to gain market share • Investment in branding to differentiate the product from rivals
Growth	• Brand and product preference develop, so sales increase • Marketing efforts to build brand preference and customer loyalty • Stabilizing prices to ensure market growth and value for money • Sales promotion and other marketing campaigns to get potential customers to switch from rival brands
Maturity	• Marketing efforts focus on holding the market position to maximize profits • Product differentiation is vital to lengthening this stage in the PLC • Promotion is widespread • Price competition can become intense • Possible extension strategies to prolong life of product, e.g. new features and benefits, other forms of differentiation, or entering new markets
Decline	• Lower prices, possibly aiming to be the lowest cost provider • Decision made either to continue with marketing efforts to sell the product (for as long as possible) or to pull it (if losses are incurred)

Extension strategies (AO3)

- Extension strategies are marketing techniques used to prolong a product's life cycle (see Figure 4.7).

- Examples include: cutting prices, product enhancements (such as 'special editions'), redesigning or repackaging the product, short-term promotions and exporting the product to overseas markets.

- They are used when a product is in a saturated market or as it enters the decline stage of the product life cycle.

- The extent to which product extension strategies are used depends on the relative costs and benefits (revenues) from implementing the plans.

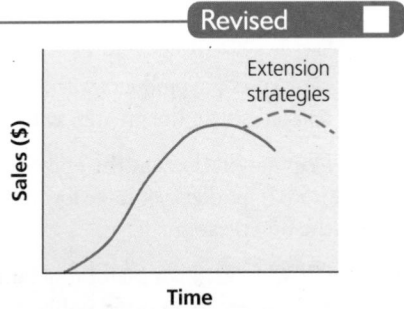

Figure 4.7 Extension strategies and the product life cycle

The relationship between the product life cycle, investment, profit and cash flow (AO2)

Table 4.7 The relationship between the product life cycle, investment, profit and cash flow

PLC stage	Investment	Profit	Cash flow
R&D	Very high R&D costs	Loss	Negative
Introduction	Very high marketing costs	Loss, but smaller	Negative, but improving
Growth	High marketing costs	High	Positive
Maturity	Lower	Profit peaks	Positive
Decline	Little, if any	Profit falls	Declines/negative

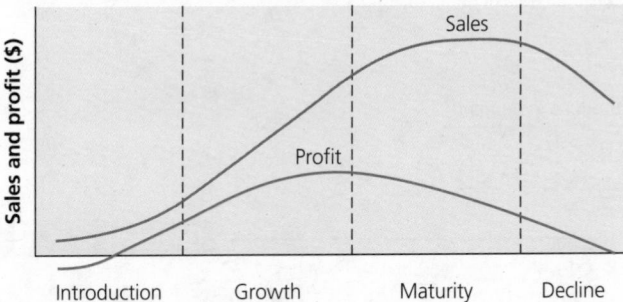

Figure 4.8 The relationship between the PLC and profit

Boston Consulting Group (BCG) matrix on an organization's products (AO3, AO4)

- The Boston Consulting Group (BCG) matrix is a marketing tool used to examine an organization's product portfolio.

- For example, the Volkswagen Group's product portfolio includes: Audi, SEAT, Skoda, Bentley, Bugatti, Lamborghini, Porsche, Ducati and Scania.

- There are two dimensions to the matrix: a product's market share and the market growth (see Figure 4.9).

- There are four quadrants in the BCG matrix:

  - ☐ *Question marks* are products that have low market share in a high growth market. Managers try to convert these products into stars, although this requires investment.

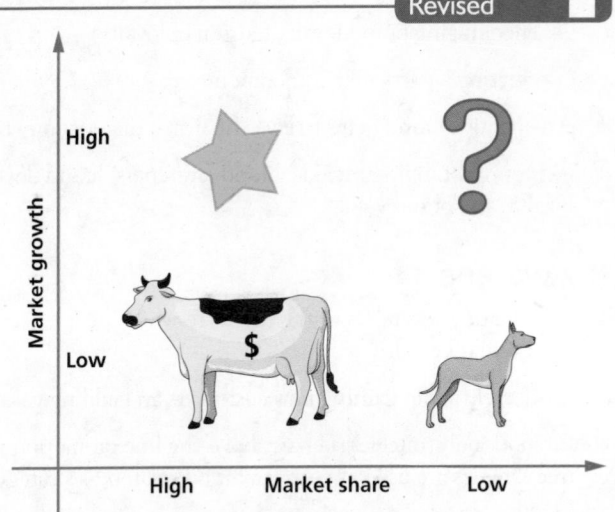

Figure 4.9 The BCG matrix

- ☐ *Stars* are products with high or increasing market share in a high growth market. They have yet to become market leaders but have the potential to become cash cows.

- ☐ *Cash cows* are products with high market share in a low growth (mature) market, so are the greatest earners of cash for a business.

- ☐ *Dogs* are products at the end of their product life cycle so operate in low growth markets yet have low market share. Hence, dogs drain cash from the organization.

- ■ The BCG matrix is a useful tool for managing a diverse range of products in an organization's portfolio, helping to provide balance to a firm's product portfolio.

Table 4.8 Categories of the BCG matrix

Stars	Question marks
● High market growth	● High market growth
● High market share	● Low market share
● Growth stage in the product life cycle (PLC)	● Introduction stage in the PLC
● Invest to turn into cash cow	● Drain cash flow
Cash cows	**Dogs**
● Low market growth	● Low market growth
● High market share	● Low market share
● Maturity stage in the PLC	● Decline stage in the PLC
● Main generators of cash	● Divest to prevent further losses

Table 4.9 Benefits of a product portfolio

- ● Developing a group of products in the portfolio can help to increase brand awareness
- ● Reduces the risks of relying on a single product
- ● Increases the revenue streams (see Unit 3.2) of the business
- ● Having a variety of products helps to limit the impact of seasonal fluctuations in demand

Aspects of branding (AO2)

Revised ☐

- ■ Branding refers to a unique name or identity for a business, e.g. Apple, McDonald's, LEGO or Toyota.

- ■ The role of branding for a business includes:

   - ☐ creating a legal identity for its goods and services

   - ☐ acting as a source of product differentiation

   - ☐ building brand awareness, i.e. recognition of the brand

   - ☐ encouraging brand loyalty (customer loyalty)

   - ☐ creating a particular corporate image.

- ■ An effective brand helps to give the firm a major competitive edge.

- ■ Aspects of branding include: brand awareness, brand development, brand loyalty, and brand value.

■ Awareness

- ■ Brand awareness refers to the extent to which people recognize and remember a particular brand.

- ■ It is largely about gaining new customers and adding value for the business.

- ■ Promotional strategies such as above-the-line promotion (see page 138) and free samples are used as part of a brand awareness strategy.

- Familiarity with a brand leads to higher sales volume of a good or service.
- Businesses often use family branding to raise brand awareness. This type of branding involves selling different products under the same brand name, e.g. Kellogg's and Heinz.

Development

- Brand development is an aspect of marketing strategy about what a brand stands for. It is also about communicating the value of a brand to customers.
- Different people are attracted to a brand for possibly different reasons, so brand development is concerned with establishing the relevant valuable aspects of the brand to different consumer profiles (see Unit 4.2).
- It is about delivering a consistent brand image that gives it a competitive edge over its rivals. An example is McDonald's use of its brand for its products, e.g. McNuggets, McMuffin, McCafé and McFlurry.
- Product endorsements and sponsorship deals are common methods of brand development.
- The market is often flooded with a large number of rival brands, thus offering customers an array of choice. Brand development is about connecting with customers to build lasting relationships and their loyalty.
- Brand development shapes people's perception of a brand, which ultimately determines its success or failure.
- Nevertheless, brand development can be extremely expensive and there is no guarantee that it will succeed. Popular brands of the past include Kodak, Compaq, Sony Ericsson and Woolworth's.

Loyalty

- Brand loyalty happens when customers repeatedly purchase their favourite brand, rather than switching to a rival brand.
- It is the result of successful brand development and marketing strategies so that consumers prefer a particular brand.
- Whilst brand awareness is generally about gaining new customers, brand loyalty is about keeping these customers and getting them to make repurchases.
- Branding becomes relatively more important than price once loyalty is developed.
- Customers purchase their preferred brand regardless of price or convenience, e.g. according to Coca-Cola's website, its customers enjoy 1.7 billion servings of its products each day.
- Loyalty programmes (rewards programmes) are often used as part of a firm's promotional strategy to foster brand loyalty. These programmes provide incentives for customers to make repeat purchases for additional benefits such as price discounts.

> **Expert tip**
>
> Branding can be a vital part of the marketing mix, with research showing that customers are largely affected by branding and not just prices. However, in some cases, customers prefer lower prices over the brand. It is important to write your answers in the context of the business in question.

Table 4.10 Benefits of brand loyalty

- It makes customers less price sensitive, so higher prices can be charged, allowing the firm to earn higher sales revenue
- It encourages repeat customers and prevents customers from switching to rival brands
- Loyal customers are likely to recommend products that they like to their family and friends
- It can lead to an increase in the value of the business as brands are intangible assets (see Unit 3.4)
- It increases the chances of success when launching new products under the same brand name

■ Value

■ There is no universally accepted definition or measure of brand value, although the most commonly used considers the estimated future earnings attributable to the brand.

■ In its simplest form, the term brand value refers to what a brand is worth to the business and its shareholders.

■ Brand value adds to (or subtracts from) the value provided by a good or service, e.g. customers buy a Ferrari or Porsche for more than the functionality of driving a car.

■ A firm's brand value can go up or down in value, based on a range of factors such as its earning potential, market share, and its corporate reputation.

■ Measuring the value of a brand is difficult and somewhat subjective.

■ Brand awareness, brand development, and brand loyalty are all dimensions of brand value.

The importance of branding (AO3)

Revised ☐

■ Branding encourages customer loyalty, i.e. repeat purchases.

■ It creates a unique identity for a product, enabling it to be distinguished from other rival products on the market.

■ It enables businesses to charge higher prices, thereby improving their profit margins.

■ Branding can enable customers to know what to expect, irrespective of where they are in the world.

■ Brands add value so customers get more than just the good or service they buy, e.g. there is an emotional value attached to purchasing certain brands.

The importance of packaging (AO3)

Revised ☐

■ Packaging is an important aspect of product differentiation, e.g. product packaging can contain the brand name and logo.

■ Similarly, packaging helps customers to identify and recognize the brand or product. Some products have a unique or distinct design to grab the attention of buyers, e.g. Toblerone chocolate bars, Tabasco sauce, Pringle's potato chips, and Coca-Cola's glass bottle.

■ It helps to shape customers' perception of a brand.

■ Packaging has a functionality role, e.g. protection of the product (physical, hygiene and transportation protection).

■ It plays an important role in promoting a product, e.g. visual appeal such as the texture and quality of the packaging, which can alter customers' perception of the product or brand.

■ Aside from the value to a business, there are legal requirements for a product's packaging, e.g. nutritional information.

Figure 4.10 Packaging in important to the marketing mix

4.5b The 4 Ps: Price

The appropriateness of the following pricing strategies (AO3)

■ Cost-plus (mark-up)

- Cost-plus pricing (also known as **mark-up pricing**) involves adding a profit element to the costs of production, i.e. the price is set above the costs by a predetermined amount.

- The **mark-up** (or the **profit margin**) is a percentage (e.g. 60% added on top of production costs) or an absolute amount (e.g. $20 above costs).

- Hence, price = cost of production + profit margin.

Table 4.11 Advantages and disadvantages of cost-plus pricing

Advantages of cost-plus pricing	Disadvantages of cost-plus pricing
• It is the simplest form of pricing strategy and suitable for literally all products	• It ignores the impact of lower prices that rival businesses may be charging
• It is very straightforward to calculate	• It does not focus on the potential level of demand but the calculated price instead
• It helps to ensure the selling price covers all production costs	

EXAM PRACTICE

4 The cost of producing one unit of output for Thornton & Greg Co. is $5. The firm uses a mark-up of 40%. Calculate its selling price for the product. [2]

5 Thornton & Greg Co. sells a different product for $1.98 for which its costs of production are $1.20. Calculate the percentage profit margin (mark-up) on the product. [2]

■ Penetration

- Penetration pricing involves setting the price low enough to enter an industry and gain market share from existing firms (often advertised as a 'special introductory price offer').

- The low pricing strategy enables the firm to create brand recognition when launching a new good or service or entering a new market.

- It is a short-term to medium-term pricing strategy as it can lead to losses or very low profit margins so is not sustainable.

> **Expert tip**
>
> Try to avoid repeating the same point in the exams as you will not get credit for doing so. When asked to explain two reasons why penetration pricing is used by businesses, some candidates have stated 'to gain more customers' and 'to increase market share'. These points are not distinct.

Table 4.12 Advantages and disadvantages of penetration pricing

Advantages of penetration pricing	Disadvantages of penetration pricing
• Allows a business to enter a market and/or to launch a new product into an existing market, acquiring market share rapidly	• If costs increase suddenly and/or rapidly, the firm could be operating at a loss
• Can discourage potential new competitors from entering due to the low prices and low profit margins	• Firms that set a low price might build a corporate image of low quality which it could find difficult to resolve when prices need to increase
• Lower prices can give the firm a competitive advantage over their rivals	• Similarly, the firm may lose some quality-conscious customers
• Attractive pricing can encourage word-of-mouth recommendations by customers	• Customers may come to expect low prices, making it difficult for the business to raise prices at a later date
• It can force the business to focus on cutting costs, raising productivity and/or improving its efficiency in order to be able to charge low prices	

■ Skimming

- Price skimming involves setting a high price when launching a new and unique product.

- It is commonly used when introducing new hi-tech products, e.g. new smartphones.

- It is used in order to maximize short-term profit margins before rival firms enter the market.

- The price is eventually lowered over time to attract customers with less disposable income and due to new entrants competing in the market.

Table 4.13 Advantages and disadvantages of skimming pricing

Advantages of skimming pricing	Disadvantages of skimming pricing
• The initially high price helps to recoup the costs of research and development (R&D) prior to launching the product	• The strategy can backfire if a close competitor launches a rival product at a lower price
• High profit margins can be earned, especially if early adopters are more concerned about quality and status of owning an original and unique product rather than the price	• The high price might put off customers, thus giving time for rival firms to launch an improved product offering better value for money
• A high price is commonly associated with high quality so can help firms to establish strong brands and products	• Price-savvy customers might not buy the product when it is newly launched, preferring instead to wait until prices are lowered
	• It is not a long term or sustainable pricing strategy

■ Psychological

- Psychological pricing involves setting prices to make them seem at least slightly lower, e.g. $499.95 instead of $500.00.

- Its purpose is to increase sales volume by portraying better value, e.g. a product priced at $15 might not sell as well as one sold at $16.99 as customers might think there is not much difference in the price, perceiving there to be a $1 difference when in fact it is closer to $2.

Table 4.14 Advantages and disadvantages of psychological pricing

Advantages of psychological pricing	Disadvantages of psychological pricing
• It makes the price seem artificially lower so can help to gain higher sales, thus generating more profit	• Some people perceive psychological pricing as unethical as it tricks people into thinking that prices are lower, which can negatively impact on the firm's image and sales
• It can work for almost any good or service by conveying better value for money	• There are calculation problems when adding up sales of a range of products sold using psychological pricing
• It can encourage impulse buying (unintended purchases) due to the perceived value	• As it is so widely used, customers are accustomed to psychological pricing so the strategy may not work in tricking customers that prices are significantly lower

■ Loss leader

- Loss leader pricing involves setting the price of a good or service below its cost of production in order to attract customers to buy the product along with others with higher profit margins.

- For example, a bakery might sell a particular product at just $0.50 each rather than the normal price of $2 in order to encourage customers to buy other products at the bakery.

- Essentially, the use of loss leaders is a form of sales promotion.

- In order to limit its losses, the firm is likely to impose a rule on the maximum number of purchases (per customer per visit) of the loss leader product.

- It is a short-term pricing tactic for a single product. As customers get used to a particular product being a loss leader, the firm introduces a different loss leader every so often.

Table 4.15 Advantages and disadvantages of loss leader pricing

Advantages of loss leader pricing	Disadvantages of loss leader pricing
• Using loss leaders can help to gain customer loyalty as people generally like bargains	• Customers may become accustomed to and expect loss leader products, which can prove to be expensive and unsustainable for some businesses
• Increased sales revenue from customers buying other goods whilst purchasing the loss leader in the retail store	• The firm makes a loss on these products and there is no guarantee that customers will purchase other products in addition to the loss leaders
• They are an effective way to get rid of older stock or merchandise	• Firms need to ensure there are sufficient stocks of the loss leader; this creates problems of stockpiling (see Unit 5.5), yet it may be necessary to prevent customer dissatisfaction

■ Price discrimination

- Price discrimination occurs when a business charges different prices to different customers for essentially the same product, e.g. adult and child cinema tickets.

- For the strategy to work, each market segment must have separate ability and willingness to pay for the good or service, e.g. charging lower prices to those living in rural areas but higher prices to those who live in central business districts.

Table 4.16 Advantages and disadvantages of price discrimination

Advantages of price discrimination	Disadvantages of price discrimination
• Enables the firm to gain higher revenues by charging higher prices in market segments which have a greater ability and willingness to pay	• Some consumers will end up paying higher prices so may be less happy
• It can help to build goodwill as lower prices are charged to those with lower ability and willingness to pay, e.g. children, the elderly and students	• Those who pay lower prices may not be less able to pay, e.g. adults could be unemployed yet retired people can be affluent
• Enables firms to manage demand and capacity, e.g. train and bus operators in many countries charge higher prices during peak hours to manage congestion	• There are often administrative costs in separating the market segments

■ Price leadership

- Price leadership occurs when one business (usually the dominant firm in the industry) sets prices which are closely monitored and followed by its rivals, e.g. Coca-Cola or Apple.

- The dominant firm is known as the **price maker** whilst the firms that follow are known as **price takers**.

- Quite often, the dominant firm (the one with the largest market share in the industry) has the lowest average costs of production, so is in a position to charge lower prices than its competitors (see section on economies of scale in Unit 1.6).

- It leaves the rivals with little choice but to follow the prices set by the market leader, by matching these prices or setting them very close to the prices of the dominant firm.

- Alternatively, dominant firms can charge higher prices than the market average if there is limited competition.

- Collusive price leadership can occur as a result of an agreement between firms to fix their prices. However, collusion is illegal in most countries.

Table 4.17 Advantages and disadvantages of price leadership

Advantages of price leadership	Disadvantages of price leadership
• Customers gain when the dominant firm sets lower prices due to its power to exploit economies of scale from operating at a large scale	• It is not in the best interest of customers if the dominant firm sets higher prices due to the lack of competition in the industry
• Low prices set by the market leader can reinforce its market share and dominant position	• The market leader can become complacent and not monitor its cost structure effectively, allowing rival firms to increase their own market share
• Market leaders that charge higher prices enjoy greater profit margins; higher prices can actually improve the profitability for all firms in the industry	• Low prices mean low profit margins, yet high prices do not equal high profits if the dominant firm does not monitor and control its operational costs
• It reduces the likelihood of a price war, which is detrimental to most firms in the long run	

■ Predatory

- Predatory pricing involves charging a low price, even below costs of production, in order to harm the sales of competitor firms and to restrict competition.

- It is used by a business that is threatened by the potential entry of a new competitor.

- In extreme cases, the existing firms with large market power may start a **price war** (when firms continually reduce their prices), forcing less established firms to leave the industry.

CUEGIS CONCEPTS

Examine how the concept of ethics has affected the pricing strategies for a business organization of your choice.

Table 4.18 Advantages and disadvantages of predatory pricing

Advantages of predatory pricing	Disadvantages of predatory pricing
• Lower prices can encourage customers to switch to buying the products of a business	• Predatory pricing is illegal in some countries, e.g. EU competition law prohibits firms from selling products at a loss deliberately to force their rivals out of business
• Sales revenue will increase following the price reductions if customers are price-sensitive	• Lower prices can trigger quality concerns about the good or service
• The low prices can act as a barrier to entry for other firms considering entering the industry	• It can encourage or force competitors to retaliate, thereby sparking a price war
	• Predatory pricing can lead to increases in market power, which is anti-competitive
	• It is unsustainable in the long run

4.5c The 4 Ps: Promotion

Revised ☐

Aspects of promotion (AO2)

Revised ☐

- Promotion is the marketing process of raising customer awareness and interest in a product or brand in order to generate sales.

- It has a key role in creating brand loyalty.

- It is the communication aspect of the marketing mix.

- The objectives of promotion include:

  ☐ building product and brand awareness

  ☐ creating customer interest

  ☐ providing product information

  ☐ stimulating demand for the product

  ☐ differentiating the product from rival products

  ☐ reinforcing and developing the brand name.

- The three key aspects of promotion are above-the-line (ATL) promotion, below-the-line (BTL) promotion and the promotional mix.

■ Above-the-line promotion

- Above-the-line (ATL) promotion is paid-for marketing communication via independent media, e.g. advertising on television or in a national newspaper.

- A third-party organization (such as YouTube, Google, a radio station or cinema) has the responsibility for and control of the process.

- Its key advantage is the potentially huge target audience as it has a very broad reach and is largely untargeted. However, the main drawback is the high expense of ATL promotion.

Table 4.19 Advantages and disadvantages of various ATL promotions

Medium	Advantages	Disadvantages
Cinema	• Captured audience of potential customers seated in the cinema • Targeted marketing based on the type of movie being screened • High impact from large screen and high-end sound system	• The impact or message may be lost or forgotten after viewers have watched the movie • Passive audience who choose to talk or consume food and drinks during the adverts
Magazine	• Access to specific customer target groups, e.g. car magazines for motor enthusiasts • Adverts have a longer shelf life as people don't tend to throw away magazines so quickly • High readership rate	• Glossy adverts in popular magazines are very expensive • Planning is difficult as adverts are often placed six months prior to publication • Advertising clutter can put off readers of magazines
Newspaper	• Most newspapers can reach a large number of people within a specific geographical area • Printed adverts can be referred to at a later date	• Adverts compete for the attention of newspaper readers • Has a relatively short life span as newspapers are usually just read once
Online	• The opportunities for online advertising continue to grow rapidly around the world • Reaches out to national and global audience • Highly accessible to customers	• There are cheaper online methods, e.g. the firm's own website, blogs or social media • Online advertising clutter, such as pop-up adverts, means online adverts can be ignored
Outdoor advertising	• Large billboard posters are highly visible and attract attention • Constant reminders as adverts are repeatedly seen by people, e.g. commuters and drivers • Digital displays can have more appeal due to the use of moving images	• Many outdoor adverts (such as billboards) are static • They can be vulnerable to vandalism or damage from severe weather conditions • Messages must be brief as large images are more effective than lots of text
Radio	• People can multi-task whilst listening to the radio, e.g. drivers • Ability to reach specific target groups, e.g. teenagers or elderly • Morning and evening commuters offer huge marketing opportunities	• No visuals, so may not be as effective as audio-visual adverts • People often regard the radio simply as background noise • Radio adverts have far less of a national reach than TV adverts
Television	• Impact of sight, sound and motion to grab viewers' attention • TV adverts can connect emotionally with viewers • Broadcast times can target specific markets, e.g. children • Huge potential to reach mass-market audience	• Very expensive so is not suitable or affordable for smaller firms • Viewers might 'channel hop', i.e. skip channels during adverts • Usually effective only when the advert is seen several times • Limited information as adverts are generally very short

■ Below-the-line promotion

■ Below-the-line (BTL) promotion refers to promotional activities that the business has direct control over, e.g. direct mail and customer loyalty schemes.

■ BTL promotion is aimed directly at a target audience rather than a generic audience, as in the case of ATL promotion.

■ Hence, BTL promotion does not use the mass media.

■ It is suitable when the business has direct contact with customers, e.g. through direct marketing, point-of-sale displays, newsletters and public relations.

■ The results and effectiveness of BTL campaigns are easier for a business to measure.

Expert tip

Students often use the terms 'advertising' and 'promotion' interchangeably. Whilst advertising is indeed a major part of promotion, the latter is much broader and includes far more than just advertising as outlined in this chapter.

Table 4.20 Advantages and disadvantages of various BTL promotions

Medium	Advantages	Disadvantages
Direct mail	• Highly targeted as the business knows the target market groups • Newsletters, letters and catalogues can help to keep customers informed and keen • Encourages customers to directly purchase from the business	• Administrative and postage costs can be high • Low readership rate as a lot of direct mail through the post is regarded as 'junk' mail • Advertising clutter can make it difficult for an advert to stand out
Public relations	• Develops positive relationships with the media and the public • Often perceived as a highly credible form of promotion • Highly cost effective when compared to the direct costs of other forms of BTL promotion	• The news media often publishes or broadcasts an edited version of the marketing message • There is no guarantee that the news media will run a story, despite efforts to put it together
Sponsorship	• Marketing advantages of being associated with the sponsoring company • Exclusive marketing exposure during sponsored events	• Negative actions of the sponsor could compromise the firm's integrity and reputation • Can be very expensive
Point of sale	• Encourages impulse (unintended) purchases • Highly visible promotion so ideal for marketing new products • Easy to monitor most popular products	• Inventory (stock) control may be problematic • May not catch the attention of customers due to so many point-of-sale displays
Email	• The internet provides wide opportunities for e-marketing • Generally inexpensive • Environmentally friendly (email marketing is paper-free) • Opt-in email subscription lists can generate good responses	• Customers might regard emails as spam (unsolicited messages) • Legal issues need to be considered, e.g. data privacy laws • Undelivered and/or unread emails due to spam filters
Loyalty programmes	• Encourage brand loyalty and frequent repurchases • The database of customer details can be used for direct marketing	• Rewards systems, such as price discounts and free gifts, can be expensive to maintain • Administrative costs can be high
Merchandising	• Promotes impulse purchases • Selling internal merchandise with the firm's logo or brand further promotes brand awareness • Provides extra revenue stream from the sale of merchandise	• The production of the firm's own merchandise can be expensive • Additional running costs are incurred, e.g. stock control • Merchandise often contributes to visual clutter
Exhibitions and trade shows	• Captive audience of potential customers at the venue • Opportunities for retail customers and consumers to see the product first-hand	• Intense competition from rival exhibitors • Limited opportunities to exhibit at trade shows throughout the year
Sales promotion	• A range of incentives to entice customers, e.g. price discounts	• It is only a short-term promotional tactic

Keyword definitions

Point of sale refers to the marketing of goods in stores where customers can purchase the goods. It is based on convenience (positioned in a way so they are easily accessible to customers, such as supermarket checkouts) and prompting impulse buying.

Merchandising refers to the use of branded products (such as toys, cups and clothing) linked to a business organization (such as a theme park, movie or music group).

CUEGIS CONCEPTS

Examine the use of loyalty schemes as a strategy for a business of your choice. As an example, you could consider one of the following industries: airlines, supermarkets, restaurants, or coffee shops.

■ Promotional mix

- ■ A promotional mix refers to the combination of different appropriate methods of ATL and BTL promotion aimed at specific target markets.

- ■ It consists of advertising, personal selling, public relations, direct marketing and sales promotion (see Figure 4.11).

- ■ All elements of the promotional mix share two common objectives: to *inform* customers about the product and to *persuade* them to buy the product over rival brands.

Figure 4.11 The promotional mix

Table 4.21 The promotional mix

Advertising	• Objective is to promote the business and its products to generate brand awareness, sales and customer loyalty
	• A range of ATL and BTL methods can be used, e.g. TV, radio, newspapers, magazines, billboards, web pages and social media
Personal selling	• Enables customers to find out more about the firm's product or service
	• May include free samples and gifts to entice customers
	• Can generate positive word-of-mouth (referrals from satisfied customers)
	• Interactions with customers can be in person, via the telephone or email, which can create personal relationships with clients
Public relations	• Public relations is about getting favourable publicity into the news media, thereby fostering a positive corporate image with the general public
	• It also involves a PR team being responsible for handling negative attention from the media or the public
	• The objective is to create customer goodwill and to build a favourable corporate image
Direct marketing	• Targets specific potential customers via telemarketing (telesales), customized letters, emails and text messages
	• Marketing efforts to sell products directly to the public, e.g. mail order or telemarketing (instead of using retailers)
Sales promotion	• Short-term marketing activities aimed at encouraging an increase in sales revenue
	• Offers specific products or services for sale, e.g. price discounts or BOGOF (buy one, get one free) deals and loyalty schemes

Keyword definition

Public relations is an organization's planned and sustained process of maintaining mutual understanding with the general public. The PR team tries to gain favourable publicity via the media and other channels, e.g. educational programmes, news conferences, community activities and sponsorship.

Expert tip

When advising a business on an appropriate promotional mix, do remember to write within the context of the organization. Students have been known to write about 'buy one, get one free' deals (for the motor car industry) and customer loyalty schemes (for health care providers); more thought and care is needed to score well in the exams!

The impact of changing technology on promotional strategies (AO3)

Technology has changed the way in which businesses use promotional strategies. Examples include viral marketing, social media marketing and social networking.

◼ Viral marketing

- Viral marketing is the spread of information about a firm's goods or services from one internet user to another, possibly creating exponential growth in a marketing message.

- It relies on the use of online channels such as blogs, microblogs, email, video-hosting websites and online forums.

- Uses social networks to generate positive online word-of-mouth marketing to raise product and brand awareness.

- The aim is to raise product and brand awareness by creating a marketing buzz around a product, e.g. the launch of a new movie.

- As consumers are the advocates of the promotional message, viral marketing can spread wider and faster than traditional adverts.

- Viral marketing works well as the target audience is 'automatically' identified, i.e. those who are interested in or attracted to the product will share the information with other like-minded people.

- It is generally suited to young customer groups and those with hand-held mobile devices.

◼ Social media marketing

- Social media marketing is the use of online tools and websites to promote products in a less formal way, e.g. using Google+ and Facebook.

- Social media entails content to be uploaded, e.g. videos, newsletters, e-books, blogs, podcasts.

- Social media, such as companies that use Facebook, is a form of direct marketing.

- It can potentially have a global reach, enabling customers to view the business from a different perspective, e.g. a company's Facebook site might include photos of staff social functions.

- It can help a business to connect with its customers on a more personal and emotional level, making their products more appealing.

- Unlike social networking, social media marketing tends to rely on one-way communication to inform and/or persuade customers to purchase the firm's products. It is intended to transmit information to a broad audience.

◼ Social networking

- Social networking refers to the use of internet-based tools and platforms to create and share online content. It enables people to connect and communicate online, e.g. through Facebook, LinkedIn, Instagram and Twitter.

- Social media and networks have encouraged many people to willingly share their opinions, ideas, feedback, photos and videos, thus providing many market research opportunities.

- Social networking facilitates viral marketing, enabling marketing messages to be communicated faster and cheaper.

- Unlike social media, social networking tends to rely on two-way communication, with customers contributing and responding accordingly. There is an act of engagement with different parties.

CUEGIS CONCEPTS

Investigate the impact of innovation (such as changing technology) on the promotional strategies for a business of your choice.

Guerrilla marketing and its effectiveness as a promotional method (AO3)

Revised

- The term **guerrilla marketing** was coined by Jay Conrad Levinson (1984) as a marketing strategy designed to promote products in a low-cost unconventional and unexpected way that makes a large impact and lasting impression on the general public.

- It is based on a high energy and imaginative approach, along with the element of surprise. Hence, it is also known as **ambush marketing**.

- Examples include the use of publicity stunts, viral videos, stencil graffiti, stickers, and flash mobs.

- It is suitable for small businesses with small budgets for promotion, to combat traditional forms of advertising and promotion. This can help to cut through advertising clutter such as junk mail, email spam and unsolicited telephone calls.

- Guerrilla marketing campaigns are often shocking, offensive, unique and memorable in order to create a general buzz. Quite often, this can lead to viral marketing.

- For some examples, visit this website: **http://goo.gl/CAKyh6** (122 must-see guerrilla marketing examples) or watch this short YouTube video clip: **http://goo.gl/O29SyE** (guerrilla marketing innovative ideas).

4.5d The 4 Ps: Place

Revised

The importance of place in the marketing mix (AO2)

Revised

- Place (or distribution), in the marketing mix, is about making the good or service available to consumers (the end users).

- An effective distribution strategy ensures consumers are able to purchase the product easily, i.e. distributing the right product to the right consumers at the right time.

- Distribution is a crucial part of the marketing mix for all businesses – there is little purpose in having a great product, sold at an attractive price if customers are unable to find a retailer nearby that sells it. The more readily available the product, the more likely it will sell well.

- Place is about the location of the consumer, not the business itself. Hence, a key function of place in the marketing mix is to provide convenience to consumers.

- It involves strategies the business uses to get its goods to the location of the customers, be it regional, national or international.

> **Expert tip**
>
> A common mistake made by students is to confuse place with location. Place refers to **distribution** in the marketing mix (where customers can purchase their products), whereas location is about the **physical position** of a business organization (i.e. where the business is situated). Place is vital to all businesses, but physical presence is not necessarily so.

The effectiveness of different types of distribution channels (AO3)

Revised

- A distribution channel refers to the process or system of getting the product to consumers, e.g. retailers, wholesalers or vending machines.

- If a manufacturer does not sell directly to the consumer, intermediaries are used, e.g. agents or distributors (see Figure 4.12):

  □ A zero-channel network uses no intermediaries so the manufacturer sells directly to the customer, e.g. farmers that sell their agricultural produce straight to consumers.

- ☐ A one-channel network involves selling to retailers.

- ☐ A two-channel network involves the goods going via wholesalers and retailers.

- ☐ A three-channel network uses an agent (perhaps to sell the product overseas) who sells the goods to wholesalers on behalf of the producer.

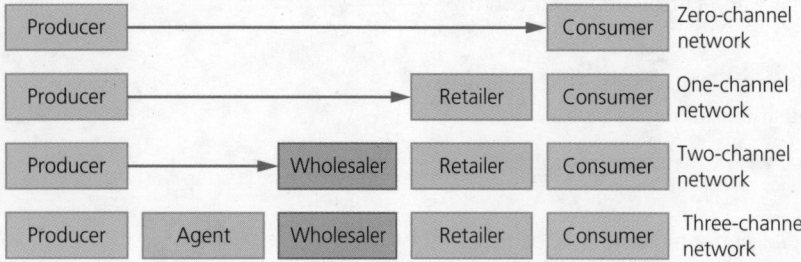

Figure 4.12 Channels of distribution

- ■ An **intermediary**, such as an agent or retailer, is a third-party business that offers distribution services between two trading parties.

- ■ Various distribution channels include direct distribution, retailers, wholesalers, mail order and e-commerce.

■ Direct distribution

- ■ Direct distribution (or a zero-channel network) involves the producer selling the good or service without using an intermediary, e.g. hair salons.

- ■ It involves the producer dealing directly with the consumers of its products.

- ■ The internet has created an alternative channel for producers to sell direct to the consumer, e.g. Amazon, Taobao and iTunes.

■ Retailers

- ■ Retailers are businesses that sell direct to customers, e.g. Walmart, Home Depot, Best Buy, 7-Eleven and Tesco.

- ■ Retailers are often multi-store outlets, offering choice and convenience for customers.

- ■ 'People' (see Unit 4.6) play a huge part in retailing as they can develop a rapport with customers in order to enhance sales.

- ■ A key drawback of using retailers is that retail stores often have to pay expensive rent (in addition to the costs of the store's decorations, furnishings and staff salaries and wages). The higher costs mean they end up charging higher prices for the manufacturer's products.

Table 4.22 Types of retailers

Chain stores	● Two or more outlets with the same business model and name
Department stores	● Multiple producers (departments) within the same retail building
	● A large and wide range of goods available
	● Convenience shopping for customers, all under one roof
Discount stores	● A wide range of products available at discount prices
	● May include some well known branded products
Supermarkets	● Large retail stores with all types of goods, usually groceries and daily products such as health and beauty products
Superstores	● Very large retail stores located in out-of-town areas (due to the amount of land needed)
	● Sell wider variety of products than supermarkets, e.g. household electronic appliances and home furniture

Expert tip

Students often confuse retailers with wholesalers and suppliers. Retailers sell to consumers, whereas wholesalers and suppliers usually sell to other businesses.

■ Wholesalers

■ Wholesalers buy large quantities of products direct from manufacturers and then sell these to customers in smaller quantities (a process known as 'breaking bulk').

■ Retailers benefit from buying smaller quantities from wholesalers rather than significantly larger volumes if bought directly from manufacturers.

■ Producers benefit from wholesalers due to lower transaction costs and fewer deliveries. Wholesalers also take care of the promotion, saving costs for the manufacturer.

■ However, they may not stock the full range of a manufacturer's products. Wholesalers may not always be conveniently located for some retailers, especially smaller ones.

■ Mail order

■ Mail order is the use of the postal system to distribute goods.

■ It traditionally relies on the use of catalogues and order forms although the internet has reduced the reliance on hard-copy catalogues and order forms.

■ It is a short distributional channel so helps to cut production costs and possibly prices for customers.

■ E-commerce

■ E-commerce is the use of the internet to conduct business transactions.

■ It has created an array of opportunities for both producers and retailers to sell to customers.

■ It is a relatively inexpensive distribution channel, providing customers with worldwide access, 24 hours a day from the convenience of their home or office.

■ With increased access to the internet and the global trend of greater use of mobile devices (such as smartphones and tablet computers), e-commerce creates a huge opportunity for businesses to use the internet as a distribution channel.

■ Unit 4.8 outlines the various forms of e-commerce, such as business to business (B2B), business to consumer (B2C) and consumer to consumer (B2C).

■ The appropriateness of different distribution channels

When selecting a distribution channel for a particular product, the following need to be considered:

■ **Type of product** – Whether the product is a producer good or consumer good (e.g. aircraft or fast food), or whether the product is technical (in which case, specialist distributors and agents may be needed to explain how the product works). Perishable goods need to reach customers quickly and/or need to be widely available in retail outlets so they can be sold rapidly. A customized product made specifically for a client would be sold using direct distribution.

■ **Frequency of purchase** – Whether the product is bought in mass markets on a daily basis (in which case, retailers such as supermarkets might be suitable) or whether it is bought infrequently (such as mattresses).

■ **The price of the product** – An expensive product with an exclusive image, such as Lamborghini or Rolex, will be sold in a limited number of retail outlets. By contrast, mass-market products such as Coca-Cola are sold in a wide range of retail outlets and other distribution channels.

■ **Location of customers** – E-commerce could be a viable distribution channel for customers located in rural areas or in overseas markets.

- **The availability of rival products** – Producers will usually compete with rivals by selling their products using the same distribution channels, thereby competing directly for consumers.

- **The size of the market** – Mass-produced goods would require a system of geographically widespread distributional channels, possibly including overseas markets.

- **The available finance** – The better the financial position of a business, the greater its distribution networks can be.

- **The degree of control expected** – The more intermediaries used, the less control a producer has over the marketing of its own products. Longer channels can cause communication problems to be more costly, whereas shorter channels enable prices to be lower.

- **Legal considerations** – There could be certain legal limitations for the sale of certain products, e.g. tobacco, alcohol and medication.

4.6 The extended marketing mix (7 Ps) *(HL only)*

Revised ☐

The 7 Ps model in a service-based market (AO2)

Revised ☐

- Bernard H. Booms and Mary J. Bitner (1981) added an extra 3 Ps to the traditional 4 Ps in the marketing mix; people, processes and physical evidence.

- The 7 Ps model, also known as the **extended marketing mix**, is applicable to the marketing of services (see Figure 4.13), whereas the traditional 4 Ps is suitable for the marketing of physical goods.

- Booms and Bitner argued that the marketing of services needs to be different to that of goods because of the unique characteristics of services: intangibility, heterogeneity and perishability.

- The marketing strategy for the provision of services must be effective as satisfied customers are the best publicity for a firm's products.

Figure 4.13 The extended marketing mix (7Ps)

People: The importance of employee–customer relationships in marketing a service and cultural variation in these relationships (AO3)

Revised ☐

- From the perspective of customers, when a service is being delivered, the person delivering it is not detached from the product itself, e.g. a rude waiter will spoil even the best of meals served in an elegant restaurant.

- People deliver a physical service with a visible result, e.g. assistants, stylists, hairdressers and nail technicians in a salon.

- Successful organizations focus on the service element of the marketing mix by investing in their people (employees) by training and developing workers to deliver good customer service.

- The attitude and behaviour of an employee directly affects the experience of the customer, be it positive or negative. This has a direct impact on whether the customer is likely to return.

- McDonald's, for example, has its own university (called Hamburger University, in Illinois, USA) where staff are trained in various aspects of restaurant management and customer service, to ensure consistency across all their branches around the world.

- The development of social networks and social media has meant that the people element of the extended marketing mix has become ever more important. The news about poor customer care spreads much faster and wider than previously possible.

Processes: The importance of delivery processes in marketing a service and changes in these processes (AO3)

Revised ☐

- Process refers to the operational aspects of a service such as the procedures, protocols, timing and sequence of activities related to the service, e.g. queuing systems in a large sports stadium.

- Processes ensure the same level of service delivery to every customer, even though the experience of each customer might be different, e.g. all customers in a restaurant should be greeted politely and be accompanied to their seats.

- Processes should also enable specific customer preferences to be accommodated (within reason), thereby providing customers with a unique experience.

- Processes include: queuing systems, payment systems (e.g. the ability to pay by credit card or online bank transfer), and after-sales care.

- McDonald's pledge to serve customers their fast food within 90 seconds (or 3.5 minutes for their drive-thru service) is an example of process in their marketing mix.

Physical evidence: The importance of tangible physical evidence in marketing a service (AO3)

Revised ☐

- The location and physical environment where the service is delivered is a significant factor affecting the level of customer satisfaction, e.g. banks should feel safe, hotels should look clean, family restaurants should appear welcoming, and florists should appear welcoming.

- Physical evidence can refer to any form of tangible representation of a service which creates customer perceptions about a service, e.g. menus, brochures, corporate stationery, certificates and awards displays, business cards, staff dress code, and company reports.

- Customers use physical evidence to gauge the level of comfort and attractiveness of a service, e.g. a calm and soothing environment will help to attract customers to a health spa.

- McDonald's restaurants, for example, are all designed to create a family-friendly environment. Their menus are designed and structured in the same way so customers feel more familiar with the physical environment within the restaurants.

- Employees are also directly affected by the physical environment, which impacts on their level of motivation. Therefore, people in the extended marketing mix can be directly influenced by physical evidence.

CUEGIS CONCEPTS

Investigate how the concepts of change and ethics have affected the extended marketing mix for an organization of your choice, such as a school, restaurant, airline or theme park.

4.7 International marketing (*HL only*)

Methods of entry into international markets (AO2)

- **Exporting** – This involves a firm selling its products to overseas buyers without having to physically expand in an overseas market.

  - ☐ The surge in e-commerce (see Unit 4.8) has encouraged more businesses to export their products to international markets.

  - ☐ It is a relatively low-risk growth option. If the export strategy is unsuccessful, the firm can withdraw with minimal costs or losses.

  - ☐ However, the international price is likely to be higher due to postage or transportation costs. The imposition of tariffs (taxes on foreign exports) can also make exports more expensive.

  - ☐ The effectiveness and profitability of this option may be reduced if the exchange rate appreciates, resulting in higher priced exports.

- **Direct investment** – This involves setting up overseas production or distribution facilities.

  - ☐ By producing overseas, the business is closer to its customers so is more aware and able to adapt to their needs and tastes, e.g. it is easier to deal with linguistic and cultural issues that might arise.

  - ☐ Direct investment allows firms to gets around the problem of exchange rate fluctuations if they rely on export markets. By operating in overseas countries, any uncertainty or possible loss of price advantages due to a higher exchange rate can be overcome.

  - ☐ Businesses sometimes directly invest in production or distribution facilities in foreign countries to avoid trade protectionist measures such as tariffs and quotas (as the goods are not classified as imports if produced locally in the foreign country).

  - ☐ Direct investment is a much higher risk growth strategy than exporting, due to the amount of capital investment required, e.g. the firm may need to raise external finance to build production facilities abroad.

  - ☐ External influences can negatively impact on the profits from direct investment, e.g. the products may be incompatible with local customs and tastes, or there could be different local rules and regulations.

- **Franchising** – This growth strategy involves using a third-party provider to supply the goods and services of the business in return for payment of a licensing fee and royalty payments.

  - ☐ It is considerably less risky and less costly than direct investment as franchisees fund the expansion by paying the licence fee and set-up costs of the franchised business overseas.

  - ☐ In addition, franchisees may already have well established customer connections and relations that can help the franchise to grow further.

  - ☐ However, franchising can result in lower quality if standards are not monitored carefully (although this is made more difficult due to operations taking place in foreign countries). This can create a negative impact on the global brand image.

- **Strategic alliance** – This growth strategy involves using foreign partners working together on a particular business venture.

- ☐ Using a local partner in an overseas market can help the business to overcome the potential problems of social, cultural and linguistic differences.

- ☐ It is a relatively safe method of entry to overseas markets as the agreement can be retracted if one of the partners fails to satisfy the terms and conditions of the agreement.

- ☐ It is a relatively cheap and quick way to expand overseas (see Unit 1.6).

- ☐ However, there is the risk that partners can enter or exit the alliance relatively easily, which can jeopardize the stability of the strategic alliance.

- **Joint ventures** (JVs) – This involves the formation of a new business with two or more other firms using their shared resources.

  - ☐ JVs are a common method of growth for companies trying to enter foreign markets.

  - ☐ Human and financial resources, management skills and ideas are shared, creating synergy in the organization.

  - ☐ JVs with foreign partner firms reduce risks when expanding to new and unknown overseas markets because they benefit from local knowledge, experience and expertise.

  - ☐ Although they are more costly to set up than strategic alliances, JVs are permanent legal entities so stakeholders have more commitment to ensure the venture is successful.

  - ☐ However, both strategic alliances and joint ventures can fail due to management and cultural incompatibilities.

The opportunities and threats posed by entry into international markets (AO3)

Revised ☐

■ Opportunities of entry into international markets

- *Profitability* – Selling to overseas markets generates higher sales revenue and the potential for higher profits, especially if the domestic market is saturated.

- *Economies of scale* – Firms can benefit from economies of scale (see Unit 1.6) by selling their products to larger markets around the world.

- *Spread risks* – Selling in overseas markets allows the business to spread its risks (diversification), e.g. if the domestic market goes into a recession, then sales from overseas markets can protect the firm's working capital and profitability.

- *Laws and legislation* – Businesses can take advantage of the more relaxed laws and regulations in some countries which would otherwise constrain their operations.

- *Competition* – There may be less competition by operating in certain countries or regions of the world. Conversely, having an overseas presence can improve the international competitiveness of the organization.

- *Production costs* – Costs of production may be lower in overseas markets, e.g. cheaper labour costs, low-priced raw material costs and lower rents.

- *Financial incentives* – Foreign governments may offer incentives for firms locating in their country (to encourage investment and employment), e.g. tax allowances.

- *Extension strategies* – Entering international markets can also help to extend a product's life cycle, thereby leading to higher profits.

> **Keyword definition**
>
> **Opportunities** are openings or prospects for an organization, in this case as they seek to expand in overseas markets.

■ Threats posed by entry into international markets

- *Social, cultural and demographic factors* – Businesses might have to change their marketing mix in order to better suit the needs of customers overseas who may have a different social and demographic profile. Cultural differences may also present some challenges so necessitate a change in the firm's marketing strategies.

- *Language barriers* – Marketing messages do not necessarily translate well across international borders, so market research and local knowledge may be required. This undoubtedly adds to the firm's operational costs.

- *Legal and political barriers* – Firms entering international markets need to ensure they comply with local laws and regulations regarding consumer protection, codes of conduct on advertising and packaging, copyrights, trademarks and patents. The political environment can also cause challenges for businesses operating in overseas markets.

- *Financial barriers* – Additional working capital may be needed to expand internationally. It will also cost more for workforce planning and to develop new distribution channels in overseas markets.

- *Competitive rivalry* – Businesses entering foreign markets may face strong competition from well established firms in these markets. Domestic and foreign firms may have already established a strong customer base and enjoy brand loyalty.

- *Exchange rate fluctuations* – Changes in the exchange rate (see Unit 1.5) can alter the competitiveness of a firm's products and prices. This directly impacts on its sales revenue and profitability.

- *Additional costs* – The above threats may necessitate additional market research in new international markets. Hence, the increase in costs can offset the potential profitability of operating in overseas markets.

> **Keyword definition**
> **Threats** present challenges for businesses as they seek to expand internationally.

The strategic and operational implications of international marketing (AO3)

Revised ▢

- International marketing has implications on the operational and strategic decisions of firms because simply extending current marketing practices is unlikely to work well in overseas markets.

- The increasing presence of multinational companies has made international marketing more of an operational and strategic priority for many businesses.

- Operational implications affect the day-to-day operations of a business, e.g. monitoring exchange rate fluctuations in foreign markets. Strategic implications refer to the longer-term operations of a business, e.g. the formation of a strategic alliance or joint venture with foreign partner firms.

- Branding becomes an integral part of an organization's international marketing strategy. Global brands have a better chance of competing in global markets.

- Ethics and etiquette become more important issues for international marketers to consider because what works well in one part of the world does not necessarily succeed in other areas, where cultures, beliefs and customs can be considerably diverse. Such an approach can increase the chances of success in overseas markets.

> **Keyword definition**
> **International marketing** is the marketing of an organization's products in foreign countries.

The role of cultural differences in international marketing (AO3)

- Organizations need to be aware of cultural differences when marketing their products internationally. What works well as a marketing mix in one country does not necessarily work well in other countries or parts of the world.

- As more businesses grow internationally, they need to be aware of the cultural sensitivities in various countries in order to avoid major damage to their reputation, sales and credentials.

- Cultural differences exist because people have different perceptions, beliefs and values. Habits and taste also vary in different parts of the world.

- Cultural differences also require firms to be fully aware of international **business etiquette** (the mannerisms and customs or traditions by which business is conducted in different countries). It also helps to prevent businesses from making marketing blunders.

- Cultural differences have provided many opportunities for businesses and industries to exploit cultural exports, e.g. the widespread use and availability of American products overseas, such as Coca-Cola drinks, McDonald's fast food and Hollywood movies.

Figure 4.14 Hollywood movies are a cultural export from the USA

The implications of globalization on international marketing (AO3)

- Globalization can be defined as the increased integration and interdependence of economies around the world, with converging habits and tastes.

- The expansion of multinational companies around the globe has contributed to the surge in international marketing.

- Having access to a greater customer base creates huge international marketing opportunities for businesses.

- Globalization has enabled businesses to exploit global production and marketing economies of scale. Technological transfer has led to similar production processes around the world.

- E-commerce and e-marketing (see Unit 4.8) have significantly reduced barriers to international trade.

- Nevertheless, international marketers need to consider cultural differences in their marketing strategies by gaining a better knowledge of local cultures and business etiquette. This approach has become known as **glocalization** – the use of a differentiated international marketing mix to meet local tastes and cultures.

CUEGIS CONCEPTS

Investigate how the concepts of culture and globalization have impacted on the marketing strategies for an organization of your choice.

4.8 E-commerce

Revised ☐

Features of e-commerce (AO1)

Revised ☐

Features of e-commerce include:

- E-commerce breaks time barriers – unlike traditional retailers, e-commerce enables customers to have 24-hour accessibility, every day of the week.

- It breaks geographical barriers – online businesses can provide customers with worldwide access and coverage.

- There are low set-up costs, thus lowering barriers to entry for new businesses.

- E-commerce websites generally have interactive functionality to engage online customers, e.g. search options, navigation, store finder, zoom features, product demos and delivery options.

- Social media links, such as Twitter, Google+ and Facebook, facilitate and encourage online purchases. Consumer reviews are increasingly popular as a means to inform customer decision making.

- Unlike retailers, e-tailers do not have physical stores or outlets. Hence, it reduces or eliminates some of the typical overheads of businesses, such as rents and utilities.

- Broad product range – unlike retailers that are constrained by physical limits on their inventory, e-commerce enables firms to stock items targeted for different market segments, e.g. men, women, teenagers, babies and young children.

- Footloose operations – online businesses no longer have to rely on locating in prime locations to entice customers so can avoid paying high rents in these locations.

- The empowerment of customers as they are able to compare prices very easily and quickly. They can also instantly share reviews about a firm's goods or services.

- Credit card payments account for the vast majority of all online purchases.

- Many businesses use e-commerce as a means to reduce their supply chains (see Unit 5.5), enabling them to get products to customers faster and more efficiently, thereby cutting costs.

- In many parts of the world, online shopping is no longer a niche market, but aimed at and used by a mass market.

> **Keyword definitions**
>
> **E-commerce** is the trading of goods and services using online electronic systems and computer networks such as the internet.
>
> **E-tailers** are businesses that operate predominantly online, such as Alibaba, Amazon, Google and eBay.

The effects of changing technology and e-commerce on the marketing mix (AO2)

Revised ☐

■ Changing technology, e-commerce and product

- With e-commerce, almost any product can be sold. To do so successfully, marketers need to clearly define the product, target it at the right audience in the online community, and not limit the potential market to a particular location or country.

- With developments in technology and e-commerce, it is easier for a firm to provide customers with up-to-date information about its products, e.g. product specifications. Customers enjoy the ease and convenience of easy access to product information.

- There is no need to print out menus, catalogues and coloured brochures, or include excessive packaging such as branded paper bags. Instead, there is more focus on functionality, e.g. protective wrapping. This helps to reduce costs and the firm's impact on the environment.

- E-commerce allows for the personalization of products, e.g. personal photos on cups, personalized messages with flowers being sent to the recipient, or printed names on t-shirts.

- E-commerce software offers customers suggestions of additional and complementary products along with the main purchase, i.e. it encourages impulse buying.

Changing technology, e-commerce and price

- E-commerce enables customers to compare prices easily due to greater price transparency, i.e. pricing information can be easily compared, so internet technologies have made pricing very competitive.

- It helps to lower prices due to price transparency, price competition and reduced operational costs (due to fewer intermediaries in the supply chain).

- Pricing may need to account for posting, packaging and delivery charges.

- Pricing is often expressed in internationally tradeable currencies, such as US dollars and euros to appeal to international buyers.

- The pricing decision can be difficult when marketing products overseas because different customers in different countries may be prepared to pay different prices. The growth of online auction websites also empowers consumers in pricing decisions.

Changing technology, e-commerce and promotion

- Information about products can be provided in more detail and in a more engaging or interactive way, e.g. the use of images and sound to promote the product.

- There is increasing use of viral marketing (see Unit 4.5), focusing on promoting products from person to person using technologies such as email, texting, microblogging or social networks.

- There is also greater reliance on the use of social media to promote a firm's products, e.g. company websites, pop-ups adverts, banners, and text messages.

- Direct marketing (see Unit 4.5) becomes easier as e-commerce technologies enable firms to communicate with customers on an individual basis.

- E-commerce has reduced the importance of packaging as a form of promotion as items are delivered through the mail.

- Unlike other methods of above-the-line (ATL) promotion, e-commerce can show customers the advantages of a firm's products in detail, with customers taking advantage of the interactive functions of internet technologies.

- Organizations can use e-marketing, such as emails and e-leaflets, to promote to the potentially huge number of customers in their database, even though the response rate is likely to be relatively low. However, e-marketing can be cost-effective for marketers.

- Marketers face the challenge of the increasing amount of advertising clutter and spam faced by customers, so e-promotions must stand out to gain the attention of the online community.

- Internet technologies have reduced the overall costs of promoting to potential customers.

> **Keyword definition**
> **Spam** refers to unsolicited and undesired electronic messaging systems, often referred to as electronic junk mail, e.g. unsolicited email, text messaging, instant messaging, fax transmissions, and pop-up adverts.

Changing technology, e-commerce and place

- E-commerce enables businesses to access large numbers of customers directly without the use of intermediaries.

- Internet technologies shorten the supply chain, hence reduce operating costs, offering improved convenience to shoppers and content being delivered in various languages. This helps to widen the customer base.

- As e-commerce relies on delivery and courier firms to distribute their products to consumers, it provides limitless opportunities for companies such as DHL and FedEx.

- E-commerce provides customers with an alternative distribution channel. As with traditional distribution methods, the challenge for online businesses is to ensure that the right product is delivered to the right consumer at the right time.

Changing technology, e-commerce and the extended marketing mix

- **People** – E-commerce is impersonal so there is a reduced need for sales staff. People, as part of the extended marketing mix, therefore become less important. Nevertheless, there is still a need for customer service staff, responsible for after-sales care and support.

- **Processes** – Internet technologies make online payments quite straightforward, although many customers are still cautious of internet fraud. Internet technologies also make it easy to reward loyal customers for repeat purchases. Any additional detailed information (such as instruction manuals) and updates about the product can be placed on the firm's website.

- **Physical evidence** – This becomes far less of an issue for marketers as e-commerce exists in the virtual world where customers do not care about the physical environment of retailers; nor are they as bothered about packaging in the marketing of a product.

The difference between the following types of e-commerce (AO2)

Business to business (B2B)

- B2B refers to e-commerce between two or more businesses, e.g. Amazon.com sells books to other book retailers.

- Trading is often based on large orders at competitive prices, often with the option of preferential trade credit (deferred payment).

- B2B offers commercial clients fast delivery times.

- B2B providers compete mainly on price.

- Social media platforms such as Facebook and Twitter have opened up two-way communications between different businesses operating in different industries.

- E-commerce enables businesses to obtain quotations from many potential suppliers and distributors with relative ease and lower costs.

- The B2B market is the largest of the three main types of e-commerce.

- To attract business customers, B2B firms often host information webinars, host booths at trade shows, attend industry networking events, and maintain a social media presence.

- In general, wholesaling is done on a B2B basis.

Business to consumer (B2C)

- B2C refers to businesses that sell directly to the general public using internet technologies.

- These businesses target their products directly at consumers (the end user), e.g. Apple's iTunes sells books, games, music and a range of apps to consumers.

- B2C was first developed by English inventor Michael Aldrich (1979) who connected televisions with computers and telephones to create teleshopping.

- B2C is widespread and it is rather rare for large consumer-based businesses not to sell their products online.

- It reduces or eliminates the need for intermediaries, thereby reducing the chain of distribution. This reduces costs because businesses can sell directly to their customers.

- Support service providers, such as PayPal, offer easy payment processing for online vendors.

- Many e-tailers, such as eBay, Amazon and Alibaba.com engage in both B2C and B2B activities.

- In general, retailing is done on a B2C basis.

Consumer to consumer (C2C)

- E-commerce platforms such as eBay and Taobao enable customers to sell directly to other customers. This type of e-commerce is called C2C.

- C2C hosting websites earn revenue by charging customers a fee and/or commission for advertising their items for sale.

- C2C is suitable for selling second-hand (used or previously owned) items, such as cars, consumer electronics, toys, CDs, DVDs, clothes and furniture.

- A common practice in C2C is online auctioning, which involves customers bidding to purchase an advertised product.

- Many businesses use online classified advertising websites (e.g. Gumtree, Uzgar and Craigslist) to allow customers to advertise and sell their products.

- Major online businesses such as Amazon allow customers to use their e-commerce platform to sell products via their websites.

- C2C has become increasingly popular due to increasingly secure and reputable online payment systems being developed, such as PayPal and AliPay.

- A key issue with C2C is the lack of quality control, especially with the trade in second-hand goods, as the C2C service provider cannot guarantee the quality of the products being sold by its customers.

The benefits of e-commerce to firms and consumers (AO3)

Revised ☐

Table 4.23 The benefits of e-commerce to firms and consumers

Benefits of e-commerce to firms	Benefits of e-commerce to consumers
• E-commerce enables firms to avoid paying high costs of rents in prime locations	• E-commerce provides ubiquity, i.e. being present everywhere – with the huge and continual growth in the use of mobile devices (e.g. laptops, smartphones and tablet computers), e-commerce can be accessed almost anywhere and at any time
• Internet technologies have cut the supply chain, thereby reducing costs and reducing the reliance on sales people and intermediaries (such as wholesalers and retailers)	• Consumers benefit from greater price transparency, enabling them to make more informed choices and decisions
• The firm can potentially reach a wider customer base across a global market	• Consumers have easy access to information from their mobile devices, e.g. address of the business, the telephone number or other contact details, and opening hours or closing times
• Social media websites, such as Twitter and Facebook, are perhaps the fastest way to get a firm's product information to customers	• Consumers benefit from a reduced supply chain as they have direct access to products and at cheaper prices
• As customers can shop 24/7 throughout the year, the business can earn significantly higher sales revenues	• They have the convenience and flexibility of shopping 24/7 on any day of the year from almost any location
• With reduced costs and the ability to be located almost anywhere, e-commerce firms can offer a broader product portfolio, thereby attracting more customers	• E-commerce offers customers convenient payment systems, e.g. credit cards, debit cards or membership accounts
• E-commerce has substantially reduced the costs of promotion, making it easier and more cost-effective to use online advertising, social media, mass emails, online videos and audio recordings	• In many cases, free shipping (delivery) is offered to e-commerce customers

The costs of e-commerce to firms and consumers (AO3)

Table 4.24 The costs of e-commerce to firms and consumers

The costs of e-commerce to firms	The costs of e-commerce to consumers
• Traditional retailers lose their ability to charge higher prices due to the presence of online providers	• There are security issues as credit and debit cards may be stolen and misused (online fraud)
• Easy access to data and product information increases the possibility of goods being easily copied by competitors	• Hackers can steal and abuse personal information (data theft)
• There is a high possibility of fraudulent trade, resulting in losses for the firm or compensation claims being made	• There is no individual interaction with customers so the service is impersonal (which many customers do not like)
• E-commerce is totally reliant on the technology working – any breakdowns will be very costly to the firm	• Customers have to wait for the delivery of the purchased products and do not necessarily know the physical condition of the products until they have been delivered
• There are additional costs to consider, e.g. the costs from hiring ICT specialists to maintain e-commerce systems, such as websites, online payment systems and technical support	• It can be expensive and time consuming for customers to return goods (perhaps because they do not match the specifications online or have been damaged in transit)
• Firms may face pressure from trade unions and other stakeholders if e-commerce leads to mass job losses	• People are bombarded with unsolicited e-marketing promotional messages (online spam)
• There is always the possibility that purchased items can get lost in the post, which further adds to the costs of the firm	• Many people do not have access to the internet nor do they feel confident in using electronic devices to buy goods and services
• Some external factors specifically hinder e-commerce firms, e.g. false descriptions of products, dishonest advertising, poor quality and late deliveries.	• Other customers are put off from the intangibility of the process of e-commerce, e.g. not being able to try on clothes or shoes
• It is not highly suitable for the sale of perishable goods (e.g. ice cream or fresh fish) or specialty products (e.g. prescription medicines or expensive wrist watches)	• Customers who shop online can often incur finance charges (interest) imposed by their credit card providers

Expert tip

When evaluating a firm's e-commerce strategy, consider a two-sided and balanced argument. Whilst its e-commerce strategy can be judged by the extent to which online sales and market share have increased, the costs of staying up to date with internet technologies and the threats of data theft and cyber-security can be very costly in the long term. Over-reliance on technology can damage relationships with customers who prefer face-to-face interactions.

CUEGIS CONCEPTS

Examine how globalization and innovation have impacted on the e-commerce strategy for a business organization of your choice.

CUEGIS CONCEPTS

Evaluate the advantages and disadvantages for a business organization of your choice of using an e-commerce strategy in a changing and globalized business world.

Unit **5** Operations management

5.1 The role of operations management
Revised ☐

Operations management and its relationship with other business functions (AO1)
Revised ☐

Operations management is about acquiring the necessary resources needed for production in the most efficient and cost-effective way. It impacts on the other functional areas of a business, as outlined in the examples below.

■ **Marketing function**

☐ Physical goods or intangible services are produced based on market research in order to meet the needs and wants of customers.

☐ The good or service needs to be promoted to existing and potential customers.

☐ The finished product also needs to be distributed using appropriate channels.

☐ A suitable pricing strategy is needed to ensure the products sell well on the market.

■ **Finance function**

☐ Costs of different production methods (see Unit 5.2), e.g. mass production, are needed to gain economies of scale although this could also require high set-up costs.

☐ Funding is needed for all aspects of operations management, e.g. product testing, research and development (see Unit 5.6) and lean production (see Unit 5.3).

☐ Production managers must be held accountable for their expenditure and budgets (see Unit 3.9).

■ **Human resources function**

☐ Production workers need to be hired and trained to work productively.

☐ Supervisors and quality controllers may also need to be hired.

☐ A crisis management team might need to be formed (see Unit 5.7).

☐ Operations managers are responsible for collaborating and working with managers from other departments to meet organizational objectives.

> **Keyword definition**
>
> **Operations management** refers to the business function of combining inputs to produce outputs (goods and services) that are valued by consumers.

Operations management in organizations producing goods and/or services (AO2)
Revised ☐

■ Operations management focuses on the management process of creating goods and services using the available resources of the organization (see Figure 5.1)

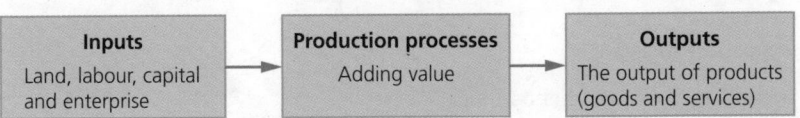

Inputs	**Production processes**	**Outputs**
Land, labour, capital and enterprise	Adding value	The output of products (goods and services)

Figure 5.1 The role of operations management

- Operations management involves planning, organizing, coordinating, and controlling all the inputs needed to produce the goods and services of a business.

- Operations management must ensure that there is value added (see Unit 1.1) in the production process. This helps to ensure firms can sell their products and earn profit for their owners.

Operations management strategies and practices for ecological, social (human resource) and economic sustainability (AO3)

Revised

- Business operations have an important role in ensuring sustainability by creating a balance between the ecological, social and economic needs of people today and those of future generations.

- Businesses are increasingly reporting their **triple bottom line**, a term coined by British entrepreneur John Elkington (1994), to evaluate their performance in a broader context of sustainable business activity. This comprises of environmental sustainability, economic sustainability and social sustainability (see Figure 5.2).

- **Sustainability** is a concept which promotes intergenerational equity, i.e. business activity is able to meet the needs of the current generation in such a way that it does not jeopardize the needs of future generations.

- Elkington's pillars of sustainability are sometimes also referred to as the three Ps of sustainability: people, planet and profit.

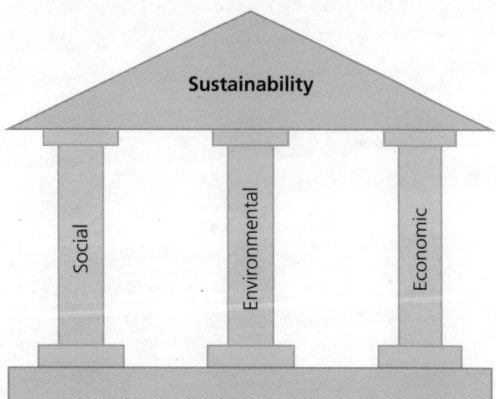

Figure 5.2 John Elkington's pillars of sustainability

Ecological sustainability

- A lack of ecological sustainability means that production will deplete the earth's natural resources for future generations, e.g. overfishing or deforestation are not ecologically sustainable.

- It requires efficient and sensible use of the planet's scarce resources so that they do not become exhausted, e.g. a recent report in *Business Insider* found that China's ban on plastic carrier bags saved the nation over 4.8 million tonnes of oil.

- The exponential population growth of the world's population puts huge pressures on the planet's finite resources. This makes ecological sustainability a key priority for many production managers.

- Examples of ecologically sustainable business practices include:

  □ **Green technologies** – Environmentally friendly innovations that consider the long-term impact on the environment, e.g. renewable energy sources such as solar power.

  □ **Recycling** – Turning waste products, such as plastic and glass bottles, into reusable materials.

> **Keyword definition**
>
> **Ecological sustainability** (or **environmental sustainability**) refers to the capacity of the natural environment to meet the needs of the current generation without risking the ability of future generations to meet their own needs.

- ☐ **Ecological footprint** – The impact of resource consumption and waste production on the natural environment, e.g. using online technologies for business meetings rather than driving to different locations.

- ☐ **Conservation** – Using the planet's scarce resources more carefully by means of renewable resources (such as trees and fish) at a sustainable rate.

- ☐ **Preservation** – Protecting the earth's resources by reducing the human impact on the physical, natural and ecological environment, e.g. rainforests.

Social sustainability

- Social sustainability enables society to optimize the quality of life for current and future generations.

- On the other hand, social hurdles prevent a community from advancing, e.g. poverty, unemployment and social exclusion (such as racism and gender inequalities).

- Elkington argued that male business leaders need to accept women as equals if there is to be social sustainability and development. Embracing social justice can bring about many business opportunities in terms of recruitment, staff retention and corporate reputation.

- Gender discrimination represents an inefficient allocation of human resources. The United Nations Development Programme (UNDP) argues that gender equality is fundamental to both economic and human development.

- From a humanitarian viewpoint, removing social inequalities gives communities a better chance of achieving sustainable development.

- In addition to creating jobs and paying taxes, many countries expect businesses to fulfil their corporate social responsibilities (CSR) (see Unit 1.3). Ignoring CSR can attract unwanted media attention. Hence, an increasing number of businesses apply CSR in their daily operations.

> **Keyword definition**
> **Social sustainability** examines the ability of businesses and people to develop in such a way that they can meet the social well-being needs of current and future generations.

Economic sustainability

- Economic sustainability requires businesses to use their resources (land, labour, capital and enterprise) efficiently and in a maintainable way. Increased global demand and consumption make it ever more difficult to sustain the output of goods and services over time.

- Economic sustainability requires businesses to be more responsible in their use of resources, e.g. using materials that are environmentally friendly, easier to recycle or that are biodegradable.

- The overuse of scarce resources is a major threat to a country's economic well-being, e.g. rapid economic development in some countries, such as China and India, has led to the rapid depletion of the world's finite resources, especially non-renewable resources.

- With the continuous rise in the world's population, the question for business leaders is whether economic growth, and its associated impact on the natural environment, is sustainable.

- However, in their endeavour to maximize profits for shareholders and due to the potentially higher costs of operating in a sustainable way, not many businesses make efficient use of available resources.

- Resistance to change or to embrace the ethos of sustainability creates further obstacles for economic sustainability.

- Nevertheless, economic sustainability as a business strategy can help firms to survive, thrive, and contribute to the economic well-being of others via the creation of jobs and wealth.

> **Keyword definition**
> **Economic sustainability** refers to development of a country that meets the economic needs of the present generation, using existing available resources, without compromising the ability of future generations to meet their economic needs.

> **CUEGIS CONCEPTS**
> For an organization of your choice, examine how the concepts of change and culture have impacted on its sustainable business operations.

5.2 Production methods

Production methods and the most appropriate method of production for a given situation (AO2)

Production refers to the manufacture or output of a physical good or intangible service. There are four main production methods: job, batch, mass and cellular.

■ Job/customized production

- Job production is the production of a special or customized good or service suited to the specific requirements of an individual customer.
- Examples of job production include: bridges, movies, private tuition, wedding dresses, wedding cakes, bespoke suits and portrait painters.
- Each order is a one-off, unique good or service.
- It is the most labour intensive method of production as it is reliant on skilled workers.
- It is also the most expensive production method, although clients pay relatively high prices for the uniqueness of the product.

Table 5.1 Advantages and disadvantages of job production

Advantages of job production	Disadvantages of job production
• It is the most flexible method of production as orders are made specifically for a customer	• High labour costs due to the need for highly skilled and experienced workers
• Due to its uniqueness, the output is likely to be of outstanding quality	• High production costs due to the large absence of economies of scale
• A high mark-up price can be charged because of the product's exclusivity and high quality	• Production is time consuming because specific requirements need to be catered for
• The skilled workers tend to be motivated by the variety and challenge of the job	

■ Batch production

- Batch production is a production method that involves identical goods being made in groups (batches) rather than in a continuous flow.
- Examples of batch production include the output of: casual clothing, cookies (biscuits), bread, shoes and furniture.
- Goods are produced in consignments (batches), undergoing the production process at the same time, before manufacturing the next batch with different specifications, e.g. 100 medium-sized red t-shirts followed by 65 small-sized blue t-shirts.
- It does not involve a system of continuous production.
- Workers are likely to be semi-skilled and output is far more capital intensive than job production.

Table 5.2 Advantages and disadvantages of batch production

Advantages of batch production	Disadvantages of batch production
• Average (unit) costs of production are lower compared with job production due to there being some economies of scale	• Less flexibility as customers have to select from a range of standardized output
• There is some flexibility to meet a variety of demands, thereby providing some choice to customers	• There is a greater need for stocks (inventories), especially raw materials
• It is useful for small businesses that cannot afford to operate continuous production lines and/or demand for the product is insufficient to justify mass production	• There is 'downtime' between batches as machinery might need cleaning and/or changing prior to the manufacture of the next batch

■ Mass/flow/process production

- ■ Mass production is used by businesses that focus on large-scale production techniques for mass market goods.

- ■ It is suitable for the large-scale production of homogeneous (identical or standardized) products such as oil, bottled water, canned soft drinks, motor vehicles, televisions, light bulbs, ball bearings and toys.

- ■ Lower prices are charged due to the standardization of output.

- ■ There is a high degree of automation as mass production is capital intensive.

- ■ The workforce can be unskilled or semi-skilled; the workers can be highly specialized.

- ■ Marketing support is essential to increase demand as mass production generates large-scale output.

- ■ It is based on specialization and the division of labour.

- ■ Whilst job production is about quality, mass production is about quantity.

> **Keyword definition**
>
> **Flow production** is the continuous and automated production process that uses capital intensive production methods to maximize output by minimizing production time. It is associated with large production runs of standardized products.

> **Expert tip**
>
> Although there are some technical differences between mass, flow and process production methods, the differences are subtle so the terms are often used interchangeably.

Table 5.3 Advantages and disadvantages of mass production

Advantages of mass production	Disadvantages of mass production
● Costs per unit of production are lower due to economies of scale	● Lower profit margins are earned due to the low prices and standardized output
● Capital intensive so manufacturing can take place for longer periods	● Limited, if any, flexibility as large quantities of identical products are created
● Automation means a low level of manpower is required in the production process, thus lowering labour costs	● Requires an efficient system of stock control as stockpiling of manufactured goods can be very expensive
● Relatively easy and cheap to hire labour for mass production	● There are likely to be very high start-up costs due to the investment in capital equipment, machinery and production systems
● Capital-intensive production means there is likely to be efficient use of machinery and equipment	● All stages of production are interdependent, so if a problem occurs in one part of the assembly line, production as a whole comes to a halt
● As mass production is capital intensive, it is comparatively easy to expand production should the level of demand for the product increase	● Workers can quickly become demotivated due to the boring and repetitive nature of the tasks

■ Cellular manufacturing

- ■ Cellular production (also known as **cell production**) involves teams working on certain parts of the production line. The production processes are broken down into units based around these teams working on a complete unit of output.

- ■ It is used by businesses that focus on mass-production techniques.

- ■ Each team (or cell) has complete responsibility for quality assurance.

> **Expert tip**
>
> In reality, many products are produced using more than one production method. For example, the engines of a Ferrari or Porsche are hand-made using job production. However, the leather is bought in batches of different hides, textures and colours. The tyres are bought in bulk from mass producers such as Michelin and Pirelli.

Table 5.4 Advantages and disadvantages of cell production

Advantages of cell production	Disadvantages of cell production
● As cells are responsible for quality assurance (see Unit 5.3), it should lead to less wastage and a lower rejection rate	● High set-up costs, e.g. machinery, equipment and stock-ordering systems
● It enables workers to operate in teams with greater autonomy, thus boosting morale, motivation and productivity	● Machinery is not used as intensively as with flow or mass production
● Workers are involved in the production process from the beginning to the end, so this creates a sense of ownership and achievement	● Costs of recruiting and training suitable staff to work in cells
● As teams are multi-skilled, they are more adaptive to changes in the business environment and the future needs of the organization	
● Team working can also create new ideas, processes and products	

EXAM PRACTICE

1 Menelao Clothing Co. designs and manufactures fashionable clothing for children in a variety of designs, colours and sizes.

 a Identify the production method that is most likely to be used by Menelao Clothing Co. [1]

 b Explain two benefits of this production method to Menelao Clothing Co. [4]

5.3 Lean production and quality management *(HL only)*

Revised ☐

Features of lean production (AO1)

Revised ☐

▪ Less waste

- Lean production, which originated in Japan, involves streamlining operations in order to reduce all forms of waste and to achieve greater efficiency.

- Lean production is about getting things right first time and using fewer resources, both of which help to reduce wastage of resources.

- The seven sources of waste (or '*muda*' in Japanese) are: defective products, overproduction, stockpiling (excessive inventories), unnecessary transportation, over-processing (over-complex or over-complicated), waiting time and excess movement by workers.

- Methods of waste minimization include: total quality management (TQM), cradle-to-cradle manufacturing and just-in-time (JIT) production.

▪ Greater efficiency

- Efficiency is about using resources more effectively to generate output, e.g. using less capital or labour to produce the same amount of output.

- Efficiency is measured by the productivity rate of resources (see Unit 5.5). For example, labour productivity can be measured by sales per person or output per worker.

- All members of the organization need to be involved for lean production to work effectively.

- Greater efficiency can be gained in several ways, including:

  ☐ staff training and development

  ☐ higher levels of staff motivation

  ☐ using improved (technologically advanced) capital.

> **Keyword definition**
>
> **Lean production** is a philosophy built into the culture of organizations that focus on less wastage and greater efficiency.

Methods of lean production (AO2)

Revised ☐

▪ Continuous improvement (*kaizen*)

- *Kaizen* is a philosophy embedded in the culture of an organization.

- It is a method of lean production and a source of competitive advantage that involves all workers committing to improving quality standards.

- It involves making small, incremental progress (rather than infrequent radical changes) to improve productivity and efficiency.

- As people tend to be resistant to change, workers might be more receptive to small, incremental changes which are less disruptive and risky than large one-off changes.

- It involves empowering workers to make their own decisions for continuous improvements.

- *Kaizen* can help to reduce costs in the long run by preventing mistakes and outputs of sub-standard quality.

- It can help to achieve greater efficiency through exploring ways to improve the productivity and efficiency of the organization's processes and operations.

- However, the implementation of *kaizen* tends to be costly and time consuming. It requires the effort and commitment of all members of the workforce to eliminate waste and to make productivity gains.

- Striving for continuous improvement usually causes increased workloads, so can lead to demotivation in the workplace.

> **Keyword definition**
> *Kaizen* is the Japanese philosophy of continuous improvement and changing for the better.

Just-in-time (JIT)

- A JIT stock control system removes the need to have buffer stocks (large quantities of stock on site held as back-up inventory).

- Deliveries of stocks such as raw materials and components are made a few hours prior to their use by the purchaser.

- Although JIT can reduce waste, there is always the risk of not having any stock if required urgently. Hence, JIT can be inflexible and expose the firm to greater risks.

- Table 5.11 (page 170) outlines the advantages and disadvantages of a JIT stock control system.

> **Keyword definition**
> **Just-in-time** (JIT) is a lean stock control system that relies on stocks (inventories) being delivered only when they are needed in the production process.

Kanban

- *Kanban* is a method of lean production that relies on using a card system to ensure that stock usage is based on actual demand from customers.

- In Japanese, it means signboard or billboard.

- It helps to prevent underproduction (which results in productive inefficiency) or overproduction (which creates waste).

Andon

- *Andon* is a method of lean production that relies on using a visual traffic light warning system to achieve greater productive efficiency.

- It uses visual displays, including digital displays, to communicate the status of production in the manufacturing process.

- The traffic light system acts as a quick visual warning for workers to help them monitor the progress of various tasks, thus achieving greater efficiency.

Features of cradle-to-cradle design and manufacturing (AO2)

Revised

- Cradle-to-cradle (C2C) involves production techniques that are waste-free and can be efficiently recycled, e.g. recyclable plastic water bottles, plastic computer keyboards or biodegradable bamboo t-shirts.

- The term was coined by Swiss architect Walter R. Stahel in the 1970s when examining production techniques that are both efficient and waste-free.

- All material inputs in C2C must be either technical (recyclable or reusable with no loss of quality) or biological (consumable or compostable in an ecologically friendly way).

- Although C2C can be time consuming and expensive to implement effectively, it can provide competitive advantages by differentiating the brand, thereby attracting and retaining customers. C2C also provides sustainable manufacturing over the long term.

- In addition, C2C can generate a positive corporate image to some specific stakeholders, such as employees and environmental protection groups.

> **Keyword definition**
>
> **Cradle-to-cradle** (C2C) is a production philosophy with the view that sustainable production involves designing and manufacturing goods so that they can be recycled to produce the product again.

Features of quality control and quality assurance (AO1)

`Revised` ☐

> **Keyword definitions**
>
> **Quality control** (QC) refers to the traditional approach to quality management by inspecting a sample of products. It involves quality controllers checking or examining a sample of products in a systematic way, e.g. once every 15 minutes on the production line, every 500th unit of output or 10% of the amount produced.
>
> **Quality assurance** (QA) is an approach to quality management that involves the prevention of mistakes in the production process, e.g. defective output, poor customer service or delays in distributing goods to customers. It involves agreeing and meeting quality standards at all stages of production to ensure customer satisfaction.

Table 5.5 Features of quality control and quality assurance

Features of quality control	Features of quality assurance
• Traditional approach of using quality controllers to check the quality of output	• QA uses workers, rather than inspectors, to check the quality of output
• QC is mainly about inspecting and detecting substandard output (defects) rather than preventing it	• All staff are responsible for quality so QA can therefore be considered as a form of job enrichment (see Unit 2.4)
• Quality controllers randomly or systematically do the inspecting or checking	• Firms have various codes of practice that notify customers of quality procedures and specifications
• It strives to ensure that products meet the quality standards set by the organization	• QA strives to achieve greater efficiency and less wastage
• Firms set an acceptable level of wastage or defects (reject rate)	• The aim is zero defects, i.e. the reject rate is zero
• QC is product-oriented rather than process-oriented	• QA is process-oriented rather than product-oriented
• QC is reactive rather than proactive, with quality checks done retrospectively	• QA is proactive rather than reactive

Methods of managing quality (AO2)

`Revised` ☐

■ Quality circle

- US government statistician Professor W. Edwards Deming (1900–93) noted that American management had typically given managers about 85% of the responsibility for quality control, with only 15% allocated to employees. He argued that this should be reversed.

- The emphasis of quality circles is preventing defects from arising in the first place, rather than quality control during post-production checks.

- Deming's ideas were originally developed by Japanese management and manufacturing techniques, with an emphasis on employees working in similar job roles being encouraged to investigate and suggest practices to improve quality.

- For quality circles to work, members must receive appropriate training in problem solving. In addition, senior management must be supportive and fund these teams appropriately, even when requests may seem trivial or budgets are limited.

> **Keyword definition**
>
> A **quality circle** is a small group of employees who voluntarily meet regularly to identify, examine and solve problems related to their work in order to improve the quality of output.

- *Kaizen* usually involves the implementation of quality circles.

- A limitation of quality circles for employees is that senior management have a clear target for blame if there are quality issues or problems.

- Almost any type of organization can set up quality circles. For example, Po Leung Kuk School in Hong Kong has five quality circles set up to promote a broad, balanced approach to learning (**http://goo.gl/TzZajy**).

■ Benchmarking

- Benchmarking involves making internal and external comparisons of predetermined criteria (industry standards) with the aim of meeting or exceeding the benchmarks.

- Internal benchmarking involves comparing business practices within the same organization. Best practice is then spread throughout the organization.

- External benchmarking involves comparing business practices outside the organizations with other firms considered to be the best in the industry. This approach can take up significant time and resources to collect, collate and interpret the data and information.

- The ultimate aim of benchmarking is to improve performance. This helps a business to maintain or develop its competitiveness.

- As a strategic management tool, it enables managers to compare the firm's performance, its processes and its products with the best of other companies within the same industry.

- It is usually conducted at regular intervals, e.g. profits per quarter or market share per year.

- Benchmarks are typically quantifiable, e.g. star ratings for the hotel industry.

- For benchmarking to be meaningful, comparisons should be made as objectively as possible. However, there is scope for subjective comparisons, e.g. customer perceptions and feedback. Importantly, it includes examining the competition from the point of view of customers.

■ Total quality management (TQM)

- Total quality management (TQM) is a philosophy about embedding awareness of quality in all organizational processes, i.e. it forms a culture of quality by empowering all workers within the organization to take responsibility for quality issues.

- An essential feature of TQM is zero defects, i.e. lean production that is efficient and without any wastage.

- TQM as a form of lean production commits the organization to continuous improvement (*kaizen*) and benchmarking of all operations relating to the quality of the product. Quality circles can also be a feature of TQM.

> **Expert tip**
>
> Do not confuse quality circles with cellular manufacturing (see Unit 5.2). Cell production involves small teams producing a complete unit of work. The focus is output, even though cell workers take responsibility for the quality of their work. However, members of quality circles form voluntarily to discuss ways to improve quality. There is no emphasis on actual output in a quality circle. Instead, it is a participative management technique that involves the input of workers in managing quality.

> **Keyword definition**
>
> **Benchmarking** is the systematic process of comparing a business or its products to its competitors, using a set of standards (called 'benchmarks'), such as sales revenue, profits, labour turnover or brand loyalty.

> **Keyword definition**
>
> **Total quality management** (TQM) is a quality management approach that aims to involve every employee in the quality assurance process. It involves organization-wide approaches to quality improvements in products, processes, people and philosophy (organizational culture).

Table 5.6 Advantages and disadvantages of TQM

Advantages of TQM	Disadvantages of TQM
Motivational impact on employees who feel more involved in decision making	It requires a change in attitudes and commitment from all staff, which can be difficult to achieve
Competitive advantages as it puts customers' needs at the centre of the production process	Staff training, including management training, and development costs can be high yet must be properly funded
Cost-effectiveness as TQM eliminates the need for inspections and the costs of reworking mistakes and defective output	Not all workers are motivated by or are suitable for job enrichment and empowerment (see Unit 2.4)
In the long term, quality is higher while costs should be reduced	Accreditation fees paid to awarding bodies such as the International Organization for Standardization (ISO)
Brand reputation of emphasis on high quality and consistency	

The impact of lean production and TQM on an organization (AO3)

Revised ☐

■ The objective of lean production and TQM is to improve the quality of a firm's goods and services. Quality is a key source of global competitiveness.

■ A quality product needs to be fit for purpose, i.e. the product fulfils its intended purpose and function, e.g. a pen should enable the user to write with it.

■ Quality is important for an organization for several reasons, such as:

☐ satisfying the needs and wants of customers

☐ raising consumer confidence regarding a business and its products

☐ improving the motivation of employees

☐ gaining a competitive advantage over its rivals

☐ lowering production costs, and hence increasing profitability.

■ Poor quality output will result in higher costs for the business due to customers seeking compensation for substandard products. Examples of poor quality include:

☐ the product breaking down unexpectedly

☐ the product being delivered late

☐ a lack of instructions or directions for use.

■ Ultimately, lean production and a culture of TQM give an organization competitive advantages over its rivals. Attracting customers and retaining their loyalty becomes easier as consumers trust reputable businesses and their brands.

The importance of national and international quality standards (AO2)

Revised ☐

■ National and international quality standards are a form of benchmark. A good or service must meet a set of predetermined criteria of quality in order to be awarded certification of quality standards recognized within the country or throughout the world.

■ ISO 9000 is the international quality standard awarded to organizations that ensure their goods and services consistently meet quality standards to meet the needs of customers.

■ It is an internationally recognized quality accolade, awarded by the International Organization for Standardization (ISO).

■ To be certified for ISO 9000, organizations must ensure there is evidence that quality is consistently improved.

Table 5.7 Advantages and disadvantages of meeting national and international quality standards

Advantages of meeting quality standards	Disadvantages of meeting quality standards
• Quality awards can provide the firm with major marketing advantages • It can help to differentiate the organization from its rivals, thus minimizing potential competition • It provides opportunities to build brand loyalty and to charge higher prices • Motivational impacts on workers who feel proud working for a business recognized for its quality	• Operational costs of meeting national or international quality standards can be very high, e.g. funding staff training or buying the necessary technology • Inspection costs must be paid to outside agencies such as the ISO • There are on-going costs of obtaining certification, licences or awards • Some customers may be put off by the higher prices

CUEGIS CONCEPTS

For an organization of your choice, investigate the impacts of change and culture on its quality management.

5.4 Location

Revised ☐

The reasons for a specific location of production (AO2)

Revised ☐

- To access cheaper and/or better quality resources, such as land, labour or raw materials.

- To be closer to customers domestically or in overseas markets to gain competitive advantages, e.g. easier access to customers and reduced transportation costs.

- To avoid trade protectionist policies (when foreign governments impose trade restrictions on imported goods) by locating in these overseas countries.

- To benefit from the local infrastructure (the essential physical and organizational structures in an economy necessary for it to function), e.g. transportation and communications networks.

- Government incentives for locating in a specific place, e.g. subsidies, grants, tax concessions or interest-free loans. Such incentives are provided to firms that locate in assisted areas (locations in need of regeneration, perhaps due to particularly high rates of unemployment, as identified by the government).

- Due to **industrial inertia** – when a business continues to stay in the same location even when there are no financial advantages for doing so, e.g. due to well established relationships with suppliers and locally-based employees.

- To benefit from clustering – when a business locates near to other organizations that function in similar or complementary markets, e.g. shoe stores and clothes retailers.

- Firms in **bulk-reducing industries** locate near the source of raw materials in order to reduce transportation costs, e.g. production plants are located near copper ore mines to reduce the weight (or bulk) and hence the transportation costs involved in making copper.

Figure 5.3 Shanghai is a popular location for firms operating in China

- Firms in **bulk-gaining industries** locate near their customers because the finished product is bulkier (heavier) than the raw materials used to make it, e.g. carbonated soft drinks.

- Qualitative factors also affect the location decision, e.g. the nature of the local infrastructure and management preferences about a particular location.

- A footloose organization is one that does not have any advantage being located in any particular area, e.g. e-commerce businesses or computer-chip makers.

- By contrast, traditional retailers such as restaurants and clothes stores need to be located near their customers.

Ways of re-organizing production, both nationally and internationally (AO3)

Revised ☐

■ Outsourcing/Subcontracting

- The outsourced firms (known as subcontractors) carry out these activities more effectively and cost-effectively, e.g. security firms, school and hospital caterers, office cleaners and ICT technical support.

- Outsourced business activities are those deemed to be non-essential tasks that can be passed on to an external provider in order to cut costs and gain from their expertise.

- Subcontractors are the people or organizations that carry out outsourced work more cost-effectively than the business itself, without compromising the quality.

> **Keyword definition**
>
> **Outsourcing** is the practice of subcontracting non-core activities of an organization to a third-party provider (an external organization) in order to improve operational efficiency and reduce costs.

Table 5.8 Advantages and disadvantages of outsourcing

Advantages of outsourcing	Disadvantages of outsourcing
• Using an outsourced provider means the business can concentrate on its core activities and competitive strategy	• Potential conflict with external parties such as subcontractors can arise
• The firm benefits from the specialized services of the outsourced partner	• There could be quality issues with subcontractors
• Improved customer service from subcontractors can attract new potential customers and strengthen brand loyalty	• The firm may have to deal with staff redundancies due to the use of outsourced providers
• It helps the firm to streamline its business operations, thereby cutting costs and improving its profitability	• There are costs of monitoring and maintaining relationships with the subcontractor

■ Offshoring

- Examples of offshored functions include: manufacturing, telesales, call centres, research and development (R&D), and accounting services.

- Offshoring can but does not necessarily involve third-party providers.

- The relocation decision requires the firm to consider both the risks and uncertainties of moving to unfamiliar territories and weigh these up against the potential rewards.

> **Keyword definition**
>
> **Offshoring** is the practice of relocating part of or all of a firm's business functions and processes overseas. These functions can remain within the business (operating in overseas markets) or outsourced to an overseas organization.

Table 5.9 Advantages and disadvantages of offshoring

Advantages of offshoring	Disadvantages of offshoring
• As with outsourcing, offshoring means the firm can concentrate on and develop its core business activity	• It is often associated with unethical practices, e.g. the exploitation of child labour in low-income countries
• Labour laws may be more relaxed overseas, making it easier to hire and fire staff	• There could be cultural issues and concerns about transferring functions to an external party
• Employee costs may be lower, resulting in lower prices for consumers and a boost in sales	• It would involve making some employees redundant, which has to be handled with care and can be costly
• Relationships with local customers can be improved as the workforce is accustomed to cultural issues and differences in the offshored country	• Overseas operations may lead to greater difficulties in conducting quality control
• Lower operational costs can lead to higher profit margins	• The firm could lose some control over workers as they are based overseas

■ Insourcing

- Insourcing involves the retention of a task, function or project within the organization.

- It is often delegated to internal stakeholders who have the expertise (such as ICT, accounting or consultancy skills) rather than outsourcing the function to an external third-party provider.

- Insourcing happens because it can sometimes be cheaper and more productive to have the work done in-house.

- It has become popular with businesses that have been dissatisfied or unsuccessful with outsourcing, e.g. substandard quality or supply chain disruptions.

- It is most suitable when the function, task or project is only temporary or when there is no significant capital investment involved.

- It is also suitable for smaller businesses and start-ups with little or no experience with outsourcing.

> **Keyword definition**
> **Insourcing** is the use of a firm's own resources to fulfil a certain role, function or task which would otherwise have been outsourced.

Table 5.10 Advantages and disadvantages of insourcing

Advantages of insourcing	Disadvantages of insourcing
• Using existing employees and resources can be cheaper than outsourcing	• Internal staff might not have the necessary skills or experience (external specialists may be more effective and productive)
• It enables a business to have better control of what it would have otherwise outsourced	• Multinationals that want to establish or maintain their international presence cannot rely on insourcing
• It helps to develop a team of skilled and experienced workers	• Implementation costs are likely to be high, affecting profits at least in the short term
• There is job creation in the local, domestic economy	

> **CUEGIS CONCEPTS**
>
> Examine how the concepts of ethics and change have impacted the international location decisions of a business you have studied.

5.5 Production planning (HL only)

Revised ☐

The supply chain process (AO2)

Revised ☐

- The supply chain process is the management process of overseeing the logistics from the manufacturing stage to the finished product being delivered to the consumer.

- It includes managing the storage and movement of raw materials, semi-finished goods and finished goods from the raw material phase to the point of consumption.

- A long supply chain and/or ineffective supply chain management can be costly as it increases the chances of things going wrong for the business.

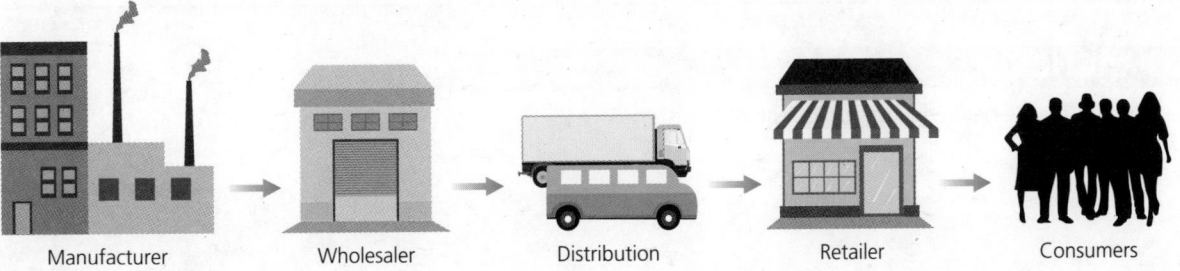

Manufacturer   Wholesaler   Distribution   Retailer   Consumers

Figure 5.4 The supply chain (an example)

The difference between JIT and just-in-case (JIC) (AO2)

- A just-in-time (JIT) stock control system is designed to eliminate the costs of holding stock, e.g. storage, maintenance and security costs.

- JIT enables a business to get hold of raw materials and components only when the need arises.

- Having access to local and reliable suppliers is essential for JIT as the system relies on an efficient stock ordering and delivery arrangement so that the inventory is ordered and arrives for the start of the operation.

- It allows businesses to avoid the costs of storage, maintenance, theft and wastage.

> ### Keyword definitions
> **Just-in-time** (JIT) is a stock control system that avoids the use of holding stocks (inventory). Instead, stocks are supplied and delivered only when needed for production.
>
> **Just-in-case** (JIC) is a stock control system that relies on having spare stocks (inventory) so that output can be raised immediately in the event of a sudden or unexpected increase in demand.

Table 5.11 Advantages and disadvantages of just-in-time

Advantages of just-in-time	Disadvantages of just-in-time
There is no need for buffer stocks, thus cost of stock management is reduced	There is complete reliance on third-party suppliers
There is no need for stockpiling, thus improving cash flow and working capital	Administrative and implementation costs of JIT are high
JIT fosters lean production and productive efficiency	There is the inability to meet unexpected changes in demand

- A just-in-case (JIC) stock control system is designed to have a reserve (buffer) stock level.

- Other costs associated with JIC can include insurance and maintenance and/or security to prevent damage or theft.

- It ensures the firm has sufficient amounts of inventory to meet the demands of customers whenever required.

- JIC is suitable for stocks that are not perishable, such as cotton, rubber, ball bearings or wine. It is less suitable for perishables, such as fresh flowers or fresh meat.

- It is not suitable for industries where customer trends and preferences are always changing, e.g. the fashion and high-tech industries.

Table 5.12 Advantages and disadvantages of just-in-case

Advantages of just-in-case	Disadvantages of just-in-case
There is flexibility to meet a sudden and unexpected rise in consumer demand	Suppliers can charge premium prices for urgent deliveries of stocks
It enables production to continue if there is a delay in deliveries from suppliers	Higher costs, e.g. storage, maintenance, security and insurance costs associated with a JIC stock control system
Customer satisfaction is maintained as they do not have to wait for stocks to arrive	There is also the risk of large stocks of obsolete and unsold products
Prevents loss of potential customers compared to if a JIC system is used	Stocks are subject to damage or theft
Firms can benefit from purchasing economies of scale (bulk buying)	There could be liquidity issues because JIC ties up valuable working capital

EXAM PRACTICE

2   Explain the difference between just-in-case (JIC) and just-in-time (JIT) stock control systems.   [4]

Stock control charts (AO2, AO4)

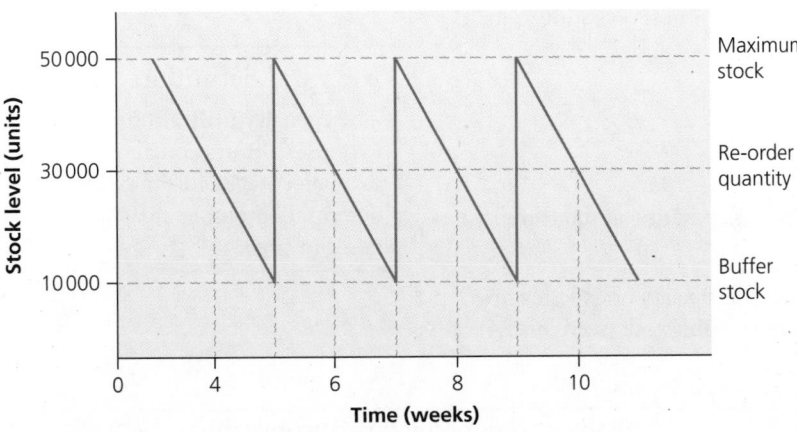

Figure 5.5 Stock control chart

- The lead time refers to the length of time it takes between a firm ordering new stock and the firm receiving the stock for production. In Figure 5.5, the lead time is one week.

- The longer the lead time, the earlier the re-order needs to be and/or the larger the re-order quantity needs to be.

- **Buffer stock** is the minimum stock level held by a firm in case of late deliveries from suppliers, damaged stock or a sudden and expected increase in demand. In Figure 5.5, the buffer stock is 10000 units.

- The **re-order quantity** is the volume of the order. In Figure 5.5, the re-order quantity is 40000 units (i.e. 50000 – 10000 units).

- The **re-order level** refers to the stock level at the time when the firm places its re-order of stock. In Figure 5.5, this occurs when the firm's stock level reaches 30000 units.

- The **usage rate** refers to the speed at which stocks (inventories) are depleted in the production process. The usage rate increases during peak periods, but drops during recessions and off-peak periods. In Figure 5.5, the usage rate is 40000 units per two weeks.

- A **stock-out** occurs when a firm has no more stock for production or sale, i.e. it is out of stock. This creates problems for the firm as production also comes to a stop. To prevent a stock-out, some businesses buy extra stock prior to peak trading periods.

- By contrast, **stockpiling** means that a business builds up excessive levels of inventory. However, holding too much stock results in working capital being tied up.

EXAM PRACTICE

3 Study the stock control diagram (Figure 5.6) for Beyond Bakeries in order to determine the following:

  a   the lead time   [1]
  b   the buffer stock   [1]
  c   the re-order quantity.   [1]

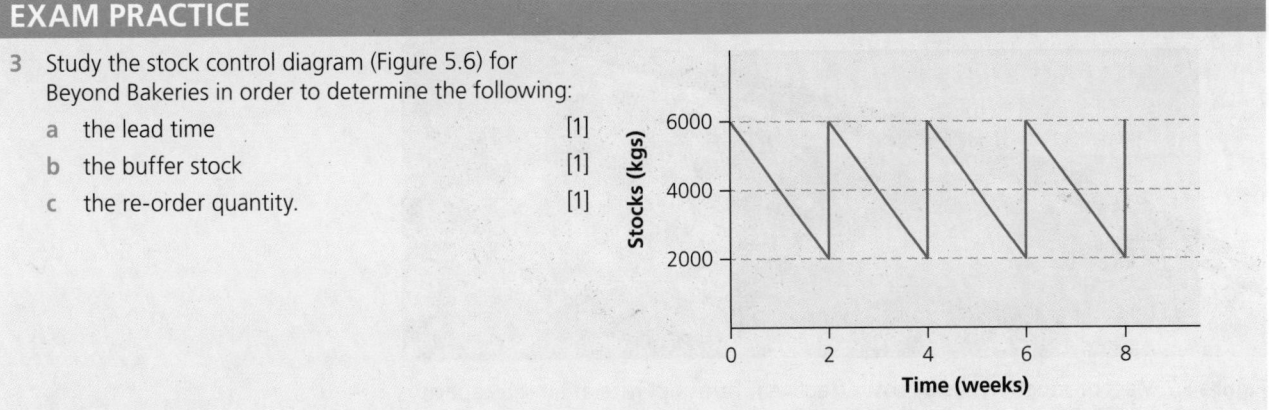

Figure 5.6 Beyond Bakeries stock control chart

Capacity utilization rate (AO2, AO4)

Revised ☐

- Capacity utilization measures the extent to which a firm is operating at its maximum potential level.

- It can be calculated by using the following formula:

$$\text{Capacity utilization} = \frac{\text{Actual output per period}}{\text{Full capacity output per period}} \times 100$$

- A firm that has a 100% capacity utilization rate is operating at full capacity, with all its resources used.

- Capacity utilization for a business operating at full capacity or experiencing high growth rates could be improved by subcontracting work (see Unit 5.4).

> **Keyword definition**
>
> The **capacity utilization rate** expresses a firm's actual output as a percentage of its maximum potential output, at a particular point in time.

Table 5.13 Advantages and disadvantages of full capacity utilization

Advantages of full capacity utilization	Disadvantages of full capacity utilization
• Average (unit) costs of production are likely to be at their lowest so the business is operating efficiently	• Employees can become overworked and stressed due to working at full capacity
• Lower costs per unit (economies of scale) will likely lead to higher profits for the firm	• Machinery and equipment are likely to deteriorate at a faster pace, thus increasing maintenance and replacement costs

EXAM PRACTICE

4   a   Calculate the capacity utilization rate for Meiji Milk Company that can produce 200 000 pints of milk in its factory each day but has an output level of 180 000 pints per day.   [2]

    b   Calculate BF Sausage Company's capacity utilization rate if it produces 2800 kilos per month but has a maximum productive capacity of 3500 kilos per month.   [2]

5   Suppose Darho Foods has fixed costs of $10 000 and a productive capacity of 5000 units per month. Calculate the change in its average fixed costs if the firm operates at only 80% capacity compared to operating at full capacity.   [4]

Figure 5.7 Mass production is only cost effective if firms operate at a high capacity

Productivity rate (AO2, AO4)

Revised ☐

- Productivity is a measure of the efficiency of production. The productivity rate measures the amount of output generated per unit of input.

- **Labour productivity**, for example, is a measure of the efficiency of workers in an organization. The most common measure of labour productivity uses the following formula to calculate output per worker:

$$\frac{\text{Total output per period (units)}}{\text{Number of employees at work}}$$

- Labour productivity can also be measured by sales revenue per worker or the volume produced per labour hour. Labour-intensive firms prefer to use this measure of productivity.

- Labour productivity matters because labour costs are usually a significant part of a firm's total costs.

- Similarly, **capital productivity** measures how efficiently a firm's fixed assets generate output for the business. Capital-intensive firms prefer to use this measure of productivity.

- The higher the productivity rate, the more efficient the firm is. This is important as there is a positive correlation between a firm's efficiency level and its profitability and competitiveness.

> **Expert tip**
>
> Whilst productivity is important, it can be difficult to measure the output in some professions, e.g. public sector workers such as teachers, nurses and doctors. For these jobs, the quality of service is regarded as more important than output or profits.

EXAM PRACTICE

6 Suppose STC produces $500 000 worth of output in one week in a total of 1000 labour-hours. Calculate the firm's labour productivity rate. [2]

7 Suppose the 25 sales staff at WIS manage to sell $120 000 worth of goods in one week. Calculate the firm's labour productivity rate. [2]

Cost to buy (CTB) and cost to make (CTM) (AO2, AO4)

Revised ☐

- A make or buy decision requires managers to compare the cost to make (CTM) with the cost to buy (CTB).

- If the CTM is greater than the CTB, then it makes financial sense for the business to buy the product instead of producing it, and vice versa.

- The CTB a product from a supplier is calculated by the formula:
  CTB = Price × Quantity.

- The CTM a product is calculated by the formula:
  CTM = Fixed costs + Variable costs.

- Quantitative methods that can be used to help with decisions about the CTM and CTB include break-even analysis (see Unit 3.3) and investment appraisal (see Unit 3.8).

- Non-quantitative factors are also considered (although these are difficult to quantify), e.g. quality control, reliability of suppliers, the impact on the workforce, experience and expertise.

> **Keyword definition**
>
> A **make or buy decision** is a management decision which involves choosing whether to manufacture a product (make) or to purchase it (buy) from an external supplier. Essentially, it is a decision about whether to insource or outsource production.

EXAM PRACTICE

8 Organix Fruit Bars can purchase equipment for in-house production costing $25 000 and manufacture the goods for $1 each. Alternatively, a local supplier can produce these for $1.50 each. Demand for the goods is forecast to be 45 000 customers. Calculate whether it is better for Organix Fruit Bars to make or buy. [3]

5.6 Research and development *(HL only)*

Revised ☐

The importance of research and development for a business (AO3)

Revised ☐

■ **Research** focuses on creating new knowledge and new products. It is a prerequisite to development.

■ **Development** is about adapting existing ideas and products to create commercially viable products. Its primary function is to improve new commercially viable products, helping to increase the firm's future earning potential.

■ R&D is important for the longevity and competitiveness of a business, irrespective of the sector in which it operates (primary, secondary, tertiary or quaternary).

■ R&D is an essential part of innovation (the commercialization of a business idea that appeals to consumers).

■ Competitive rivalry in an industry can drive firms to spend more on R&D in order to survive in the long term.

■ Market leaders often use R&D expenditure as a barrier to entry so that they can continue to dominate the industry, e.g. airline manufacturers such as Airbus and Boeing.

> **Keyword definition**
>
> **Research and development (R&D)** is the systematic process of discovering new knowledge about products, processes and markets, and then applying the knowledge to make new and improved products, processes and services to fulfil market needs.

> **Expert tip**
>
> Although the terms 'research' and 'development' are usually used together, make sure you are able to distinguish the meanings of the two terms. Answers in the exam can be enhanced by using real-world examples of innovations.

Table 5.14 Advantages and disadvantages of R&D

Advantages of R&D	Disadvantages of R&D
• It can improve a firm's productivity rate (see Unit 5.5) • It can enhance a firm's corporate image, e.g. brand perception as an innovator • It can help to gain a first-mover advantage or achieve a competitive advantage • Premium prices can be charged • R&D expenditure can prolong a product's life cycle (see Unit 4.5) • R&D does not necessarily lead to higher prices, as the discovery of more efficient production methods can help to cut prices	• There is an opportunity cost of spending large sums of money on R&D • There is no guarantee that the R&D expenditure will be recouped due to the high failure rate of product launches • R&D can be very time consuming in some industries, e.g. pharmaceuticals • Rivals might spend more money on R&D, thus wiping out any advantages of the firm • R&D is not always applicable for all firms, such as those that make budget laptops, as R&D can result in higher costs and prices

The importance of developing goods and services that address customers' unmet needs (AO2)

Revised ☐

■ Many product ideas fail to get commercialized because:

  ☐ There are legal and administrative barriers which discourage R&D expenditure.

  ☐ The amount of money needed to fund successful R&D is often unaffordable.

  ☐ The market for the product might be too small to justify the amount of R&D expenditure.

  ☐ The product does not meet the needs or desires of the market, perhaps due to a lack of market research (see Unit 4.4).

■ Market research enabled Samsung, for example, to become the market leader in the smartphone industry as the company developed phones with larger screen sizes (something that Apple failed to recognize as an unmet customer need).

- R&D addresses the fact that not all unmet needs are known by the customers. Steve Jobs famously said that Apple would create a product that everyone would want despite no one knowing they would want it (the iPod, which went on to revolutionize the whole music industry).

- To test whether a new product addresses the unmet needs of customers, businesses often develop a **prototype**. This refers to trial products prior to final development of a product for launching on the market.

Types of innovation (AO2)

Revised ☐

The types of innovation are often referred to as the 4 Ps of innovation: product, process, positioning and paradigm.

- **Product innovation** is about research and development that focuses on creating new products or improving existing ones.

- **Process innovation** is about R&D that focuses on new or significantly improved methods of production or work practices. It refers to changes in the way that production takes place, i.e. how production takes place.

- **Position innovation** is about R&D that focuses on changing customer perceptions of an existing product, e.g. Nissan's GT-R sports car offers supercar performance at a premium price, changing customer perceptions that Nissan only produces mass-market cars.

- **Paradigm innovation** refers to a change in the concept of a product, so is an extreme form of innovation, e.g. the smartphone revolutionized the use of mobile phones due to its multi-functionality such as being a camera, gaming device and multi-media player. Paradigm innovation is associated with radical and extensive innovations that involve high risks to the business.

> **Keyword definition**
>
> **Innovation** is the successful commercial creation of a new business idea, which adds value to the organization. It strives to create or fulfil existing needs and desires that are not currently being satisfied.

The difference between adaptive creativity and innovative creativity (AO2)

Revised ☐

- **Adaptive creativity** is about adjusting and improving something that already exists. This takes place incrementally, e.g. Apple's iPad Mini was developed from the original, larger sized iPad.

- **Innovative creativity** is about creating a new product or process, e.g. Apple's iTunes Store changed the way consumers around the world buy their music, movies and games. It can occur radically.

- The underlying difference between adaptive creativity and innovative creativity is the pace and degree of change involved in the innovation process.

> **Expert tip**
>
> Whilst innovative creativity can create huge competitive advantages for a business, radical changes do not always work better than incremental changes, especially if such changes cause huge disruptions, anxieties and uncertainty for employees.

How pace of change in an industry, organizational culture and ethical considerations may influence research and development practices and strategies in an organization (AO3)

Revised ☐

- Change in an industry can influence R&D practices. For example:

  - ☐ It can create demand for new products, e.g. hybrid or electric fuelled cars.

  - ☐ Customers might turn away from rival brands if the firm is highly innovative and sells products that are more appealing to buyers.

  - ☐ The life cycle of many products is short, so innovation through R&D can ensure the business embraces change and survives the impacts of the external environment.

- Organizational culture determines the degree of risk that a business is willing to take in R&D. It also regulates business practices, e.g. a firm that pursues its corporate social responsibilities is likely to focus on innovations that benefit a greater number of stakeholders.

- Unethical business practices mean that governments need to protect the intellectual property rights of inventors and innovators. For example:

  - □ A **patent** gives exclusive rights to the registered owner to use an invention for a finite period of time.

  - □ **Copyrights** protect the published works of artists, composers, musicians, photographers, authors and movie directors by creating legal rights to these creations. Copyrighted materials carry the © symbol.

  - □ A **registered trademark** is a sign or symbol that enables a firm to distinguish its products from those of other traders, e.g. brands and logos. Once registered, these trademarks are the exclusive property of the trademark holder for a finite period of time.

- As the pace of change quickens in many hi-tech industries, questions about the ethics of R&D have been raised. Product recalls (see Units 5.7 and 5.3) and over-consumption are just two examples of the issues arising from innovation in the business world.

> **CUEGIS CONCEPTS**
>
> Investigate how the innovative culture of an organization such as Google or Apple has shaped its corporate strategy.

5.7 Crisis management and contingency planning (*HL only*)

`Revised` ☐

The difference between crisis management and contingency planning (AO2)

`Revised` ☐

- Crisis management is about how a business responds to a crisis, especially one that threatens its survival.

- Contingency planning involves formulating risk assessments in order to be better prepared for crises, should they ever occur.

- Examples of crises include: financial crises, economic recession, severe weather conditions, power failure, major product recalls, the outbreak of infectious diseases, a fire, employees on strike, and natural disasters.

- Crisis management is about dealing with actual threats and disasters a business faces.

- Crisis management is about the way in which an organization responds during a crisis situation.

- Contingency planning helps to prepare a business to deal with crises if they occur. This differs from crisis management, which is about responding to a real crisis.

- Contingency planning is about scenario planning, i.e. examining 'what if' scenarios and developing business continuity plans to minimize the impact of a crisis if it occurs.

- Contingency planning involves formulating management actions to minimize the negative impacts of potential crises.

> **Keyword definitions**
>
> **Contingency planning** is the development of predetermined strategies to deal with a crisis should it occur.
>
> **Crisis management** is the response taken by a business in the event of an actual crisis occurring.

> **Expert tip**
>
> Be sure to know the link between crises and contingency plans. Although contingency plans can help a business to deal with a crisis, the crisis itself is unpredictable so is disruptive and costly to the organization (otherwise it would not be classed as a crisis).

Factors that affect effective crisis management (AO2)

Revised ☐

The fundamental factors affecting the effectiveness of crisis management include: transparency, communication, speed and control.

■ Transparency

■ Transparency is about the ethical obligation of businesses to be honest and to inform their stakeholders of the truth during a crisis.

■ Most risks in business are quantifiable, e.g. the costs of theft or fire damage to a factory. However, not all risks are easily quantifiable, e.g. the costs following the outbreak of an infectious disease. This is because non-quantifiable risks are prohibitively expensive to calculate and highly unlikely to happen.

■ Transparency about the truth can help a business to maintain its integrity, reputation and public perception, especially if the crisis was beyond the firm's control.

■ Employees, the general public and the media are far more forgiving if a business owns up to its mistakes and responds with transparency and honesty.

■ Communication

■ During and after a crisis, public relations (PR) plays an important role in communicating with and reassuring all stakeholders.

■ Prompt and effective communication with stakeholders is vital in a crisis, e.g. contacting the emergency services, informing employees, notifying insurers and communicating appropriately with the media.

■ Speedy and honest communication is important to prevent a possible loss of goodwill and a public relations crisis.

■ Within the organization, a specialist media or PR team is often used to communicate with the general public, politicians and the mass media.

■ Communicating corporate social responsibility (see Unit 1.3) is an important part of crisis management. It might not always be necessary to communicate with the general public, although all responses and actions must be implemented in a socially responsible way.

■ Speed

■ A speedy response is essential to contain the crisis and to ensure it is not prolonged or worsened by causing collateral damage.

■ A swift strategy applied with common sense can prevent huge expenses resulting from a crisis, e.g. BP was too slow in responding to an oil spillage in the Gulf of Mexico in 2010, resulting in the company losing 3.19 million barrels of oil and being fined a record $14 billion.

■ Speed is far less of an issue if the organization has adequate preparation and simulation through its contingency planning.

■ Speed also means the business acts quickly before a biased or untruthful version of the issue gets reported by others in the media, which could potentially lead to even greater problems that the organization has less control over.

■ Speed also helps to pre-empt or prevent a crisis from actually occurring.

■ A speedy response, backed by honest actions, helps to return the business to normality.

■ Control

■ Crises can be preventable. For example, contingency planning not only helps a business to be better prepared in the event of a real fire, but to prevent fires from actually occurring.

■ Quantifiable risks are measurable risks, e.g. the damage or theft of commercial property. These risks mean that control is a vital factor that affects the effectiveness of crisis management.

■ To ensure effective control, it is important for the business to select a suitable team to handle a crisis.

■ Control of the situation is vital, especially as bad news will spread extremely quickly via social networks and social media (see Unit 4.8).

> **Keyword definition**
>
> **Quantifiable risks** are financially measurable threats that can jeopardize the survival of an organization, e.g. there is a statistically low chance of a fire breaking out in a hospital, but a much higher likelihood of taxi drivers being involved in a motor accident.

Advantages and disadvantages of contingency planning for a given organization or situation (AO2)

`Revised` ☐

Table 5.15 Advantages and disadvantages of contingency planning

Factor	Advantages	Disadvantages
Cost	● Business continuity becomes top priority during a crisis, not costs ● Contingency funds and emergency financial aid can help to deal with the costs of a crisis ● Effective planning can help to minimize losses incurred	● The costs of dealing with a crisis can be huge ● It uses up valuable management time and resources ● Having insurance does not necessarily cover unquantifiable risks associated with crises
Time	● A properly prepared contingency plan is essential for being prepared to manage a crisis	● The incident planned for might never happen, so planning can be a waste of time and money
Risks	● Enables businesses to be better prepared to deal with setbacks should a crisis ever occur ● Planning helps to reduce the risks arising from a crisis	● The plans cannot fully prepare firms for the actual impacts of natural disasters ● It is not realistic for businesses to account for all possible risks
Safety	● Contingency planning can ensure the safety of employees in the event of a crisis ● It also helps to protect and reassure customers	● There are opportunity costs involved to ensure contingency plans cover all aspects of a crisis ● Implementation costs of ensuring safety in the workplace

EXAM PRACTICE

9 In 2015, global car giant Toyota recalled 181 000 of its vehicles in Australia, equipped with faulty airbags supplied by Takata. The recall was announced to prevent increasing the risk of injury to drivers and passengers. Toyota acted quickly to reassure customers that the faulty airbags would be replaced free of charge, with the process taking about 90 minutes per vehicle.

   a Identify two stakeholder groups from the case study. [2]

   b Explain what is meant by a product recall and why it is an example of a crisis. [3]

   c Explain why crisis management and contingency planning are important to global multinational companies such as Toyota. [4]

CUEGIS CONCEPTS

Investigate the role of ethics and organizational culture in contingency planning and crisis management for a business of your choice.

Glossary

Above-the-line (ATL) promotion is paid-for marketing communication via independent media.

The **acid test ratio** is a liquidity ratio that measures a firm's ability to meet its short-term debts. It ignores stock because some inventories are difficult to turn into cash in a short time frame.

Adaptive creativity is about adjusting and improving something that already exists.

An **adverse variance** exists when the difference between the actual and budgeted figure is disadvantageous to the business.

Aims are long-term goals of an organization, formulated by the senior management team.

Andon is a method of lean production that relies on using a visual traffic light warning system to achieve greater productive efficiency.

Appraisal refers to the formal assessment of an employee's performance with reference to the roles and responsibilities set out in the job description.

Arbitration involves an independent arbitrator deciding on an appropriate outcome.

The **average rate of return** (ARR) is an investment appraisal technique that calculates the average annual profit of an investment project expressed as a percentage of the initial amount invested in the project.

The **balance sheet** shows the value of an organization's assets and liabilities at a particular point in time.

Batch production is a production method that involves identical goods being made in groups (batches) rather than in a continuous flow.

Below-the-line (BTL) promotion refers to promotional activities that the business has direct control over.

Benchmarking is the systematic process of comparing a business or its products to its competitors, using a set of standards (called 'benchmarks'), such as sales revenue, profits, labour turnover or brand loyalty.

The **Boston Consulting Group (BCG) matrix** is a marketing tool used to examine an organization's product portfolio.

Brand awareness refers to the extent to which people recognize and remember a particular brand.

Brand development is an aspect of marketing strategy about what a brand stands for. It is also about communicating the value of a brand to customers.

Brand loyalty happens when customers repeatedly purchase their favourite brand, rather than switching to a rival brand.

Brand value refers to the estimated future earnings attributable to a particular brand.

Break-even exists when a business sells enough goods and/ or services in order to cover all its costs of production.

The **break-even point** (BEP) is where the total costs of production equal the total revenue.

A **budget** is a plan of the costs and revenues with the purpose of achieving the objectives of a business in a given time period, usually one year.

Buffer stock is the minimum stock level held by a firm in case of late deliveries from suppliers, damaged stock or a sudden and expected increase in demand.

Bureaucracy refers to the administrative systems of a business, such as the set of rules and procedures and formal hierarchical structures in an organization.

Business angels are wealthy individuals who invest in high-risk business projects with high profit potential.

A **business plan** is a formal document that details how an organization intends to meet its objectives.

The **capacity utilization rate** expresses a firm's actual output as a percentage of its maximum potential output.

Capital expenditure is the spending on fixed assets and capital equipment of a business.

Cash flow is the movement of money in and out of an organization.

Cell production involves teams working on production processes that are broken down into units based around the teams working on a complete unit of output.

Centralization refers to organizational structures where the majority of decision making is in the hands of a very small number of people at the top of the hierarchical structure.

The **chain of command** is the formal line of authority through which orders and decisions are passed down from senior management at the top to operational workers at the bottom of the hierarchy.

Charities are not-for-profit organizations that operate in an altruistic way with the objectives of promoting a worthwhile cause.

Closure is an extreme method used by employers to deal with workers taking industrial action by stopping all business operations.

Collective bargaining is the process by which employers' and employees' representatives negotiate on the terms and conditions of employment.

Commercial marketing is the use of marketing strategies to meet the needs and wants of customers in a profitable way for the benefit of the owners of the business.

Companies (or **corporations**) are commercial business with limited liability and owned by their **shareholders**.

Conciliation involves two parties in a dispute, such as employee and employer representatives, agreeing to use the services of an independent mediator to help resolve their differences.

Consumer profile refers to the demographic and psychographic characteristics of consumers in different markets.

Consumers are the people who use a good or service.

Contingency planning is the development of predetermined strategies to deal with a crisis should it occur.

Contribution per unit refers to the amount of money a business earns from selling each unit of output.

Cooperatives are for-profit social enterprises owned and run by their members, such as employees, managers and customers.

Copyright as a form of intellectual property right gives the owner legal rights to a creative piece of work.

Corporate culture is the set of values, attitudes, norms and beliefs in an organization.

Corporate social responsibility (CSR) refers to an organization's duties to its internal and external stakeholders by behaving in a way that positively impacts society as a whole.

A **cost centre** is a department or division within an organization that is responsible and held accountable for its own costs.

Cost-plus pricing (also known as **mark-up pricing**) involves adding a profit element to the costs of production.

Cost of goods sold (COGS) refer to the direct costs of production. COGS can include raw materials, components, packaging and direct labour costs.

Cradle to cradle involves production techniques that are waste-free and can be efficiently recycled.

Creditors are the suppliers that have given trade credit so need to be repaid in the near future.

Creditor days ratio measures the average number of days a business takes to repay its creditors.

Crisis management is the response taken by a business in the event of an actual crisis occurring.

Culture clash exists when there is a difference between the values and beliefs of individuals within an organization.

Current assets are short-term, liquid assets of the business that are intended to be used up within the year, i.e. cash, debtors and stock.

Current liabilities are short-term debts that need to be repaid within 12 months of the balance sheet date, i.e. overdrafts, creditors and short-term loans.

The **current ratio** is a short-term liquidity ratio which calculates the ability of a business to meet its debts within the next 12 months.

Customers are the buyers of a good or service. Buyers and users are not necessarily the same.

Cyclical variations refer to the recurrent fluctuations in sales revenues linked to the business cycle cause.

Debtors are customers who have received goods or services, but have yet to pay for them.

The **debtor days ratio** measures the average number of days a business takes to collect debts from its customers who have bought goods and services on trade credit.

Decentralization refers to organizational structures which include the delegation of decision-making authority throughout an organization, away from a central authority.

De-layering is the process of removing one or more layers in the organizational hierarchy to make the structure flatter.

Delegation is the process of entrusting and empowering a subordinate to successfully complete a task, project or job role.

Depreciation is the decline in the value of a fixed asset over time, mainly due to usage (wear and tear) and newer models or better technologies being available.

Differentiation is the act of making a business or its products distinct from its rivals in the industry.

A **discount rate** is a number used to reduce the value of a sum of money received in the future in order to determine its present value.

Diseconomies of scale arise when unit costs increase due to the organization being too large, e.g. problems with communication and coordination.

Dismissal refers to the termination of a worker's employment due to their incompetence or breach of employment contract.

A **distribution channel** refers to the process or system of getting the product to consumers, e.g. retailers, wholesalers or vending machines.

Dividends are the payments that a company pays to its shareholders from its net profit after interest and tax.

E-commerce is the trading of goods and services using online electronic systems and computer networks such as the internet.

Economies of scale are the cost-saving benefits of operating on a large scale, i.e. the reduction in unit costs of production as an organization grows.

Employee representatives are individuals or organizations (such as a trade union) who act as the collective voice of the workforce.

Employer representatives are the individuals or organizations that represent the senior management team in the collective bargaining process.

An **entrepreneur** is someone who is willing to take financial risks by investing in a business idea.

Expenses are the indirect costs of production, such as rent, insurance and management salaries.

Extension strategies are marketing techniques used to prolong a product's life cycle.

External economies of scale refer to the fall in unit costs of production for all organizations as the industry experiences growth.

External growth (also known as **inorganic growth**) occurs when a business relies on third-party organizations for growth, e.g. mergers, acquisitions, and franchising.

Extrapolation is a sales forecasting technique that makes future predictions of sales based on trends identified from using past data.

A **favourable variance** exists when the difference between the actual and budgeted figure is beneficial to the business.

A **flat** (or **horizontal**) **organization** has few layers of management.

Flow production is the continuous and automated production process that uses capital intensive production methods to maximize output by minimizing production time.

Fixed assets are long-term assets (lasting more than 12 months) used to produce goods and services, e.g. land, buildings, vehicles, equipment, tools, and machinery.

Franchising refers to an agreement between a business (the franchisor) giving the legal rights to other organizations (the franchisees) to sell products under the franchisor's brand name.

Franchising is a growth strategy that involves using a third-party provider to supply the goods and services of the business in return for payment of a licensing fee and royalty payments.

Fringe benefits (or **perks**) are any type of remuneration awarded to employees in addition to their basic pay.

The **gearing ratio** reveals the degree to which a business is financed by loan capital by comparing loan capital and the total capital employed.

Globalization can be defined as the increased integration and interdependence of economies around the world, with converging habits and tastes.

Goodwill refers to the established reputation and networks of a business, enabling it to be worth more than the market value of its quantifiable assets.

Go-slows involve staff working at the minimum allowable pace without the workers being sanctioned for breaching their employment contract.

Gross profit is the amount of profit from ordinary trading activities. It is calculated by taking away the value of COGS from the sales revenue.

Gross profit margin (GPM) is a profitability ratio that shows a firm's gross profit expressed as a percentage of its sales revenue.

Guerrilla marketing is a marketing strategy designed to promote products in a low-cost unconventional and unexpected way that makes a large impact and lasting impression on the general public.

Hierarchical structures refer to the management structure of an organization based on the number of layers of formal authority, usually presented in a diagram or chart.

Human resource planning is the management process of anticipating and meeting an organization's current and future staffing needs.

Hygiene factors are aspects of a job that can lead to workers being dissatisfied. These factors need to be addressed in order to prevent dissatisfaction, but do not motivate.

Industrial democracy is the practice of involving and empowering people in the workplace.

Innovation is the successful commercial creation of a new business idea, which adds value to the organization.

Innovative creativity is about creating a new product or process.

An **intangible asset** is a non-physical asset that adds value to an organization, e.g. patents, copyrights and trademarks.

An **intermediary** is a third-party business that offers distribution services between two trading parties.

Internal economies of scale refer to the fall in unit costs of production for a single organization as it experiences growth, e.g. managerial and financial economies of scale.

Internal growth (also known as **organic growth**) occurs when an organization expands using its own resources, without involving other organizations.

Internal sources of finance come from within the business using its own resources.

International marketing is the marketing of an organization's products in foreign countries.

Insourcing is the use of a firm's own resources to fulfil a certain role, function or task which would otherwise have been outsourced.

Investment refers to the capital expenditure of a business, e.g. the spending on fixed assets such as premises, equipment and machinery.

Investment appraisal is a quantitative decision-making tool used to assess and justify the capital expenditure of a firm in terms of whether it will be financially worthwhile.

Job production is the production of a special or customized good or service suited to the specific requirements of an individual customer.

A **joint venture** (JV) is an arrangement between two or more separate parties to pool their resources together to form a new legal entity.

Just-in-case (JIC) is a stock control system that relies on having spare stocks (inventory) so that output can be raised immediately in the event of a sudden or unexpected increase in demand.

Just-in-time (JIT) is a lean stock control system that relies on stocks (inventories) being delivered only when they are needed in the production process.

Kaizen is the Japanese philosophy of continuous improvement and changing for the better.

Kanban is a method of lean production that relies on using a card system to ensure that stock usage is based on actual demand from customers.

Labour turnover measures the rate of change of human resources within an organization, per period of time.

The **lead time** refers to the length of time it takes between a firm ordering new stock and the firm receiving the stock for production.

Lean production is a philosophy built into the culture of organizations that focus on less wastage and greater efficiency.

Liquidity ratios are the financial ratios that look at a firm's ability to pay its debts.

Lock-outs occur when the employer temporarily prevents employees from working during an industrial dispute.

Loss leader pricing involves setting the price of a good or service below its cost of production in order to attract customers to buy the product along with others with higher profit margins.

A **make or buy decision** is a management decision which involves choosing whether to manufacture a product (make) or to purchase it (buy) from an external supplier.

Marketing is the process of anticipating, identifying and satisfying the needs and desires of customers in a profitable way.

The **marketing mix** is a business tool used within a marketing plan referring to the set of actions that an organization uses to market its goods, services or brands: product, price, promotion and place.

Marketing objectives are the specific goals of the marketing department in order to help achieve the overall objectives of the organization.

A **marketing plan** is a document that outlines a firm's marketing objectives and strategy for a stated period of time.

Marketing planning is the systematic process of conducting a marketing audit, setting marketing objectives, and devising marketing strategies in terms of the marketing mix to achieve those objectives.

Market leaders are firms with the largest market share in a given industry.

Market orientation is an outward-looking marketing approach that focuses on meeting the specific wants and needs of customers.

Market research is the systematic process of collecting, collating, analysing and interpreting data and information about existing and potential consumers, competitors and markets.

A **market segment** is a distinct group of customers with similar characteristics and similar needs or wants.

Market segmentation is the process of splitting a market into distinct consumer groups to better understand their needs.

Market share refers to a firm's portion of the total value of sales revenue in a particular industry.

Mass marketing is marketing strategy aimed at all consumers in a market without trying to differentiate them into separate market segments.

Microfinance providers are a type of banking service provided to unemployed or low-income earners who would otherwise struggle to gain external finance.

A **mission statement** is a clear and concise declaration of an organization's fundamental purpose, i.e. a succinct description of what the organization does, in order to become what it want to be.

Motivators are factors which help staff to gain job satisfaction, e.g. recognition and opportunities for personal advancement.

The **moving average** is a quantitative method used to discover the underlying trend by levelling out variations in a data set.

A **multinational company** (MNC) is an organization that operates, owns, or controls production and/or service facilities in two or more countries.

Net assets are the overall value of a firm's assets after all liabilities are accounted for.

Net present value (NPV) is an investment appraisal technique that calculates the real value of an investment project by discounting the value of future cash flows.

Net profit margin (NPM) measures a firm's overall profit (after all costs have been deducted) as a percentage of its sales revenue.

Niche marketing is a corporate strategy based on identifying and serving a relatively small market segment.

A **non-governmental organization** (NGO) is a type of non-profit social enterprise that is neither a part of a government nor a traditional for-profit business but run by voluntary groups.

Non-sampling errors are market research mistakes that are not attributed to human errors.

A **no-strike agreement** is a contractual agreement whereby a trade union pledges not to use strike action as a form of industrial action.

Objectives are the targets an organization is trying to achieve, e.g. to maximize shareholder value.

Offshoring is the practice of relocating part of or all of a firm's business functions and processes overseas. It can but does not necessarily involve third-party providers.

Off-the-job training is training conducted by specialists away from the workplace.

On-the-job training is training conducted within the workplace while the employee is working.

Operations management refers to the business function of combining inputs to produce outputs (goods and services) that are valued by consumers.

Outsourcing is the practice of subcontracting non-core activities of an organization to a third-party provider (an external organization) in order to improve operational efficiency and reduce costs.

An **overtime ban** is a directive to workers from the employees' representative in a trade dispute to refuse working beyond their contracted hours.

A **partnership** is a commercial business organization owned by two or more people.

A **patent** is the exclusive right granted to an organization by the government to make use of an invention or process for a particular period of time.

The **payback period** (PBP) is the amount of time it takes for a business to recover the initial cost of an investment project.

Penetration pricing involves setting the price low enough to enter an industry and gain market share from existing firms.

Piece rate is a payment system, which rewards workers based on their level of output.

Place (or **distribution**), in the marketing mix, is about making the good or service available to consumers (the end users).

Point of sale refers to the marketing of goods in stores where customers can purchase the goods.

Predatory pricing involves charging a low price, even below costs of production, in order to harm the sales of competitor firms and to restrict competition.

Price discrimination occurs when a business charges different prices to different customers for essentially the same product, e.g. adult and child cinema tickets.

Price leadership occurs when one business (usually the dominant firm in the industry) sets prices which are closely monitored and followed by its rivals.

Price skimming involves setting a high price when launching a new and unique product.

Primary market research (or **field research**) is the systematic process of collecting, recording, analysing and interpreting new data and information about a specific issue of direct interest to the business.

The **productivity rate** measures the amount of output generated per unit of input.

The **product life cycle** (PLC) refers to a marketing theory that illustrates the different stages a typical product goes through from its launch to its eventual withdrawal from the market.

Product orientation is an inward-looking marketing approach that focuses on making products that a business knows how to make rather than focusing on the needs and wants of potential customers.

A **product position map** is a visual representation of customers' perception of a product, relative to its competitors, e.g. its price and quality.

Profit is the positive difference between a firm's total sales revenue (TR) and its total costs (TC). It is the reward for successful risk-taking in a business.

The **profit and loss account** shows the net profit (or loss) after all costs have been deducted from the organization's revenues.

A **profit centre** is a department or division within an organization that is responsible and held accountable for both its own costs *and* revenues.

Project-based organization refers to the organization of human resources around specific projects that need to be completed.

Promotion is the marketing process of raising customer awareness and interest in a product or brand in order to generate sales.

A **promotional mix** refers to the combination of different appropriate methods of ATL and BTL promotion aimed at specific target markets.

Psychological pricing involves setting prices to make them seem at least slightly lower, e.g. $499 instead of $500.

Public–private partnerships (PPP) are organizations jointly established by the government and at least one private sector organization.

Public relations is an organization's planned and sustained process of maintaining mutual understanding with the general public.

Qualitative research is based on opinions, feelings and perspectives. It generates in-depth, non-numerical information.

Quantitative research is based on facts and figures, i.e. numerical patterns, correlations and results, such as how many people prefer a particular brand over its rivals. The results of quantitative research are usually predictive rather than descriptive.

Quality assurance (QA) is an approach to quality management that involves the prevention of mistakes in the production process.

A **quality circle** is a small group of employees who voluntarily meet regularly to identify, examine and solve problems related to their work in order to improve the quality of output.

Quality control (QC) refers to the traditional approach to quality management by inspecting a sample of products. It involves quality controllers checking or examining a sample of products in a systematic way.

Quantifiable risks are financially measurable threats that can jeopardize the survival of an organization,

Random variations are unpredictable and erratic fluctuations in sales revenues, caused by irregular factors.

Redundancy occurs when a business can no longer afford to hire a certain number or group of workers or because the job ceases to exist, perhaps due to seasonal or technological factors.

The **re-order level** refers to the stock level at the time when the firm places its re-order of stock.

The **re-order quantity** is the volume of an order in a just-in-case stock control system.

Retained profit is the amount of net profit remaining after all costs are paid and shareholders have been compensated. It is an important internal source of finance.

The **return on capital employed** (ROCE) ratio measures a firm's efficiency and profitability in relation to its size (as measured by the firm's capital employed).

Research and development (R&D) is the systematic process of discovering new knowledge about products, processes and markets in order to fulfil market needs.

Revenue expenditure refers to the need for businesses to finance their daily and routine operations.

Revenue streams refer to the various sources of income for a business, e.g. sales revenue, royalties and rental income.

Sales forecasting is a quantitative technique used to predict the level of sales revenue that a firm expects to earn over a certain period of time.

Sales revenue or **sales turnover** refers to the income from the sales of goods and services.

Sampling is the practice of selecting a small group of customers from the population of a certain market for the purpose of market research.

Sampling errors are the mistakes that arise from sampling design.

Seasonal variations are expected periodic fluctuations in sales revenues over a given time period.

Secondary market research (or **desk research**) is the collection, collation and interpretation of existing data and information from previously available sources

Share capital is the value of equity in a company funded by shareholders.

A **social enterprise** is an organization that uses commercial business practices to improve communities, the environment and human well-being rather than focusing on profits for external shareholders.

Social marketing refers to marketing activities designed to influence the behaviour of the general public in order to benefit the wider community.

Social media marketing is the use of online tools and websites to promote products in a less formal way, e.g. using Google+ and Facebook.

Social networking refers to the use of internet-based tools and platforms to create and share online content.

The **span of control** describes the number of subordinates who are directly accountable to a manager.

Stakeholders are individuals, organizations or groups with a direct interest in the operations and performance of a particular business or organization.

A **STEEPLE analysis** examines the influences in the external environment in which a business operates, i.e. social, technological, economic, ethical, political, legal, and environmental factors.

A **stock exchange** (or **stock market**) is the marketplace where people and businesses buy and sell second-hand company stocks and shares, and a place for buying and selling shares in public limited companies.

A **stock-out** occurs when a firm has no more stock for production or sale, i.e. it is out of stock.

Stockpiling means that a business builds up excessive levels of inventory.

The **stock turnover ratio** measures the number of days it takes a business to sell its stock or the number of times the business replenishes its stock during a given period of time.

Strategic alliances (SAs) are formed when two or more businesses join forces to benefit from growth without any fundamental changes to their own long-term strategies.

Strike action involves employees refusing to work, thereby preventing the organization from continuing to operate.

The **supply chain process** is the management process of overseeing the logistics from the manufacturing stage to the finished product being delivered to the consumer.

Sustainability is business activity that meets the needs of the current generation without jeopardizing the needs of future generations.

A **takeover** is a form of external growth that occurs when one company buys a controlling interest in another company.

A **tall (or vertical) hierarchical organizational structure** has many levels of management, with narrow spans of control.

Targeting is the practice of devising of an appropriate marketing mix and marketing strategies for different market segments.

A **target market** is a particular market segment that a business aims to focus its marketing effort on.

Target price is the amount charged to customers in order to reach break-even (or any desired target profit).

Target profit is the desired or expected profit from a business, i.e. how much profit it aims to earn.

Target profit output (or **target profit quantity**) refers to the sales volume (quantity) needed in order to reach the target profit.

Total quality management (TQM) is a quality management approach that aims to involve every employee in the quality assurance process.

Trademarks are the legal protection for an organization's registered symbol (logo), word (brand), or phrase (slogan).

Training is the process of teaching a particular new skill or knowledge in order to develop a person's competence in the workplace.

A **trade union** (or labour union) is established to protect the interests of its members, e.g. to negotiate with employers for improved pay and conditions at work.

Triple bottom line refers to John Elkington's framework used to evaluate a firm's performance in the context of sustainable business activity. It comprises of environmental, economic and social sustainability.

A **unique selling point** (USP) is any aspect of a business, brand or a product that makes it distinctive (stand out) from those offered by their competitors.

Unlimited liability means that the owner (or owners) of a business is personally liable for all of its debts.

The **usage rate** refers to the speed at which stocks (inventories) are depleted in the production process.

Value added is the process of creating a product that is worth more than the cost of the inputs used to produce it.

Venture capital comes from external firms that invest in business start-ups and/or expanding small businesses with significant growth potential.

Viral marketing is the spread of information about a firm's goods or services from one internet user to another, possibly creating exponential growth in a marketing message.

A **vision statement** is an optimistic and inspiring declaration that defines the purpose and values of an organization and where it wants to be in the future.

Working capital (or **net current assets**) is the amount of money available for the day-to-day running of a business.

Work-to-rule involves workers complying with every single rule, policy and procedure of the organization in order to purposely disrupt output.